WORLD HISTORY

Selected Course Outlines and
Reading Lists from American
Colleges and Universities

World History

edited by
Steven Adams, Michael Adas
and Kevin Reilly

New Enlarged and Updated Edition

 Markus Wiener Publishers
Princeton

New enlarged and updated edition, 1998

For information write to:
Markus Wiener Publishers
231 Nassau Street, Princeton, NJ 08542

Library of Congress Cataloging-in-Publication Data

World history: selected course outlines and reading lists from
    American colleges and universities/edited by Steven Adams,
    Michael Adas, and Kevin Reilly.—4th updated and enlarged edition.
    (Selected course outlines and reading lists from American
colleges and universities)
    Includes bibliographical references.
    ISBN 1-55876-136-5 (paper)
    1. History—Outlines, syllabi, etc.   2. History—Bibliography.
3. History—Study and teaching (Higher)—United States.
I. Adams, Steven, 1962– .   II. Adas, Michael, 1943– .
III. Reilly, Kevin, 1941– .   IV. Series: Selected reading lists and
course outlines from American colleges and universities.
D21.W926   1998   98-28365
907.1'273—dc21   CIP

Printed in the United States of America

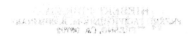

Table of Contents

I.

Graduate and Professional Courses

Graduate and Professional Courses

Michael Adas
Rutgers University
Seminar in Comparative & Global History: Race, Gender and Class under Colonialism.

Rutgers University
Department of History
Fall 1995

510:607
Seminar in Comparative & Global History
Race, Gender and Class under Colonialism
Professor Michael Adas
Tuesday 1:10 - 4:10
Van Dyke Hall 011

Sept. 5 - Orientations: Varieties of Colonialism & Colonial Societies
SLIDE SHOW·

Supplemental Readings:
D.K. Fieldhouse, *The Colonial Empires* (1965)
L. Hartz, ed.,*The Founding of New Societies* (1964)
E. Said, *Orientalism* (1978)
W. Baumgart, *Imperialism* (1982)
N. Thomas, *Colonialism's Culture* (1994)
N. Dirks, ed., *Colonialism & Culture* (1992)

Sept. 12 - Social Theory & Colonial "Realities": Race, Gender, Class
Readings:
T. Holt, "Marking: Race, Race-making and the Writing of History"
(1995)
J. Scott, "Gender: A Useful Category of Historical Analysis"
(1986)
J. Haggis, "Gendering Colonialism or Colonizing Gender" (1990)
A. Gramsci, Selections on Hegemony from the *Prison Notebooks*
(1930s)
R. Williams, "Hegemony" (1977)
J. Lears, "The Concept of Cultural Hegemony" (1985)
M. Adas, *Machines as the Measure of Men*, intro.

3

Supplemental:
> S. Gregory & R. Sanjek, *Race* (1995)
> P. van den Berghe, *Race and Racism* (1967)
> H.L. Gates, ed., *"Race," Writing & Difference* (1985)
> J. Kelly, *Women, History and Theory* (1984)
> L. Nicholson, *Gender & History* (1986)
> C. Hall, *White, Male and Middle Class* (1992)
> Walter Adamson, *Hegemony & Revolution*(1980), esp. chapter six.
> R. Williams, *Marxism & Literature & Keywords* (1976), esp.
>> sections one & two.
> K. Marx, relevant sections from the *Grundrisse & The Communist Manifesto* in *The Portable Karl Marx* or D. Caute, ed, *Essential Writings* R. Dahrendorf, *Class and Class Conflict in Industrial Society* (1957)

Sept. 19 - Before the Industrial Revolution
> **Readings:**
>> J. Taylor, "The Web of Colonial Society"
>> G. Brooks, "The *Signares* of Saint-Louis & Gorée"
>> C. Boxer, "Brazil and the Maranhão"
>> M. Adas, *Machines*, chapter 1 & 2.

> **Supplemental:**
>> P. Spear, *The Nabobs* (1963), chapters 1 & 2.
>> J. Taylor, *The Social World of Batavia* (1983), chapters 1 & 3.
>> C. Boxer, *Race Relations in the Portuguese Colonial Empire* (1963)
>> W. Cohen, *The French Encounter with Africans* (1980), chapters 1-3.
>> L. Blussé, *Strange Company* (1988)
>> M. Crowder, *Senegal: A Study of French Assimilation Policy* (1969)

Sept. 26 - "High" Imperialism and The Great Transition
> **Readings:**
>> P. Spear, "Race Relations"
>> M. Berger, "Imperialism & Sexual Exploitation" & R. Hyam, "A Reply"
>> C. Knapman, "White women ... the ruin of empires?"
>> Ann Stoler, "Rethinking Colonial Categories"
>> M. Adas, *Machines*, chapter three.

Graduate and Professional Courses

Supplemental:
    P. Curtin, *The Image of Africa* (1964), chs 2, 9-10
    J. Taylor, *Social World of Batavia*, chapters 4-6.
    M. Sinha, "Gender and Imperialism," in M. Kimmel, ed., *Changing Men* (1987)
    B. Gartrell, "Colonial Wives: Villains or Victims?" & Janice Brownfoot, "Memsahibs in Colonial Malaya" in H. Callan & S. Ardener, *The Incorporated Wife* (1984)
    Lata Mani, "Contentious Traditions" *Cultural Critique* 7 (Fall, 1987)
    G. Bearce, *British Attitudes Towards India* (1961)
    F. Hutchins, *The Illusion of Permanence* (1967)
    W. Cohen, *French Encounter*, 3,4

Oct. 3 - Colonial Society at Its Apex
Readings:
    A. Stoler, "Making Empire Respectable"
    M. Adas, *Machines*, chapter four.
    The following essays from Chaudhuri & Strobel, eds., *Western Women & Imperialism*:
    S. Blake, "A Woman's Trek"
    J. Clancy-Smith, "The `Passionate Nomad' Reconsidered"
    H. Callaway & D. Helly, "Crusader for Empire"
    M. Sinha, "Chatams, Pitts and Gladstones in Petticoats"

Supplemental:
    L. Fleming, "A New Humanity"; and S. Jacobs, "Give a Thought to Africa," & D. Birkett, "White Woman's Burden" in Chaudhuri & Strobel.
    H. Callaway, *Gender, Culture & Empire* (1987)
    Essays by D. Kirkwood & I. Clark, in Callan & Ardener
    B. Parry, *Delusions and Discoveries* (1972)
    P. Curtin, *The Image of Africa* (1965), esp. chapters 15, 16
    K. Ballhatchet, *Race, Sex & Class under the Raj* (1980)
    M. Pratt, *Imperial Eyes* (1992)
    P. Brantlinger, *Rule of Darkness* (1988)
    H. Cairns, *Prelude to Imperialism* (1965)
    W. Cohen, *French Encounter*, remaining chapters
    M. Strobel, *European Women and the Second British Empire* (1991)
    And the essays by A. JanMohamed, Brantlinger, and S. Gilman, in Gates, *"Race"*

Graduate and Professional Courses

Oct. 10 - Interactions between Colonizer & Colonized
Readings:
    The following essays from Chaudhuri & Strobel:
      M. Hatem, "Through Each Other's Eyes"
      B. Ramusack, "Cultural Missionaries"
      A. Burton, "The White Woman's Burden"
      K. Hansen, *Distant Companions* (Pbk)
      M. Adas, *Machines*, chapter five
Supplemental:
      D. Prouchaska, *Making Algeria French* (1990)
      R. Hyam, *Empire and Sexuality* (1990)
      T. Mitchell, *Colonizing Egypt* (1988)
      A. Stoler, "Sexual Affronts & Racial Frontiers" *CSSH* (July, 1992)
      J. Boone, "Vacation Cruises; or, the Homoerotics of Orientalism" *PMLA* (January, 1995)
      G. Fredrickson, *White Supremacy* (1981)
      C. Knaplund, *White Women in Fiji* (1986)
      L. White, *The Comforts of Home: Prostitution in Colonial Nairobi* (1990)
      D. Arnold, *Colonizing the Body* (Berkeley, 1993)

Oct. 17 - Gender, Race & Class in Resistance to Colonization
Readings:
      M. Sinha, "Gender and Imperialism"
      D. Engels, "The Limits of Gender Ideology"
      P. Chatterjee, "Colonialism, Nationalism & Colonized Women"
      L. Ahmed, "The Discourse of the Veil"
      J. van Allen, "'Aba Riots' or Igbo 'Women's War'?"
Supplemental:
      F. Fanon, *Black Skin, White Masks* (1967)
      _____, *The Wretched of the Earth* (1963)
      P. Chatterjee, *Nationalist Thought and the Colonial World* (1986)
      A. Nandy, *The Intimate Enemy: Loss and Recovery under Colonialism* (1983)
      N. Wa Thiong'o, *Decolonising the Mind* (1981)
      D. Haynes & G. Prakash, *Contesting Power* (1991)
      J. R. Hargreaves, *Decolonization in Africa* (1988)
      D. A. Low, ed., *Congress and the Raj* (1977)

Oct. 24 to the Winter Break: Individual paper presentations & critiques.

Graduate and Professional Courses

Kenneth J. Andrien
The Ohio State University
Seminar in World History: Historical Approaches to Colonialism and Post-Colonialism.

THE OHIO STATE UNIVERSITY

Kenneth J. Andrien
Office: 210 Dulles Hall
Office Telephone: 292-0324
Department Telephone: 292-2674 (messages)
E-Mail: Andrien.1@osu.edu
Office Hours: Monday, Wednesday, 1:00-2:00; Friday, 9:00-10:00; and by appointment

History 810.01: Seminar in World History

Historical Approaches to Colonialism and Postcolonialism

COURSE DESCRIPTION:

Within the historical discipline many scholars have sought reintegrative and comparative approaches to studying the past. This trend has led a number of historians to reexamine the field's relationship to other disciplines, particularly in the humanities and social sciences. This course is designed to bring together graduate students from a number of specialized backgrounds to participate in a research course that encourages them to place their own scholarly interests within a "global" perspective. This year the focus of the course will be *Historical Approaches to Colonialism and Postcolonialism.*

The first part of History 810 will be devoted primarily to reading and analyzing some influential works dealing with colonial and postcolonial studies. At the end of the term, each student will produce a prospectus for his/her research paper. By the end of the second term, the students will complete this research paper applying a more global or comparative approach to a topic in their major field of specialization.

REQUIRED READINGS:

Partha Chatterjee, *Nationalist Thought in the Colonial World: A   Derivative Discourse*
Ranajit Guha, *Elementary Aspects of Peasant Insurgency in Colonial India*
Karen Ordahl Kupperman, ed., *America in European Consciousness,1492-1750*
Gyan Prakash, *After Colonialism: Imperial Histories and Postcolonial Displacements*
Patricia Seed, *Ceremonies of Possession in Europe's Conquest of the New World, 1492-1640*

All of the books are available at the Student Book Exchange at 1806 North High Street

Graduate and Professional Courses

Patricia Seed, "Colonial and Postcolonial Discourse," *Latin American Research Review*, 26:3 (1991): 181-200.
Hernan Vidal, "The Concept of Colonial and Postcolonial Discourse," *ibid.*, 113-19.
Walter Mignolo, "Colonial and Postcolonial Discourse: Cultural Critique or Academic Colonialism," *ibid.*, 120-34.
Rolena Adorno, "Reconsidering Colonial Discourse for Sixteenth- and Seventeenth-Century Spanish America," *ibid.*, 135-45.
Patricia Seed, "More Colonial and Postcolonial Discourses, *ibid.*, 146-52.
Ranajit Guha, "The Small Voice of History," *Subaltern Studies IX*, (1996): 1-12.
Gyan Prakash, "Subaltern Studies as Postcolonial Criticism," *American Historical Review*, 99-5 (1994): 1475-90.

COURSE REQUIREMENTS:

I. Each student must attend every class and participate in discussions of the weekly reading assignments. If any student misses a class, he/she must write a five page review of the assigned readings, summarizing the content of the assignment and his/her critical assessment of the work and duplicate it for the other members of the class.

II. Our class will also meet jointly to discuss the assigned readings with Spanish and Portuguese 858 on the following dates: January 23 (in 250 Dulles Hall), January 27 and February 17 (in 214 Central Classroom Building) between 4:30 and 6:30.

III. Every student must write two critical reviews, on Patricia Seed, *Ceremonies of Possession* and on Ranajit Guha, *Elementary Aspects of Peasant Insurgency*. The review on Seed is due on 4 February and the second on Guha is due on 25 February.

IV. The final assignment is a project prospectus that proposes, defines, and defends a seminar paper topic to be completed during the spring term. The prospectus should be approximately ten pages and include a preliminary bibliography. It is due on the last day of class, 11 March.

SCHEDULE OF ASSIGNMENTS:

January 7: Discussion of Course goals, requirements, and procedures

Graduate and Professional Courses

January 14: Introduction to Colonialism and Postcolonialism: Patricia Seed, "Colonial and Postcolonial Discourse," *Latin American Research Review*, 26:3 (1991): 181-200; Hernan Vidal, "The Concept of Colonial and Postcolonial Discourse," *ibid.*, 113-19; Walter Mignolo, "Colonial and Postcolonial Discourse: Cultural Critique or Academic Colonialism," *ibid.*, 120-34; Rolena Adorno, "Reconsidering Colonial Discourse for Sixteenth- and Seventeenth-Century Spanish America," *ibid.*, 135-45; and Patricia Seed, "More Colonial and Postcolonial Discourses, *ibid.*, 146-52. Ranajit Guha, "The Small Voice of History," *Subaltern Studies IX*, (1996): 1-12.

January 23: New Approaches to Colonial History: Patricia Seed, *Ceremonies of Possession in Europe's Conquest of the New World, 1492-1640* with Spanish and Portuguese 858 in 250 Dulles Hall

January 27: New Approaches to Colonial History, II: Karen Ordahl Kupperman, ed., *America in European Consciousness, 1492-1750* with Spanish and Portuguese 858 in 214 Central Classroom Bldg.

February 4: Subaltern Studies: Gyan Prakash, "Subaltern Studies as Postcolonial Criticism," *American Historical Review*, 99-5 (1994): 1475-90. Ranajit Guha, *Elementary Aspects of Peasant Insurgency in Colonial India*

February 11: Subaltern Studies II: Partha Chatterjee, *Nationalist Thought in the Colonial World: A Derivative Discourse*

February 17: Colonial and Postcolonial Studies: Gyan Prakash, *After Colonialism: Imperial Histories and Postcolonial Displacements* with Spanish and Portuguese 858 in 214 Central Classroom Bldg.

February 25: Consultations about Seminar Paper Topics

March 4: Discussion of student projects

March 11: Discussion of student projects

Graduate and Professional Courses

Jerry H. Bentley
University of Hawaii
Seminar in World History.

Seminar in World History

Fall 1996   HIST 609   Jerry H. Bentley

World history is a fast-emerging and exciting subfield of the broader discipline of history. The purpose of this reading seminar is to provide an introduction to the most important literature, themes, theories, concepts, and methods of world history as a field of research and scholarship. The works listed in this syllabus all deal with world history in one sense or another of the term: they explicitly compare experiences across the boundary lines of societies and cultural regions, they analyze processes of cross-cultural interaction, or they examine large-scale patterns that influence historical development on a transregional or global scale. Some works represent efforts at macrohistory in that they deal with the whole world or large parts of it. Most, however, examine the workings of large-scale processes in local or regional contexts. Many bring the results of basic research to bear on global themes.

Each member of the seminar will read one book for each of the weekly themes and will prepare incisive book analyses, with copies for all other members, of at least eight books during the course of the semester. In addition, each member of the seminar will provide an introduction to the literature and will help facilitate discussion for one of the weekly themes. Course grades will be based on class discussion and book analyses.

Date   Themes and Readings

29 Aug.   Introduction and organization

5 Sept.   **Conceptions of world history**

H. G. Wells, *The Outline of History*
Oswald Spengler, *The Decline of the West*
Arnold Toynbee, *A Study of History*
William H. McNeill, *The Rise of the West*
Marshall G.S. Hodgson, *Rethinking World History*
Bruce Mazlish and Ralph Buultjens, eds., *Conceptualizing Global History*
Stephen K. Sanderson, *Social Transformations*
P.A. Sorokin, *Social and Cultural Dynamics*
Paul Costello, *World Historians and Their Goals*
Jerry H. Bentley, *Shapes of World History in Twentieth-Century Scholarship*

12 Sept.   **Modernization analysis**

W.W. Rostow, *The Stages of Economic Growth*, 3rd ed.
-----, *How It All Began*
Cyril E. Black, *The Dynamics of Modernization*
-----, et al., *The Modernization of Japan and Russia*
-----, ed., *Comparative Modernization*
Reinhard Bendix, *Nation-Building and Citizenship*, enlarged ed.
-----, *Kings or Peoples*
S.N. Eisenstadt, ed., *The Protestant Ethic and Modernization*
Barrington Moore, *Social Origins of Dictatorship and Democracy*
Daniel Chirot, *Social Change in the Modern Era*
E.L. Jones, *Growth Recurring*
-----, *The European Miracle*, 2nd ed.
-----, Lionel Frost, and Colin White, *Coming Full Circle*
Peter N. Stearns, *The Industrial Revolution in World History*

19 Sept.   **Dependency and world-system analysis**

Immanuel Wallerstein, *The Modern World-System*, 3 vols. to date
-----, *Geopolitics and Geoculture*
Andre Gunder Frank, *World Accumulation*
-----, *Dependent Accumulation and Underdevelopment*
----- and B. Gills, *The World System: Five Hundred Years or Five Thousand?*
Eric Williams, *Capitalism and Slavery*
Walter Rodney, *How Europe Underdeveloped Africa*
J.M. Blaut, *The Colonizer's Model of the World*
Eric Wolf, *Europe and the People without History*

Graduate and Professional Courses

Janet L. Abu-Lughod, *Before European Hegemony*
Giovanni Arrighi, *The Long Twentieth Century*
L.S. Stavrianos, *Global Rift*
Fernand Braudel, *The Perspective of the World*
Daniel Chirot, *Social Change in the Twentieth Century*
Alan K. Smith, *Creating a World Economy*
Alvin So and Stephen Chiu, *East Asia and the World-Economy*

26 Sept. **Cross-cultural trade: premodern**

Philip D. Curtin, *Cross-Cultural Trade in World History*
C.G.F. Simkin, *The Traditional Trade of Asia*
S. Ratnagar, *Encounters: The Westerly Trade of the Harappa Civilization*
Michael Rowlands et al., eds., *Centre and Periphery in the Ancient World*
Ying-shih Yü, *Trade and Expansion in Han China*
J. Innes Miller, *The Spice Trade of the Roman Empire*
Vimala Begley and Richard Daniel de Puma, eds., *Rome and India*
Liu Xinru, *Ancient India and Ancient China*
Richard Hodges, *Mohammed, Charlemagne and the Origins of Europe*
K.N. Chaudhuri, *Asia before Europe*
-----, *Trade and Civilisation in the Indian Ocean*
S.D. Goitein, *A Mediterranean Society*
Janet L. Abu-Lughod, *Before European Hegemony*
E.W. Bovill, *The Golden Trade of the Moors*
Kenneth Hall, *Maritime Trade and State Development in Early Southeast Asia*

3 Oct. No class meeting today

10 Oct. **Cross-cultural trade: early modern**

Philip D. Curtin, *Cross-Cultural Trade in World History*
James D. Tracy, ed., *The Rise of Merchant Empires*
-----, ed., *The Political Economy of Merchant Empires*
K.N. Chaudhuri, *Trading World of Asia and the English East India Company*
Jonathan Israel, *Dutch Primacy in World Trade*
Niels Steensgaard, *The Asian Trade Revolution of the Seventeenth Century*
Anthony Reid, *Southeast Asia in the Age of Commerce*
Leonard Blussé, *Strange Company*
Leonard Blussé and F.S. Gaastra, eds., *Companies and Trade*

R. Ptak and D. Rothermund, eds., *Emporia, Commodities, and Entrepreneurs*
Holden Furber, *Rival Empires of Trade in the Orient*
A. Das Gupta and M.N. Pearson, eds., *India and the Indian Ocean*
Michael Pearson, *Before Colonialism*
-----, *The Portuguese in India*
Sanjay Subrahmanyam, *The Portuguese Empire in Asia*
_____, *The Political Economy of Commerce*
_____, *Improvising Empire*
M.A.P. Meilink-Roelofsz, *Asian Trade and European Influence*
Om Prakash, *The Dutch East India Company and the Economy of Bengal*
Stephen F. Dale, *Indian Merchants and Eurasian Trade*
Nicholas Thomas, *Entangled Objects*

17 Oct.   **Migrations and diasporas**

J.P. Mallory, *In Search of the Indo-Europeans*
Irving Rouse, *Migrations in Prehistory*
Wang Gungwu, ed., *Global History and Migrations*
Philip D. Curtin, *The Rise and Fall of the Plantation Complex*
John K. Thornton, *Africa and Africans in the Making of the Atlantic World*
Mechal Sobel, *The World They Made Together*
Patrick A. Manning, *Slavery and African Life*
Barbara Solow, ed., *Slavery and the Rise of the Atlantic System*
Richard Price, *First-Time*
-----, *Alabi's World*
Allison Blakely, *Blacks in the Dutch World*
Paul Gilroy, *The Black Atlantic*
Martin L. Kilson and Robert I. Rotberg, eds., *The African Diaspora*
Joseph E. Harris, ed., *Global Dimensions of the African Diaspora*
Hugh Tinker, *A New System of Slavery*
David Northrup, *Indentured Labor in the Age of Imperialism*
P.C. Emmer, ed., *Colonialism and Migration*
Lynn Pan, *Sons of the Yellow Emperor*
Gabriel Sheffer, ed., *Modern Diasporas in International Politics*

24 Oct.   **The age of European imperialism**

Daniel R. Headrick, *The Tentacles of Progress*
-----, *The Tools of Empire*
Carlo Cipolla, *Guns, Sails, and Empires*
D.K. Fieldhouse, *The Colonial Empires*

Graduate and Professional Courses

-----, *Economics and Empire*
V.G. Kiernan, *From Conquest to Collapse*
-----, *Imperialism and its Contradictions*
R. Robinson and J. Gallagher, *Africa and the Victorians*
J. Gallagher, *Decline, Revival, and Fall of the British Empire*
C.A. Bayly, *The Imperial Meridian*
-----, *Indian Society and the Making of the British Empire*
Bernard S. Cohn, *Colonialism and Its Forms of Knowledge*
Sidney Mintz, *Sweetness and Power*
Michael Adas, *Prophets of Rebellion*
-----, *Machines as the Measure of Men*
Margaret Strobel, *European Women and the Second British Empire*
N. Chaudhuri and M. Strobel, eds., *Western Women and Imperialism*

31 Oct.   **Post-colonial perspectives**

Edward W. Said, *Orientalism*
-----, *Culture and Imperialism*
Carol Breckenridge, ed., *Orientalism and the Postcolonial Predicament*
Talal Asad, ed., *Anthropology and the Colonial Encounter*
James Clifford, *The Predicament of Culture*
----- and G. Marcus, eds., *Writing Culture*
Bernard McGrane, *Beyond Anthropology*
Nicholas Thomas, *Colonialism's Culture*
Paul Gilroy, *The Black Atlantic*
-----, *There Ain't No Black in the Union Jack*
Mary Louise Pratt, *Imperial Eyes*
Stevan Harrell, ed., *Cultural Encounters on China's Ethnic Frontiers*
Vicente L. Rafael, *Contracting Colonialism*
Timothy Mitchell, *Colonising Egypt*
Peter Hulme, *Colonial Encounters*
Henry Louis Gates, Jr., ed., *"Race," Writing, and Difference*
Benedict Anderson, *Imagined Communities*, 2nd ed.
Homi K. Bhabha, *Location of Culture*

7 Nov. **Cross-cultural encounters**

Mary W. Helms, *Ulysses' Sail*
Jerry H. Bentley, *Old World Encounters*
Walter Burkert, *The Orientalizing Revolution*
Martin Bernal, *Black Athena*

14

Graduate and Professional Courses

Edward H. Schafer, *The Golden Peaches of Samarkand*
-----, *The Vermilion Bird*
Stuart B. Schwartz, ed., *Implicit Understandings*
Sabine MacCormack, *Religion in the Andes*
James Axtell, *The European and the Indian*
-----, *The Invasion Within*
Jacques Lafaye, *Quetzalcóatl and Guadalupe*
John Leddy Phelan, *The Hispanization of the Philippines*
John E. Wills, *Embassies and Illusions*
Rhoads Murphey, *The Outsiders*
Masao Miyoshi, *As We Saw Them*
Jean and John Comaroff, *Of Revelation and Revolution*
Greg Dening, *Islands and Beaches*

14 Nov.　**Technology and science**

Arnold Pacey, *Technology in World Civilization*
Richard W. Bulliet, *The Camel and the Wheel*
Lynn White, Jr., *Medieval Technology and Social Change*
Daniel R. Headrick, *The Tentacles of Progress*
-----, *The Tools of Empire*
William H. McNeill, *The Pursuit of Power*
Geoffrey Parker, *The Military Revolution*
David B. Ralston, *Importing the European Army*
Peter N. Stearns, *The Industrial Revolution in World History*
Toby E. Huff, *The Rise of Early Modern Science*
Michael P. Adas, *Machines as the Measure of Men*

21 Nov.　Thanksgiving holiday

28 Nov.　**Biological and ecological exchanges**

Andrew Watson, *Agricultural Innovation in the Early Islamic World*
Alfred W. Crosby, *Ecological Imperialism*
-----, *The Columbian Exchange*
-----, *Germs and Seeds and Animals*
William Cronon, *Changes in the Land*
Timothy H. Silver, *A New Face on the Countryside*
Donald Worster, *Rivers of Empire*

15

-----, ed., *The Ends of the Earth*
William H. McNeill, *Plagues and Peoples*
-----, *The Global Condition*
Richard H. Grove, *Green Imperialism*
William M. Denevan, ed., *The Native Population of the Americas in 1492*
Philip D. Curtin, *Death by Migration*
Clive Ponting, *A Green History of the World*

5 Dec. **Frontiers**

Frederick Jackson Turner, *The Frontier in American History*
Walter Prescott Webb, *The Great Frontier*
William H. McNeill, *The Great Frontier*
-----, *Polyethnicity and National Unity in World History*
Owen Lattimore, *Inner Asian Frontiers of China*
Thomas J. Barfield, *The Perilous Frontier*
Stevan Harrell, ed., *Cultural Encounters on China's Ethnic Frontiers*
Barry Cunliffe, *Greeks, Romans and Barbarians*
Richard Eaton, *The Rise of Islam and the Bengal Frontier*
Richard White, *The Middle Ground*
Frances Karttunen, *Between Worlds*
David J. Weber, *The Spanish Frontier in North America*
Patricia Nelson Limerick, *The Legacy of Conquest*
----- et al., eds., *Trails: Toward a New Western History*
Nancy M. Farriss, *Maya Society under Colonial Rule*
Inga Clendinnen, *Ambivalent Conquests*

12 Dec. **Spread of religious faiths**

Arthur Darby Nock, *Conversion*
Jerry H. Bentley, *Old World Encounters*
Johannes Geffcken, *The Last Days of Greco-Roman Paganism*
Ramsay MacMullen, *Christianizing the Roman Empire*
S.N.C. Lieu, *Manichaeism in the Later Roman Empire and Medieval China*
Jacques Gernet, *Buddhism in Chinese Society*
Liu Xinru, *Ancient India and Ancient China*
Arthur W. Wright, *Buddhism in Chinese History*
E. Zürcher, *The Buddhist Conquest of China*
Clifford Geertz, *Islam Observed*

Graduate and Professional Courses

Richard W. Bulliet, *Conversion to Islam in the Medieval Period*
Daniel C. Dennett, *Conversion and the Poll Tax in Early Islam*
S.M. Ikram, *Muslim Civilization in India*
Nehemiah Levtzion, ed., *Conversion to Islam*
Michael Gervers and Ramzi Jibran Bichazi, eds., *Conversion and Continuity*
Speros Vryonis, *The Decline of Medieval Hellenism in Asia Minor*
Robert W. Hefner, ed., *Conversion to Christianity*
Jacques Gernet, *China and the Christian Impact*
George Elison, *Deus Destroyed*

Graduate and Professional Courses

Philip D. Curtin
The Johns Hopkins University
Seminar in Comparative World History.

Seminar in Comparative World History
100.724
Spring Semester - 1998
Ten to Noon - Thursday

Studies in Comparative and World History

The general format of the seminar in this semester will consist of meetings to discuss works in the fields of world and comparative history.

For purposes of discussion, the subject matter will be divided into particular kinds of comparison, with some fuzzy borders between divisions. Most of these subject-matter fields will be discussed at only one meeting.

Each week, two or more students will present discussion-openers on one of the listed problematic questions—-or on a subject of his own choosing, but they should clear unlisted problems with the instructor. Whatever the stated problem, each discussion opener should include an analysis of the kind of comparative history dealt with----including an evaluation of the way each author has handled the techniques of comparative history. With few students this semester, we will have a briefer kind of discussion opener than usual, a sketch rather than a written expression.

Bibliogrphy: Comparative Method

Bendix, R., "The Comparative Analysis of Historical Change," in T. Burns and S. B. Saul, *Social Theory and Economic Change*, pp. 67-86.

Bloch, Marc, "A Contribution Toward a Comparative History of European Societies," in J. E. Anderson (ed.), *Land and Work in Medieval Europe* (Berkeley: University of California Press, 1967)

Frederickson, George,"Comparative History," in Michael Kammen (ed.), *The Past Before Us: Contemporary Historical Writing in the United States* (Ithaca: Cornell University Press, 1980).

Grew, Raymond, "The Case for Comparing Histories," *AHR*, 85:763-78 (1980).

Grew, Raymond, "Comparative History in Theory and Practice," *CSSH*, 22(April 1982)

Hill, Alette Olin, and Boyd H. Hill, Jr., "Marc Bloch and Comparative History," *AHR*, 85:823-57 (1980).

Marsh, Robert, *Comparative Sociology.*

Graduate and Professional Courses

Smelser, Neil J., *Comparative Methods in the Social Sciences*
Warner, R. Stephen, "The Role of Religious Ideas and the Use of Models in Max Weber's
Comparative Studies of Non-Capitalist Societies, *JEH*, 30:74-99 (1970).

Memoires on the Teaching of Non-Western History:
Vansina, Jan, *Living with Africa*
Williams, John A., *Classrooms in Conflict: Teaching Controversial Subjects in a Diverse Society*
(1994).

February 5 - World Histories: The Classics

Possible discussion openers:
1. What is Toynbee's proper place in the historiography of world history, seen from the end of the
   twentierh century? (Toynbee, McNeill biography, Bentley article)
2. Hodgson and Gellner have come to world history after an earlier career in non-Western
   studies. Should either approach be preferred to the western-centered view of Braudel?

February 12 - World Histories: New Approaches

Possible discussion openers:
1. The Standards in World History for American high schools suggest that the West should be
   slightly overemphacized at about 40 percent of the total allocation for world history. This
   is about right for an American audience, either in general or in world history courses at
   universities? If not, how should it be different?
2. Is it the distinction between "global" and "world" history useful? (Mazlish and Buultjens)
3. Is the "expansion of Europe" a viable departure for the study of non-Western history? (Emmer
   and Wesseling)

More-or-Less World Histories
Adas, Michael (ed.), *Islamic and European Expansion: The Forging of a Global Order*
(Philadelpia: Temple, 1993).
Beyer, Michael, and Charles Bright, "World History in a Global Age," *AHR*, 100:1034-1060
(1995)
Toynbee, Arnold J., *A Study of History*, 10 vols. (1934-54).
Braudel, Fernand, *Civilization and Capitalism*, 3 vols. (1967-79) First published in French as
Civilisaton materielle et capitalisme (1967), *Les jeux de l'echange* (1979), and *Le temps
du monde* (1979).
Bentley, Jerry H., *Shapes of World in History in Twentieth-Century Scholarship* (Washington:
American Historical Association, 1996).
Emmer, Pieter C., and H. L. Wesseling (eds), *Reappraisals in Overseas History: Essays on Post-
war Historiography about European Expansion* (Leiden).

Goody, Jack, *The East in the West* (New York: Cambridge Press, 1996).

Keegan, John, *History of Warfare* (1995).

Ferro, Marc, Colonization: *A Global History* (St-Hyacinthe, Quebec: World Heritage Press, 1997).

Mazlish, Bruce, and Ralph Buultjens (eds.), *Conceptualizing Global History* (Boulder: Westview Press, 1993).

Prazniak, Roxann, *Dialogues across Civilizations: Sketches in World History from the Chinese and European Experience* (Boulder: Westview, 1996)

Wolf, Eric, *Europe and the People Without History*

Wells, H. G., *The Outline of History* (1920).

Fletchner, Joseph, "Integrative History: Parallels and Interconnections in the Early Modern Period, 1500-1800," *Journal of Turkish Studies*, 9:37-57 (1985).

Gamble, Clive, *Timewalkers: The Prehistory of Global Colonization* (Cambridge: Harvard Press, 1994).

Gellner, Ernest, *Plough, Sword, and Book: The Structure of Human History* (London, 1988).

Geiss, Imanuel, *Geschichte griffbereit*, 6 vols. (Dortmund: Harenberg Lexikon-Verlag, 1993)

Hodgson, Marshall G. S., *Rethinking World History: Esays on Europe, Isalam and World History* (New York: Cambridge, 1993).Edited by Edmund Burke III.

Lewis, Bernard, "Other People's History," *The American Scholar*, 50:397-405 (1990)

Jones, E. L., *Growth Recurring: Economic Change in World History* (Oxford,Clarendon Press, 1988)

Powelson, John P., *Centuries of Economic Endeavor: Parallel Paths in lapan and Europe and their Contrasts with the Third World* (Ann Arbor: University of Michigan Press, 1994)

National Center for History in the Schools, *National Standards for World History: Exploring Paths to the Present* (Los Angeles: National Cent er for History in the Schools, University of Calfornia, Los Angeles, 1994).

From this point onward, the schedule is tentative. We have nine class sessions left, one of which should be reserved for students presenting part of their own work, at any stage. This leaves eight sessions for the discussion of world and comparative history. The list below gives tentative bibliographies and discussion openers for eleven possible sessions. Eight can be chosen from this list, with unlisted discussions a possibility as well. Any of these discusions can be expanded to two weeks or more, if class interest justifies it.

Week A - Regional Histories on a World Scale

Possible discusion openers:

1. How can one decide which "world system" has more explanatory value? Wallerstein's, Frank and Gills, or neither?

2. Do Chaudhuri's two volumes on the Indian Ocean demostrate that an Indian-ocean-centered approach to history is valid and useful, or merely that comparative history is valid and useful, or neither?

Regional Histories:

Abu-Lughod, Janet L., *Before European Hegemony*

Adas, Michael (ed.), *Islamic and European Expansion: The Forging of a Global Order* (Philadelphia: Temple University Press, 1993).

Adas, Michael (ed.), AHA Essays on Global and Comparative History---Stearns, Curtin, McNeill, Tucker, Abu-Lughod, Tilley, Adas, Strobel.

Bentley, Jerry, *Old World Encounters: Cross-Cultural Contact and Exchanges in Pre-Modern Times* (New York, OUP, 1993).

Benton, Lauren, "From the World-Sytems Perspective to Institutional World History: Culture and Economy in Global Theory," *JWH*, 7:216-295.

Canny, Nicholas, *Europeans on the Move: Studies on European Migration, 1500-1800* (Oxford: Clarendon Press, 1994)

Canny, Nicholas and Anthony Pagden, *Colonial Identity in the Atlantic World, 1500-1800* (Princeton, Princeton University Press, 1987).

Chaudhuri, K. N., *The Trading World of Asia* (1978)

Chaudhuri, K. N., *Asia Before Europe: Economy and Civilisation of the Indian Ocean from the Rise of Islam to 1750* (1990).

Frank, Andre Gunder, *The Centrality of Central Asia* (Amsterdam: VU Boekhandel, 1992). [See also Daniel Ballard and others, "'The Centrality of Central Asia': A Dialogue with Frank," *Studies in History*, 8(new series): 43-122 (1992).]

Frank, A. G., and Barry K. Gills, *The World System: Five Hundred Years or Five Thousand* (London: Routledge, 1993).

Hodgson, Marshall G. S., *The Venture of Islam* (more approachable though Rethinking World History, edited by Burke).

Jones, Eric, Lionel Frost, and Colin White, *Coming Full Circle: An Economic History of the Pacific Rim* (Boulder: Westview, 1993)

Karras, Alan L., and John R. McNeill (eds.), *Atlantic American Societies: From Columbus through Abolition 1492-1888* (New York: Routledge, 1992).

Liss, Peggy K., *Atlantic Empires: The Network of Trade and Revolution, 1713-1826* (Baltimore, 1983).

McPhearson, Kenneth, *The Indian Ocean: A History of People and the Sea* (New York: Oxford University Press, 1993).

Offen, Karen, Ruth Roach Price, and James Rendall (eds.), *Writing Women's History: International Perspectives* (Bloomington: Indiana University Press, 1991)

Shaffer, Lynda Norene, *Maritime Southeast Asia to 1500* (Armonk, NY: M. E. Sharpe, 1995)

Thornton, John K., *Africa and Africans in the Making of the Atlantic World, 1400-1680* (New York: Cambiridge Univerdsity Press, 1992).

Tracy, James D., *The Rise of Merchant Empires: Long-Distance Trade in the Early Modern World 1850-1750* (1990).

_____, *The Political Economy of Merchant Empires: State Power and World Trade, 1350-1750* (1991).

Trigger, Bruce G., *Early Civilizations: Ancient Egypt in Context* (Cairo: American University in Cairo Press, 1993).

Wallerstein, Immanuel, *The Modern World System*

Wink, Andre, *Al-Hind: The Making of the Indo-lslamic World. Volume 1. Early Medieval India and the Expansion of Islam* (New York: Brill, 1990). Five volumes projected.

Week B- Comparative Revolutions

Possible discussion openers:

1. Crane Brinton wrote about Western revolutions---how far wrong did he go in failing to bring in non-Western examples, or did it make any difference? (Compare Brinton, Paige, Moore, and Wolf).
2. Marx was a classic theorist of revolution. How valid is Skocpol's implied revision?
3. Have the works on comparative revolution inspired by the Vietnam experience aged well over recent decades?

Comparative Revolution

Brinton, Crane, *Anatomy of Revolution*

Dunn, John, *Modern Revolutions: An Introduction to the Analysis of a Political Phenomenon*

Moore, Barrington, Jr., *The Social Origins of Dictatorship and Democracy*

Paige, Jeffrey, *Agrarian Revolution*

Skocpol, Theda, *States and Social Revolutions: A Comparative Analysis of France, Russia, and China* .

Walton, John, *Reluctant Rebels.*

Walt, Stephen M., *Revolution and War* (Ithaca: Cornell University Press, 1996).

Wolf, Eric R., *Peasant Wars of the Twentieth Century*

Comparative Studies in Society and History, Volume 29, pp. 417-513. A series of comparative articles on peasant resistance and revolt in Indonesia, France, Mexico, El Salvador, and Sri Lanka.

Commentaries on comparative revolutions

Adas Michael, "Social History and the Revolution in African and Asian Historiography," *Journal of Social History*, 19:335-348 (1985).

David Geggus, "The French and Haitian Revolutions and Resitance to Slavery in the Americas: An Overview," *Revue franaise d'histoire d'outre-mer*, 76: (1989).

Nzongola-Ntalaja, *Revolution and Counter-Revolution in Africa: Essays in Contemporary Politics* (London: Zed Books, 1987).

Week C - Technological History

Possible Discussion Openers:

Graduate and Professional Courses

1. Is the "industrial revolution" a part of the history of technology, or is it so important that industrial marchines are only a small part?(Jones, Growth Recurring, and others)
2. "The industrial revolution is clearly a world-wide event, while the ancient agricultural is a set of piecemeal changes in many different societies---changes that became world-wide only after human intercommunication increased greatly. In the long run of history, that intercommunication rather than the agricultural techniques communicated was the truly world-revolutionay event." Is this a correct evaluation of the differences between the industrial and agricultural revolutions?(Bruce Smith, Mark Cohen, and John Hather) .
3. How is the "military revolution" related to the "industrial revolution," especially in regard to the timing of each? (Parker and McNeill)

Histories of Technology

Cohen, Mark, "The Epidemiology of Civilization," in Judith E. Jacobsen and John Firor, *Human Impart on the Environment: Ancient Roots and Current Challenges* (Boulder: Westview, 1992)

Cohen, Mark Nathan and George Armelagos (eds.), *Paleopathology at the Origins of Agriculture* (Orlando: Academic Press, 1984).

Cohen Mark Nathan, *The Food Crisis in Prehistory: Overpopulation and the Origins of Agriculture* (New Haven, Yale University Press, 1977).

Cohen, Robin (ed.), *The Cambridge Survey of World Migration* (Cambridge: Cambridge University Press, 1995).

Hather, John (ed.), *Tropical Archaebotany: Applications and New Directions* (New York: Routledge, 1994).

Headrick, Daniel, *Tools of Empire*

-------, *The Tentacles of Progress.*

-------, "Botany, Chemistry, and Tropical Development," *JWH*, 7:1-10 (1996).

Jones, E. L., *The European Miracle*

Jones, E. L., *Growth Recurring: Economic Change in World History* (Oxford, Clarendon Press, 1988).

Livi-Bacci, Massimo, *A Concise History of World Population* (Cambridge,Mass.: Blackwell, 1992).

Kindleberger, Karl A., *World Economic Primacy: 1500-1990* (New York: Oxford University Press, 1996).

O'Brien, Patrick Karl, "Intercontinental Trade and the Development of the Third World since the Industrial Revolution," *Journal of World History*, 8:75-133 (1997).

Powelson, John P., *Centuries of Economic Endeavor: Parallel Paths in Japan and Europe and their Contrasts with the Third World* (Ann Arbor: University of Michigan Press, 1994)

Singer, Charles, E. J. Holmyard, and A. R. Hall, *A History of Technology*, 5 vols. (1954-58)

McNeill, William, *The Pursuit of Power*

Parker, Geoffrey, *The Military Revolution*

Smil, Vaclav, *Energy in World History* (Boulder: Westview Press, 1994).

--------, *Cycles of Life: Civilization and the Biosphere* (New York: Scientific American Library, 1997)

Smith, Bruce D., *The Emergence of Agriculture* (New York: Scientific American Library, 1994)

Stearns, Peter N., *The Industrial Revolution in World History* (Bounder: Westview, 1993)

Watson, Andrew M., *Agricultural Innovation in the Early Islamic World: the Diffusion of Crops and Farming Techniques, 700-1100* (Cambridge: Cambridge University Press, 1983).

Week D - Comparative Slavery

Possible discussion openers:

1. How much does Cooper's criticism leave of the main interpretive thesis advanced by Kopytoff and Miers?'
2. Is Russian or South-East Asian slavery too far removed from the familiar picture of the plantation complex to make it valuable for comparative analysis?
3. How should the differences interpretation between Orlando Patternson, Meillassoux, and Kopytoff be resolved?

Comparative Slavery

Cooper, Frederick, "The Problem of Slavery in African Studies," *JAH*, 20:103-125 (1979).

------, "Race, Ideology, and the Perils of Comparative History," *AHR*, 101:1122 1138 (1996). (Begins with a survey of the historiography of comparative slavery.)

Hellie, Richard, *Slavery in Russia: 1450-1725* (Cambridge: Harvard University Press, 1982)

Kolchin, Peter, *Unfree Labor: American Slavery and Russian Serfdom* (Harvard, 1987).

Klein, Martin L., *Breaking the Chains: Slavery, Bondage, and Emancipation in Africa and Asia* (Madison: University of Wisconsin Press, 1993)

Lovejoy, Paul, and Toyin Falola (eds.), *Pawnship in Africa* (Boulder: Westview Press, 1993).

Lovejoy, Paul E. and Nicholas Rogers, *Unfree Labour in the Development of the Atlantic World* (London: Frank Cass, 1994).

Meillassoux, Claude, *The Anthropology of Slavery: The Womb of Iron and Gold* (Chicago: Chicago University Press, 1991). or for quick review see Joseph Miller, "The World According to Meillassoux: A Challenging but Limited Vision," *IJAHS*, 22:473-495 (1988).

Morrissey, Marietta, *Slave Women in the New World: Gender Stratification in the Caribbean* (Lawrence: University of Kansas Press, 1989)

Miers, Suzanne and Igor Kopytoff, *Slavery in Africa*

Miers, Suzanne, and Richard Roberts (eds.), *The End of Slavery in Africa* (1989)

Palmie, Stephan (ed.), *Slave Cultures and the Cultures of Slavery* (Knoxville: Universitty of Tenessee Press, 1995).

Patterson, Orlando, *Slavery and Social Death: A Comparative Study* (Cambridge, MA, 1982).

------, *Freedom, Vol. 1. Freedom in the Making of Western Culture* (New York: New York University Press, 1990).

Phillips, William D., Jr., *Slavery from Roman Times to the Early Transatlantic Trade* (Minneapolis, 1985)
Reid, Anthony (ed.), *Slavery, Bondage and Dependency in Southeast Asia* (St. Lucia, Queensland University Press, 1983).
Watson, James L. (ed.), *Asian and African Systems of Slavery* (Oxford: Blackwell, 1980).

Week E - Environmental History

Possible discussion openers:
1. Are Alfred Crosby, John MacKenzie, or Richard Grove successful in making a case for some kind of biological "imperialism?"
2. Is historical epidemiology a proper heading for the understanding of environmental history, or is it really a branch of the history of medicine, hence a specialized field within the broader history of science and technology? (Curtin, Migration, and McNeill, Plagues and Peoples)

Environmental Studies

Beinart, William and Peter Coates, *Environment and History: The Taming of Nature in the USA and South Africa* (New York: Routlege, 1995)
Crosby, Alfred W., Jr., *The Columbian Exchange: Biological and Cultural Consequences of 1492.*
-------, *Ecological Imperialism: The Biological Expansion of Europe, 900-1900.*
-------, *Germs and Seeds and Animals: Studies in Ecological History* (Armonk: M.E. Sharp, 1994)
Curtin, Philip D., *Death by Migration: Europe's Encounter with the Tropical World in the Nineteenth Century*
Dean, Warren, *Brazil and the Struggle for Rubber: A Study in Environmental History* (New York, CUP, 1987). Strongly revisionist of the previous views of the rise and fall of Brazilian rubber. Real cause of failure was a leaf blight. Study takes a strongly biological approach and looks at the history of science in projects and failures in Brazil and elsewhere.
Grove, Jean M., *The Little Ice Age* (New York: Methuen, 1988). A study of the climatic change over the past millennium, based on recorded changes in the positions and extent of glaciers everywhere in the world.
Grove, Richard, *Green Imperialism: Colonial Scientists, Ecological Crises and the History of Environmental Conecern* (Cambridge: Cambridge University Press, 1994)
Kiple, Kenneth F. (ed.), *The African Exchange: Toward a Biological History of Black People* (Durham: Duke University Press, 1987).

Larson, Clark Spencer, "Bioarchaeological Interpretations of Subsistence Economy and Behavior from Human Skeletal Remains," *Advances in Archaeological Method and Theory*, 10:339-445 (1987).

MacKenzie, John M. (ed.), *Imperialism and the Natural World* (Manchester, Manchester U. Press, 1990).

Ponting, Clive, *A Green History of the World: The Environment and the Collapse of Great Civilizations* (New York: St. Martin's Press, 1991)

McNeill, William, *Plagues and Peoples*

Richards, John F. and Richard P. Tucker (eds.), *World Deforestation in the Twentieth Century* (Durham, NC: Duke University Press, 1988). Has chapters by different authors on Kenya, Togo, Sahelian Africa, India, Thailand, and the US and USSR.

Smil, Vaclav, *Energy in World History* (Boulder: Westview Press, 1994).

-------, *Cycles of Life: Civilization and the Biosphere* (New York: Scientific American Library, 1997)

Turner, B. L. II, William C. Clark, Robert W. Kates, John F. Richards, Jessica T. Mathews, and William B. Meyer (eds.),*The Earth As Transformed by Human Action: Global and Regional Changes in the Biosphere over the Past 300 Years* (New York, Cambridge University Press, 1990)

Wrigley, T. M. L., M. J. Ingram, and G. Farmer (eds.), *Climate and History: Studies in Past Climates and their Impact on Man* (New York, Cambridge Press, 1981).

Week F - Cross-Cultural Images

Possible discussion openers:

1. In what ways were non-Western images of the West different from Western Images of the non-West? (See Adas in comparison with selected articles in Schwartz)
2. Is it proper or useful to study cross-cultural images held by ordinary people, as opposed to those that made a difference---the "official mind" of Gallagher and Robinson?
3. Are the images of the non-West in pictures different from those in words? (Could take Africa as a case in point and compare Curtin and Honour, or other material of this sort)

Image Studies

Adas, Michael, *Machines the Measure of Man*

Blakeley, Allison, *Blacks in the Dutch World: The Evolution of Racial Imagery in a Modern Society* (Bloomington: Indian University Press, 1993)

Cohen, William, *The French Encounter with Africans*

Curtin, Philip D., *The Image of Africa*

Curtin, Philip D. (ed.), *Africa and the West: Intellectual Responses to European Culture*

Devisse, Jean, and Michel Mollat, *The Image of the Black in Western Art: Volume 2 From the Chrsitian Era to the "Age of Discovery,"* 2 parts (New York: William Morrow, 1979).

Gordon, David C. *Images of the West: Third World Perspectives* (Savage, Md., Rowan and Littlefield, 1989).

Honour, Hugh, *The Image of the Black in Western Art: Volume 4, From the American Revolution to World War I,* 2 parts (Cambridge, Mass.: Harvard University Press, 1989).

Kartunen, Frances, *Between Worlds: Interpreters, Guides, and Suvivors* (New Brunswick: Rutgers Press, 1994).

Keen, Benjamin, *The Aztec Image in Western Thought*

Lewis, Bernard, *The Muslim Discovery of Europe* (New York: 1982)

Thompson, Ann*, Barbary and Enlightenment: European Attitudes toward the Magreb in the Eighteenth Century* (New York: Brill, 1987).

Raychaudhuri, Tapan, *Europe Reconsidered: Perceptions of the West in Nineteenth-Century Bengal* (Delhi: OUP, 1988)

Pagden, Anthony, *European Encounters with the New World* (New Haven: Yale Press, 1993)

Said, Edward, *Orientalism*

Schwartz, Stuart (ed.), *Implicit Understandings: Observing, Reporting, and Reflecting on the Encounters Between Europeans and Other Peoples in the Early Modern Era* (Cambridge: Cambridge Univerfsity Press, 1994). See especially aritcles by Anthony Reid and Ronald Toby

Spitzer, Leo, *Lives in Between: Assimilation and Marginality in Austria, Brazil, West Africa, 1780-1945* (Cambridge: Cambridge University Press, 1989).

Thompson, Lloyd, *Romans and Blacks* (London, Routledge, 1989).

Wachtel, Nathan, *The Visions of the Vanquished: The Spanish Conquest of Peru through Indian Eyes* (New York, Harper and Row, 1977).

Week G - Frontier Studies

Possible discussion openers:

Is such a thing as a general frontier theory possible, or are the frontier theoriests talking about too many different things under the same name?

1. Discuss this problem in relation to Kopytoff and Lattimore.
2. Discuss this problem in relation to Turner, Eccles, and Hennesy.
3. Discuss this problem in relation to two or more authorities of you own choice.

Frontier Studies

Adelman, Jeremy, *Frontier Development: Land, Labour, and Capital on the Wheatlands of Argentina and Canada, 1890-1914* (Oxfod: Clarendon Pess, 1994).

Careless, J. M. S., *Frontier and Metropolis: Regions, Cities, and Indentities in Canada before 1914* (Toronto: University of Toronto Press, 1989).

Duncan Baretta, Sylvio R., and John Markoff, "Civilization and Barbarism: Cattle Frontiers in Latin America," *Comparative Studies*, 20:587-618 (1978).

Ferguson, R. Brian, and Neil L. Whitehead (eds.), *War in the Tribal Zone: Expanding States and Indigenous Warfare* (Seattle: University of Washington Press, 1992)

Eccles, W. J., *The Canadian Frontier, 1534-1760*

Hennesy, Alistair, *The Frontier in Latin American History*

Jagchid, Sechin, *Peace, War, and Trade along the Great Wall: Nomadic-Chinese Interaction through Two Millennia* (Bloomington: Indiana University Press, 1989).

Kopytoff, Igor, *The African Frontier*

Lamar, Howard and Leonard Thompson, *The Frontier in History: North America and Southern Africa Compared* (New Haven: Yale Press, 1931)

Lattimore, Owen, *Inner Asian Frontiers of China*

-------, *Studies in Frontier History*

McNeill, Willliam, *The Great Frontier: Freedom and Hierarchy in Modern Times* (Princeton: Princeton University Press, 1983).

Rausch, Jane, *Where Cultures Meet: Frontiers in Latin American History* (Wilmington: Wilmington: SR Books, 1994)

Solberg, Carol E.,*The Prairies and the Pampas: Agrarian Policy in Canada and Argentina, 1880-1930* (Stanford: Stanford University Press, 1987)

Spicer, Edward, *Cycles of Conquest*

Turner, Frederick Jackson, *The Frontier in American History*

Wolfskill, George, and Stanley Palmer (eds.), *Essays on Frontiers in World History* (Austin: University of Texas Press, 1981).

Week H - Millennarian and Nativist Movements

Possible discussion openers:

1. To what extent is Thrupp or Worsley led astray by concentrating to a single culture area? What,if anything, would a cross cultural treatment have added?

2. Talmon concentrates on narrowly-defined "Millennarian" movements, while Adas used a more relaxed definition concentrating on anti-Western "nativist" revivalism. Would the answer be different in either case if a different kind of definition had been used.

Millennarian and Nativist Movement

Adas, Michael, *Prophets of Rebellion: Millennarian Protest Movements agaiinst the European Colonial Order.*

Burridge, Kenelm, *New Heaven New Earth: A Study of Millennarian Activities.*

Mair, L. P., "Independent Religious Movements on Three Continents," *CSSH,* 1:223-36 (1959).

Talmon, Yonina, "Millennarian Movements," *Archives europeenes de sociologie,* 7:159-200 (1966).

Thrupp, Sylvia L. (ed.), *Millennial Dreams in Action: Essays in Comparative Study*

Wallace, Anthony F. C., "Revitalization Movements," *American Anthropologist,* 58:264-81 (1956).

Worsley, Peter, *The Trumpet Shall Sound: A Study of "Cargo" Cults in Melanesia*

Week I - Urban History

Possible discussion openers:

1. Is it possible that Adams and Bairoch are in basic agreement, in spite of diffferences in nationality, previous specialization, and disciplinary training?
2. Do economic principles that cut through parochial cultural differences make possible the comparative study of urbanization (or of the relations between cities) in ways that are not the case for comparative revolutions or comparative slavery?

Urban History

Adams, Robert McC., *The Evolution of Urban Society.*

Bairoch, Paul, *Cities and Economic Development: From the Dawn of History to the Present* (Chicago: University of Chicago Press, 1988).

Broeze, Frank (ed.), *Brides of the Sea: Port Cities of Asia in the 16th-20th Centuries* (Honolulu, HA: University of Hawaii Press, 1989).

Lampard, Eric, "The Nature of Urbanization," in Derek Fraser and Anthony Sutcliffe, *The Pursuit of Urban History* (London: Arnold, 1983).

McClain, James L. and others, *Edo and Paris: Urban Life and the State in the Early Modern Era* (Ithaca: Cornell University Press, 1994).

Rozman, Gilbert, *Urban Networks in Russia, 1750-1800*

-------, *Urban Networks in Ch'ing China and Tokugawa Japan*

Skinner, G. William, The *City in Late Imperial China* (Stanford, 1977)

Week J - Cross-Regional Studies - Feudalism, Plantations, and Hydraulic Civilizations

Possible discussion openers:

1. It seems probable that the study of the Atlantic plantation complex or the slave trade is the study of a single institution that happens to have an inter-continental spread. Is this comparative history, or does something have to be added to make a genuine comparison?
2. How much is left of Oriental Despotism after Witfogel's critics have had their say?
3. Is either feudalism or cross-cultural trade a suitable subject for comparative analysis? If one, or the other, or both fail to meet the test---why?

Feudalism, Plantations, and Hydrolic Civilizations

Coulborn, Rushton (ed.), *Feudalism in History*

Curtin, Philip D., *Cross-Cultural Trade in World History*

-------, *The Atlantic Slave Trade: A Census*

-------, *The Rise and Fall of the Plantation Complex: Essays in Atlantic History*

Graduate and Professional Courses

Fredrickson, George, *White Supremacy: A Comparative Study of American and South African History*

Greenberg, Stanley, *Race and State in Capitalist Development: Comparative Perspectives. Deals with South Africa, Alabama, Israel, and Ulster.*

Pieterse, Jan P. Nederveen, *Empire and Emancipation: Power and Liberation on a World Scale* (New York, Praeger, 1989).

Witfogel, Karl, *Oriental Despotism*

Lewis, Archibald, *Nomads and Crusaders, A.D. 1000-1368* (Bloomington, Indiana Press, 1988).

Week K - Societies Ruled by Cultural Aliens

Possible discussion openers:

1. Few of these works compare two or more societies under Western Rule. Is this because two cultures are already enough to deal with at one time, or would a general assessment also be possible?

2. How does Farris's analysis differ from the earlier approach of Gibson?

3. How do the Andeanists (Spalding and Stern) differ from the MesoAmericanists (Farris and Gibson)?

Bacon, Elizabeth, *Central Asia Under Russian Rule*

Curtin, Phlip D., *Two Jamaicas*

Farris, Nancy, *The Maya under Spanish Rule*

Gibson, Charles, *The Aztecs under Spanish Rule: A History of the Indians of the Valley of Mexico, 1519-1810*

Phelan, John L., *The Hispanization of the Philippines*

Spalding, Karen, *Huarochiri: An Andean Society under Inca and Spanish Rule*

Stern, Steve J., *Peru's Indian Peoples and the Challenge of Spanish Conquest: Huamanga to 1640*

Bayly, C. A. and D. H. A. Kloff (eds.), *Two Colonial Empires: Copmparative Essays on the History of India and Indonesia in the Nineteenth century*

SAN DIEGO STATE UNIVERSITY
WORLD HISTORY FOR TEACHERS
SYLLABUS

History 496G

R. Dunn
Spring 1997

Course Description: This course for upper division undergraduate students explores topics in world history from early times to the eighteenth century C.E. The course is not a survey but rather addresses a number of questions about large-scale patterns of change in the global past and the development of civilizations within broad contexts of human interaction. The class also considers the problems and challenges of defining, conceptualizing, and organizing the study of world history. The course will give special attention to issues that prospective teachers are likely to face in teaching grades six and seven world history in California public schools. We will read and critically examine both the *California History - Social Science Framework* and the *National Standards for World History.* This is not, however, a course on social studies classroom methods and strategies but focuses on the subject matter content of world history and on the challenge of making world history intelligible. Therefore, the class should be of interest not only to Liberal Studies majors and students enrolled in the Social Science Single Subject Waiver program, but also to History or Social Sciences major or minors and any other students interested in better understanding the broad sweep of the human past.

To start probing the human past in world-scale terms, think about framing several kinds of questions on each topic we will consider. The following kinds of questions should prove useful to you as both student prospective teacher. All these types of questions have a dyanmic, probing quality. All require serious thought and study, and the answer to most of them will have a tentative quality. Any reasonable answer must also be supported by evidence.

Definitional Question: What is culture? What is a culture?" What is "civilization?" How is the "world" defined when we speak of world history?

Evidential Question: How does Jerry Bently support the assertion that the development of a civilization can only be understood in relation to neighboring peoples and societies?

Explanatory Question: How can we best understand the rapid expansion of Islam in the seventh and eighth centuries?

Graduate and Professional Courses

Policy or Decision Question: Should public money support schools that teach Afrocentric world history curriculum?

Speculative Question: Did China nearly achieve an industrial revolution between the 11th and 13th centuries?

Examinations: We will have a 15-20 minute quiz every week beginning with week two. All these tests, fourteen in all, will require writing a short essay. Questions will invariably relate to the language of a chapter heading or subheading included in the reading for that week. This procedure will be explained further in class. No make-ups of these weekly tests will be given for any reason. (Please do not ask!) Rather in calculating final grades, a student's two lowest quiz grades (including "zero" grades for absence) will be dropped.

On February 17 we will also have a 15-20 minute map quiz. Students must achieve a score of 76 out of 100 points on the question or repeat it on March 3 near the end of the class period. If a student does not pass the test the second time, the higher of the two grades will count toward the final grade. Any student who passes the test the first time may retake it to improve his or her grade. Study guides for the map quiz will be provided.

We will have a two-hour comprehensive final examination dealing with very broad issues that the course has addressed.

Class Format: The class will consist of informal lectures, discussions, and panel sessions on topics in world history. Because the class meets only once a week continuous attendance is essential. Come to class every time. (When I don't see you, I get worried!)

Papers and Discussions: Each week five or six students (depending on course enrollment) will submit and 3-4 page paper addressing a question posed on the syllabus. These same students will also give five minute presentations to the class on the question or questions that their paper addresses. All students will make notes on each presentation and prepared to discuss with the presenter the issues raised. All students in the class are expected to participate each week. All students will submit two papers and give two presentations during the semester. The principal aims of these paper assignments, presentations, and discussions are 1) to help you develop presentation skills, 2) to help you enhance your understanding of history as a critical discipline, 3) to introduce you to the new field of world history as a way of approaching the human past, 4) and to stimulate you to think about the challenges of teaching world history, not as a collection of "facts" or ideas about "other cultures," but as a complex set of patterns and processes that made the world what it is today.

All papers must be printed or typewritten and meet college-level standards of spelling, grammar, and style. I strongly urge you to purchase copies of both Kate Turabian, *A Manual for Writers of Term Papers*, and Strunk and White, *The Elements of Style*.

Graduate and Professional Courses

Weighting of Grades: Since all tests with the exception of the map quiz are essay type, the following proportionment of grades in only an approximation. A trend of improvement in exam scores will be taken into consideration in arriving at a final grade. Exams are not graded on a curve. Plus and minus grades will be awarded:

map quiz	5%
weekly quizzes	35% (12 recorded.grades x approx. 3% each)
first paper	10%
second paper	15%
final exam	15%
attendance, panel discussions, and participation	20%

Office: AH 4123, tel 594-6391 email dunn@mail.sdsu.edu
     Office Hours Wed. 9-12 and by appointment

Required Readings to Purchase:

> Richard Bulliet, et al., *The Earth and Its Peoples: A Global History*, vols. 1 & 2
> Jerry H. Bentley, *Old World Encounters: Cross-Cultural Contacts and Exchanges in Pre-Modern Times*
> Ross E. Dunn, *The Adventures of Ibn Battuta, a Muslim Traveler of the Fourteenth Century*
> Marshall G. S. Hodgson (Ed. Edmund Burke III), *Rethinking World History: Essays on Europe, Islam, and World History*
> Council on Islamic Education, *Teaching about Islam and Muslims in the Public School Classroom*
> National Center for History in the Schools, *National Standards for History*, Basic Edition
> California State Department of Education, *California History - Social Science Framework*

Week 1   Jan. 27

> Introduction
> Film: *Black Athena*

Week 2   Feb. 3

> What is the difference between world history that is teleological and world history that is not?
> Paper: How did all the continents of the Earth (excepting Antarctica) come to be populated by human beings?

Bulliet, ch. 1
Hodgson, ch. 1 (3-28)
Dunn, "Draft World History: Chapter 1" (handout)
Standards, pp. 14-24 and 137-139
Framework, pp. 57-58

Week 3   Feb. 10

Was agriculture discovered or was it invented?
Paper: Why did civilizations arise, when nobody seemed to need them for hundreds of thousands of years?

Bulliet, ch. 2
Standards, pp. 140-145
Framework, p. 58

Week 4   Feb. 17

Map Quiz

What has been the significance of encounters in world history between pastoral nomads and settled peoples?
Paper: How did the Afrasian region change during the Bronze Age (second millennium BCE)?

Bulliet, chs. 3 and 4
Standards, pp. 146-153

Week 5   Feb. 24

Is there a history of the Indo-Mediterranean region?
Paper: How should ancient Greece be viewed: The beginning of Western civilization, a Mediterranean civilization, an Indo-Mediterranean civilization, none of the above, a combination of the above?

Bulliet, ch. 5
Framework, pp. 58-59

Week 6   Mar. 3

What did the Roman and Han empires mean for the history of Afrasia?

Paper: Why are cross-cultural exchange and social conversion worth understanding as concepts in teaching and learning world history?
Make-up Map Quiz

> Bulliet, chs. 6 and 7
> Bentley, chs. 1 and 2
> Standards, pp. 146-153 (review)
> Framework, pp. 59-61

Week 7   Mar. 10

What was Islam and how did it reach so far across Afrasia so fast?
Paper: In what ways is the California History - Social Science Framework for sixth-grade world history? In what ways is it not?

> Bulliet, chs. 8 and 10
> Bentley, ch. 3
> Teaching about Islam, pp. 1-27
> Standards, pp. 154-163
> Framework, pp. 61-63

Week 8   Mar. 17

How did international trade contribute to the development of a trans-Hemispheric system of human interchange?
Paper: To understand changes in the world today, what do we need, if anything to understand about China between the 11th and 13th centuries?

> Bulliet, ch. 11
> Teaching about Islam, pp. 28-71
> Standards, pp. 164-173
> Framework, pp. 64-65

Spring Break

Week 9   March 31

What factors characterized Europe's growth and expansion from the 5th to the 13th centuries?
Paper: Why did Western and Central Europe develop "late" as an urban civilization?

> Bulliet, ch. 9

Framework, p. 66
Hodgson, ch. 7

Week 10   April 7

Were the Americas a "world apart?"
Paper: How did the fact that the peoples of the Americas did not share in the cultural exchanges of Afrasia make a difference in the course of Western Hemispheric history before 1500?

Bulliet, chs. 12 and 13
Framework, p. 65 (review)

Week 11   April 14

Did the modern age begin with the Mongols?
Paper: Who were the Mongols? The usual barbarians, savage monsters, great empire builders, intermediaries in cultural exchange? All or some of the above?

Bulliet, chs. 14 and 15
Bentley, ch. 4
Standards, pp. 164-173 (review)
Dunn, chs. 1-5

Week 12   April 21

Was the 14th a century of Afrasian crisis?
Paper: What significance did the Black Death have as a world-scale event?

Bulliet, ch. 16
Dunn, chs. 6-14

Week 13   April 28

What was the "great world convergence" and why did it happen?
How did the importance of Europeans in world history change between 1400 and 1600?

Bulliet, chs. 17-18
Bentley, ch. 5
Standards, pp. 174-184
Framework, pp. 66-68

Week 14   May 5

What was the Atlantic system of human interchange? How and why did it arise?
Paper: According to Hodgson, what was the great Western Transmutation? Did
something unique happen in Europe and in its relationship to the rest of the world
between the 16th and 18th centuries?

Bulliet, chs. 19-20
Hodgson, ch. 4

Week 15   May 12

Did the balance of world power "tip" between 1500 and 1800?
Paper: In what ways is the California History - Social Science Framework for seventh-
grade world history? In what ways is it not?

Bulliet, ch. 21 and 22

Carter V. Findley
The Ohio State University
Studies in World History.

Instructor: C. V. Findley
Office Hours: M, 3:30-5 & by appt
Hist. 700
e-mail: findley.1@osu.edu
Office: Dulles 238
Telephone: 292-5404

HISTORY 700: STUDIES IN WORLD HISTORY
[Autumn 1996, R, 1:30-3:30, Derby Hall 62, call no. 08551-7·]

COURSE OBJECTIVES
    Many historians, reacting to the specialization of the recent past and to challenges coming from other disciplines, seek reintegrative approaches to the study of history and are examining anew its relations with other fields in the humanities and social sciences. The goal of this course is to bring together history graduate students from a variety of specialized backgrounds to participate in this reintegrative effort by examining several different approaches to the formulation of a global perspective, as well as some of the challenges recently directed against macroconceptual approaches to history and other fields of study.
    To pursue this goal, we shall begin with world system theory, which has been the most influential and most contested approach to the conceptualization of world history in recent years. We shall examine influential works that develop this line of analysis from several disciplinary perspectives. Then we shall branch out to consider alternative ways of thinking about global interrelatedness, as well as attacks that some theorists have raised against the very idea of overarching conceptualizations of the kind world history represents.

COURSE REQUIREMENTS
    In this course, we shall all normally read the same books each week. Classes will be devoted primarily to discussions of the issues raised in the books. Different students will be asked to serve as facilitators in different weeks. Facilitators will come to class prepared to launch the discussion with a presentation of about fifteen minutes on the implications of that week's book for world history. In addition, each student will be asked to prepare a term paper, the basic format for which will be a review of the literature on one of the approaches to world history dealt with in the course.
    40% average of grades for analytical papers (about 5 pages) on weekly assignments, to be completed by none on Wednesday, with one copy to the instructor's mailbox and one for each member of the class deposited in a box at a location to be determined.
    20% facilitation of in-class discussions (rotational)

40% one paper (15-20 pages, typewritten, double-spaced, or equivalent), on a subject agreed on in advance with the instructor.

E-MAIL NETWORKS

Many of the subjects to be discussed in this course are currently the subjects of intense, ongoing debate over the e-mail networks for world history and world system studies. Members of the class are urged to sign up for these lists, and to follow and participate in the discussion. Information on how to do so will be made available in class. From time to time, the instructor will also forward selected messages to the members of the class.

ASSIGNED READINGS

The following titles have been ordered at SBX. In addition, an order has been placed to put one copy of each on closed reserve in the Main Library Reserve Room.

Wallerstein, Immanuel, *The Modern World-System*, 3 vols., San Diego, Academic Press, 1974-1989

Abu-Lughod, Janet L., *Before European Hegemony: The World System A.D. 1250-1350*, New York, Oxford U. Press, 1989

Wolf, Eric R., *Europe and the People Without History*, Berkeley and Los Angeles, U. of California Press, 1982

Braudel, Fernand, *Capital and Civilization, 15th-18th Century*, III: *Perspective of the World*, trans. Siacn Reynolds, New York, Harper and Row, 1984

Crosby, Alfred W., *Ecological Imperialism: The Biological Expansion of Europe, 900-1900*, New York, Cambridge U. Press, 1986

McNeill, William H., *The Pursuit of Power: Technology, Armed Force, and Society since A.D. 1000*, Chicago, U. of Chicago Press, 1982

Adas, Michael, *Machines as the Measure of Men: Science, Technology, and Ideologies of Western Dominance*, Ithaca, Cornell U. Press, 1989

Steven Best and Douglas Kellner, *Postmodern Theory: Critical Interrogations*, New York, Guilford Press, 1991

Other titles mentioned in the weekly assignments below (mostly articles) have not been ordered through the bookstore, but have been placed on reserve in the Main Library Reserve Room.

COURSE SCHEDULE

26 Spt.   Organizational Meeting; Clarification of Course Goals

3 Oct. Wallerstein, *Modern World System*, I, intro & chs. 2, 5, 6 & 7
        Wallerstein, *Modern World System*, II, intro & chs. 2, 3, & 6

Graduate and Professional Courses

10 Oct.	Wallerstein, *Modern World System*, III, entire
17 Oct.	Abu-Lughod, *Before European Hegemony* reviewed by Immanuel Wallerstein in *International Journal of Middle East Studies*, XXIV, 1 (1992), 128-31
24 Oct.	Wolf, *Europe and the People without History*
31 "	Braudel,*Civilization and Capitalism*, III: *Perspective of the World*, pp. 17-157, 177-235, 280-429, 480-535, 556-588, 619-632 (at least)
7 Nov.	Crosby, *Ecological Imperialism*, entire
14 Nov.	McNeill, *The Pursuit of Power: Technology, Armed Force, and Society since A.D. 1000*, Chicago, 1982, or Adas, *Machines as the Measure of Men*
21 "	Said, *Culture and Imperialism* Lewis D. Wurgraft, "Identity in World History: A Postmodern Perspective," in *World Historians and their Critics*, theme issue 34 of *History and Theory: Studies in the Philosophy of History*, edited by Philip Pomper, et al., 1995
28 Nov.	THANKSGIVING
5 Dec.	Best and Kellner, *Postmodern Theory* Geyer, Michael, and Charles Bright, "World History in a Global Age," *American Historical Review*, C, 4 (1995), 1034-60
12 "	Papers Due

Peter B. Golden
Rutgers University, Newark
Colloquium in Comparative History: The Islamic World in a Global Setting.

History 510:575
Colloquium in Comparative History
The Islamic World in a *Global Setting*
Thurs. : 2:30-5:30

Prof. Peter B. Golden
Spring, 1996

The purpose of this course is to introduce students to some of the current problems/points of discussion in the history of Islamic societies and their contacts with the Non-Islamic world. Readings will focus on the role of the Islamic lands in the pre-Modern World System, the problems of state formation in a frontier society, the articulation of social and economic systems (such as slavery), the encounter with Europe, Islamic societies as conquerors, colonizers and colonized. There are no prerequisites for this course.

Background reading
Marshall G. S. Hodgson, The *Venture of Islam:* Conscience *and History* in a *World* Civilization, 3 vols. (Chicago : University of Chicago Press, 1973)

Ira Lapidus, A History *of Islamic Societies* (Cambridge : Cambridge University Press, 1988)

R. M. Eaton, Islamic *History as Global History* (American Historical Association, Essays on Global and Comparative History, ed. M. Adas, Washington, D.C., 1990)

Discussion Topics and Reading Assignments

General Orientation
J.H. Bentley, *Old World Encounters. Cross-Cultural Contacts and Exchanges* in Pre-Modern Times (New York: Oxford University Press, 1993)

Optional:
S.A.M. Adshead, Central Asia in *World History* (New York: St. Martin's Press, 1993)

The Medieval Islamic World System
S.D. Goitein, A *Mediterranean Society,* Vol. 1, Economic Foundations (Berkeley: University of California Press, 1967)

A.M. Watson, Agricultural Innovation in the Early Islamic Period (Cambridge: Cambridge University Press, 1983)

Graduate and Professional Courses

Optional:
J. Abu-Lughod, Before European Hegemony. *The World* System *A.D. 1250-1350* (New York: Oxford University Press, 1989)

Slavery in Islamdom
B. Lewis, Race and Slavery in *the Middle East* (New York-Oxford: Oxford University Press, 1990)

The Ottoman Empire: Frontier Society and World Power
C. Kafadar, Between *Two Worlds. The Construction of the* Ottoman State (Berkeley : University of California Press, 1995)

P. Brummett, Ottoman *Seapower* and Levantine Diplomacy in *the Age of Discovery* (Albany: State University of New York Press, 1994)

Optional:
M.F. Köprülü, The *Origin of* the Ottoman State, trans. G. Leiser (Albany: State University of New York Press, 1992)

R.P. Lindner, Nomads and Ottomans in *Medieval* Anatolia (Indiana University Uralic and Altaic Series, vol. 144, Bloomington, Ind., 1983).

H. Inalcik, The Ottoman Empire: *The Classical Age, 1300-1600* (London: Weidenfeld & Nicolson, 1973)

Islam in South and Southeast Asia
D.E. Streu sand, The Formation *of the Mughal* Empire (Delhi : Oxford University Press, 1989)

R. Eaton, *The Rise of* Islam and *the Bengal Frontier 1204-1760* (Berkeley: University of California Press, 1993)

A. Reid, *Southeast Asia in the Age of Commerce 1450-1680,* vol. 2 : Expansion and *Crisis* (New Haven: Yale University Press, 1993)

Graduate and Professional Courses

The World of the Indian Ocean
K.N. Chaudhuri, Trade *and Civilization in* the Indian Ocean. An Economic *History* from *the Rise of* Islam to *1* 750 (Cambridge : Cambridge University Press, 1985)

K.N. Chaudhuri, *Asia Before Europe.* Economy and *Civilization of the* Indian Ocean from *the Rise of Islam to* 1750 (Cambridge : Cambridge University Press, 1990)

P. Risso, Merchants and Faitk Muslim Commerce and *Culture in the* Indian Ocean (Boulder, Colo. : Westview Press, 1995)

Muslim Encounters with Europe
B. Lewis, *The Muslim Discover-y of Europe* (New York: Norton, 1986)

T. Mitchell, *Colonizing Egypt* (Berkeley: University of California Press, 1988)

Graduate and Professional Courses

Allen M. Howard
Rutgers University
Colloquium in World History: The Atlantic.

510:541 COLLOQUIUM IN WORLD HISTORY: THE ATLANTIC   Spring, 1998

Instructor: Allen M. Howard

Office: Van Dyck 007A, Rutgers University
Hours: Tues. 1:00-1:45; Wed. 1:00-2:00 and by arrangement.
E-mail: <ahoward@rci.rutgers.edu> ph.:732-932-7142

This course is designed to provide participants with a foundation in some of the more important theoretical, comparative, and integrative issues in World History, and also with an understanding of particular aspects of the history of Western Africa, the circum-Caribbean, and to a lesser extent other areas of the Atlantic. Thus while class members are debating general questions, they will be supporting and illustrating their analysis with cases. The course is designed for people who will be minoring in World/ Comparative History, teaching a course in World History, or expanding a regional or topical course. For some, it may also prove relevant substantively or conceptually for dissertation research.

Atlantic history involves the flow of people, culture, ideas, commodities, and diseases; it looks at the many ways in which the regions have been interconnected and affected one another. The course examines the large systemic forces--particularly economic--that have shaped the Atlantic, but also looks at how people have challenged structures of economic, racial, and gender domination and have "made" history. Much of the problematic in world history involves the tensions between the local, regional, and global, and the also variations on common patterns. We do not approach the big questions of Atlantic history in only one mode: during some weeks we take a more historiographic approach, looking at how the literature has changed over time; in other weeks we try to construct themes and variations by looking at cases; in other weeks we mainly consider how to teach key issues. Topical bibliographies will be handed out. Because of its sweep, no one person can encompass all the relevant cases or theory. We will be most successful if each course member brings her or his own knowledge of particular places and readings to bear upon the big questions. Please suggest readings for the course and bibliographies.

Beginning January 28th, class members are asked to write a short paper each week responding to the readings; those papers should address a major issue that runs through the readings--analytic, historiographic, pedagogic. The papers are due on the day of discussion. For each week questions guiding the readings will be handed out in advance. In most weeks two people will serve as discussion leaders; ideally, discussants will meet in advance to prepare presentations. In certain weeks, readings are very numerous and no one is expected to cover all; some are core works and will be read by the whole group, others will be divided among class members according to interests.

Each class member will lead discussion 3-4 times during the semester and will write a 4-5 page analytic paper based on a topic relevant to that week's theme. Finally, everyone will either:

44

a) write a broad, integrative paper focusing on a major problem in Atlantic History, or b) create a syllabus for a course in Atlantic History, plus a paper discussing themes in the syllabus. A draft of a) or b) will be presented during the last session of the course, when we will also examine texts, major interpretive writings, etc.

The following books are available for purchase at the Recto and Verso Bookstore, 80 Albany St., New Brunswick (just north of the George St.-Albany St. intersection):

Abu-Lughod, J. Before European Hegemony. The World-System A.D. 1250-1350.
Adas, M., ed., Islamic and European Expansion. The Forging of a Global Order.
Barnes, S. Africa's Ogun: Old World and New.
Curtin, P. D. The Rise and Fall of the Plantation Complex. Essays in Atlantic History.
Gilroy, P. There Ain't No Black in the Union Jack.
Lovejoy, P. Transformations in Slavery.
Thornton, J. Africa and Africans in the Making of the Atlantic World, 1400-1680.

Each class member should build up detailed knowledge of one area of West or West Central Africa. A selection of recommended readings will be provided on a separate list. A few books will be available for purchase; these include:

S. Greene, Gender, Ethnicity, and Social Change on the Upper Guinea Coast. A History of the Anlo-Ewe.
D. Wright, The World and a Very Small Place in Africa.

Jan. 21   CONCEPTUALIZING WORLD HISTORY; ISLAM AND WORLD HISTORY

A. G. Frank and Barry K. Gills, "The 5,000-Year World System. An Interdisciplinary Introduction," in Frank and Gills, eds. The World System. 500 Years or 5000?, 3-55.

L. Shaffer, "Southernization," Journal of World History 5:1 (1994), 1-22.

J. Abu-Lughod, "The World System in the Thirteenth Century: Dead-End or Precursor," in Adas, Expansion, 75-102.

R. M. Eaton, "Islamic History as World History," in Adas, Expansion, 1-36.

S. Stern, "Africa, Latin America, and the Splintering of Historical Knowledge: From Fragmentation to Reverberation," in F. Cooper, et al.. Confronting Historical Paradigms, 3-20.

L. Benton, "From the World Systems Perspective to Institutional World History: Culture and Economy in Global Theory," in Journal of World History, 7:2 (1996), 261-295.

Jan. 28   CONTINUATION OF Jan. 21; WEST AFRICA BEFORE 1500

In this week we: 1) examine Abu-Lughod's approach more fully; 2) assess the reasons for including parts of West (and East) Africa in the 13th and 14th-century system; and 3) begin to build detailed knowledge of sub-regions in West Africa, as preparation for studying the Atlantic slave trade and the carry-over of culture to the Americas.

J. Abu-Lughod, Before European Hegemony. The World-System A.D. 1250-1350. All should skim ch. 1, read 102-134, 212-247, 312-373.Discussion leaders could read additional sections.

J. O. Voll, "Islam as a Special World-System, Journal of World History 5:2 (1994), 213-226.

N. Levtzion, "The Early States of the Western Sudan," in J. F. A. Ajayi and M. Crowder, eds., History of West Africa Vol I. 3rd ed., 129-166.

P. Lovejoy, Transformations in Slavery, 23-35.

Discussion leaders should present more of the texture of her argument using regional case studies in the book and also some of the criticisms of Abu-Lughod's project based on commentaries accompanying her early article:

J. Abu-Lughod, "The Shape of the World System in the Thirteenth Century," and commentaries, Studies in Comparative International Development 22:4 (1987-88), 3-53.

It is important for course members to build up a foundation in one area in West and West Central Africa, especially an area whose people and cultures have been significant in the history of the Americas. Selected readings will be available; these include the following:

Western Sudan, Senegambia and neighboring areas (Mande-speakers in particular):

G. Connah, "An Optimal Zone: The West African Savanna," African Civilizations, 97-120.

G. Brooks, "Social and Cultural Paradigms," in Landlords and Strangers. Ecology, Society and Trade in Western Africa, 1000-1630, 33-57.

P. McNaughton, The Mande Blacksmiths, 11-21.

Graduate and Professional Courses

Bight of Benin and neighboring areas (Yoruba-speakers in particular):

G. Connah, "Brilliance Beneath the Trees: the West African Forest and its Fringes," African Civilizations, 121-149.

R. Smith, Kingdoms of the Yoruba (3rd ed.), 13-41, 87-98.

R. F. Thompson, "Black Saints Go Marching In," Flash of the Spirit, 3-18.

Congo/Angola area (Kongo-speakers in particular):

D. Birmingham, "Society and Economy before A. D. 1400," in D. Birmingham and P. Martin, eds., History of Central Africa, 1-29.

J. Vansina, "The Southwest: The Growth of States," in Paths in the Rainforest, 146-158.

R. F. Thompson, "The Sign of the Four Moments of the Sun," Flash of the Spirit, 103-127.

Feb. 4 QUESTIONS ABOUT THE "TRANSITION TO CAPITALISM," THE ECONOMIC DEVELOPMENT OF EUROPE, AND EUROPEAN EXPANSION ABROAD

F. Fernandez-Armesto, Before Columbus: Exploration and Colonisation from the Mediterranean to the Atlantic, 1229-1492, 43-60, 169-202, 212-217.

R. S. Duplessis, Transitions to Capitalism in Early Modern Europe, 3-13, 28-45, 88-101, 111-140, 190-206, 237-252, 286-309

I. Wallerstein, The Modern World System I: Capitalist Agriculture and the Origins of the European World-Economy in the Sixteenth Century, read 15-63, read 85-104, skim 105-129, read 165-221, skim 225-297, read 325-344.

L. Kaba, "Archers, Musketeers, and Mosquitoes: The Moroccan Invasion of the Sudan and the Songhay Resistance (1591-1612)," JAH (Journal of African History) 22 (1981), 457-475.

A. W. Crosby, Ecological Imperialism, 70-103, 269-308.

S. Stern, "Feudalism, Capitalism, and the World-System in the Perspective of Latin America and the Caribbean," in Cooper, et.al., Paradigms, 23-83. For Stern's original article and critical comments on it, see AHR 93:4 (1988), 829-897.**

Graduate and Professional Courses

W. H. McNeill, "The Age of Gunpowder Empires, 1450-1800, in Adas, Expansion, 103-139.

The so-called "Brenner debate" provides a context for the above. For those who wish more background, see: R. Brenner, "Agrarian Class Structure and Economic Development in Pre-Industrial Europe" (skim for main points)
    E. Le Roy Ladurie, "A Reply to Robert Brenner"
    R. H. Hilton, "A Crisis of Feudalism"

Feb. 11   TEACHING THE DEBATES ABOUT 1492, 1519, AND THEREAFTER: ENCOUNTER/EXCHANGE/EXPLOITATION/GENOCIDE

I. Clendinnen, Aztecs. An Interpretation, 15-44, 68-83, 111-140; optional 236-263.

A. Crosby, "The Columbian Voyages, the Columbian Exchange, and Their Historians," in Adas, Expansion, 141-164.

H. J. Viola and C. Margolis, Seeds of Change. A Quincentennial Commemoration, survey for contents and tone.

B. Bigelow, "Two Myths Are Not Better Than One," Monthly Review (July-Aug., 1992), 28-48. A discussion leader should review Rethinking Columbus.

R. Shafer, "Exchange\Encounter Theory and the Myths of America" and "A Response," Monthly Review (Dec., 1992), 40-51.

D. Stannard, American Holocaust. The Conquest of the New World, 195-258.

F. Karttunen, "After the Conquest: The Survival of Indigenous Patterns of Life and Belief," Journal of World History 3:2 (1992), 239-256.

This will be one of the weeks devoted to discussing teaching strategies and materials. Discussion leaders should read M. Leon- Portilla, The Broken Spears. The Aztec Account of the Conquest of Mexico (2nd ed.), and may wish to draw upon other primary sources useful for teaching, e.g. P. Hulme and N. L. Whitehead, Wild Majesty. Encounters with Caribs from Columbus to the Present Day.

Someone may wish to compare the arguments in the readings of Feb. 4, Feb. 11 and certain later weeks with those in a teaching survey or textbook: See P. Stearns, M. Adas, and S. Schwartz, World Civilization: The Global Experience; E. Wolf, Europe and the People without History; R.Strayer, et.al., The Making of the Modern World. Connected Histories, Divergent Worlds (1500 to the Present); K. Reilly, The West and the World; R. W. Bulliet, et.al., The Earth and Its People. A Global History, II.

Feb. 18   AFRICAN INVOLVEMENT IN THE SLAVE TRADE AND IMPACTS UPON
AFRICA; QUESTIONS OF TRANSFORMATION AND UNDERDEVELOPMENT

P. D. Curtin, Plantation Complex, 3-45, 113-143. Those without a background in the material of Feb.
18-Mar. 11 will find it beneficial to read all of Curtin as soon as possible.

J. Thornton, Africa and the Africans, xi-xxxviii, 1-125.

W. MacGaffey, "Dialogues of the Deaf: Europeans on the Atlantic Coast of Africa," in S. B.
Schwartz, ed. Implicit Under-standings: Observing, Reporting, and Reflecting on the Encounters
between Europeans and Other Peoples in the Early Modern Era, 249-267.

P. Lovejoy, Transformations in Slavery, 1-22, 35-65, 66-87, 88- 107,108-134.

W. Rodney, How Europe Underdeveloped Africa, 95-113.

D. Henige, "Measuring the Immeasurable: The Atlantic Slave Trade, West African Population and
the Pyrrhonian Critic," JAH 27(1986), 295-313.

We will debate the arguments in a number of major articles that present different case studies and
theses about slavery and the slave trade. A separate list will be provided, but the articles include W.
Rodney, "African Slavery and Other Forms of Social Oppression on the Upper Guinea Coast in the
Context of the Atlantic Slave-Trade," JAH 7 (1966), 431-43, and J. D. Fage, "Slavery and the Slave
Trade in the Context of West African History," JAH 10 (1969), 393-404.

During this week or in one of the next two weeks, leaders may wish to review and discuss documents
for use in teaching: see, for example, P. D. Curtin, Africa Remembered and R. E. Conrad, Children
of God's Fire. A Documentary History of Black Slavery in Brazil.

Feb. 25   GENDER, CLASS, ETHNICITY, AND RACE IN THE ERA OF SLAVERY

Curtin, Plantation Complex, 46-110.

Thornton, Africa and Africans, 162-182.

P. Manning, Slavery and African Life, 60-85. This is a major book and was required the last time
the course was taught; one discussant should read it in entirety and present its theses.

C. C. Robertson and M. Klein, eds., "Women's Importance in African Slave Systems," in Robertson
and Klein, eds. Women and Slavery in Africa, 3-25.

Graduate and Professional Courses

H. S. Klein, "African Women in the Atlantic Slave Trade," in Robertson and Klein, Women and Slavery, 29-38.

D. Eltis and S. Engerman, "Was the Slave Trade Dominated by Men," The Journal of Interdisciplinary History 23:2 (1992), 237-258.

B. L. Mouser, "Women Slavers of Guinea-Bissau," in Robertson and Klein, Women and Slavery, 320-239.

G. E. Brooks, "The Signares of Saint-Louis and Goree: Women Entrepreneurs in Eighteenth-Century Senegal," in N. J. Hafkin and E. G. Bay, eds. Women in Africa. Studies in Social and Economic Change, 19-44.

D. L. Schafer, Anna Kingley; see also "Anta Majigeen Ndiaye, A Wolof Woman in Florida and Haiti: A Biographical Examination of African Cultural Patterns in New World Settings" (unpub.)

R. Dunn, Sugar and Slaves: The Rise of the Planter Class in the English West Indies, 1624-1713, 84-116, 263-281.

F. Cooper, Plantation Slavery on the East African Coast, 253-268.

B. Bush, Slave Women in Caribbean Society, xi-50.

B. Moitt, "Women, Work and Resistance in the French Caribbean during Slavery, 1700-1848' in V. Shepherd et.al., Engendering History. Caribbean Women in Historical Perspective, 155-175.

S. M. Socolow, "Economic Roles of Free Women of Color of Cap Francais," in D. B. Gaspar and D. C. Hine, More than Chattel: Black Women and Slavery in the Americas, 279-297.

M. Karash, ""Slave Women on the Brazilian Frontier in the 19th Century," in Gaspar and Hines, More than Chattel, 79-96.

J. E. Mason, "Paternalism Under Siege. Slavery in Theory and Practice During the Era of Reform, c. 1825 through Emancipation," in N. Worden and C. Crais, eds., Breaking the Chains. Slavery and its Legacy in the Nineteenth-Century Cape Colony, 45-77.

D. G. White, Ar'n't I a Woman. Female Slaves in the Plantation South, 119-141.

Mar. 4 AFRICAN RELIGIOUS INFLUENCES AND DYNAMICS IN ATLANTIC COMMUNITIES

Thornton, Africa and Africans, 183-271.

H. S. Klein, "Creation of a Slave Community and Afro-American Culture" African Slavery in Latin America and the Caribbean, 163-187.

Barnes, S. Africa's Ogun, Old World and New, xiii-25, 39-64, 263-289, 105-146, 173-198, 353-367.

J. M. Murphy, Working the Spirit, 114-144.

J. D. Y. Peel, Ijeshas and Nigerians, 164-174.

Anyone unfamiliar with the Frasier-Herskovits debate may wish to read J. Raboteau, Slave Religion, 44-92 and/or J. E. Holloway ed., Africanisms in American Culture.
Groups may wish to study religious change in West Africa, especially the importance of Islamic reform movements, missionary Christianity, and syncretistic beliefs and practices.

Mar. 11 IDEOLOGIES AND STRUGGLES FOR LIBERTY; ABOLITION AND ITS AFTERMATH

Curtin, Plantation Complex, 144-206

Thornton, Africa and Africans, 272-303.

M. Craton, "From Caribs to Black Caribs," in G. Y. Okihiro, ed., In Resistance. Studies in African, Caribbean, and Afro-American History, 96-116.

P. Linebaugh and M. Rediker, "The Many-headed Hydra: Sailors, Slaves, and the Atlantic Working Class in the 18th Century," Journal of Historical Sociology 3:3 (1990), 225-252.

S. W deGroot, "A Comparison between the History of Maroon Communities in Surinam and Jamaica," in Heuman, Out of the House of Bondage, 173-184.

Bush, Slave Women, 51-82, 162-167.

D. Geggus, "The Haitian Revolution" in F. Knight and C. Palmer, eds., The Modern Caribbean, 21-50.

Graduate and Professional Courses

P. H. Wood, "'The Dream Deferred': Black Freedom Struggles on the Eve of White Independence," in G. Y. Okihiro, ed. In Resistance, 166-187.

D. Tomich, "Contested Terrains. Houses, Provision Grounds...in Post-Emancipation Martinique," in M. Turner, ed. From Chattel Slaves to Wages Slaves, 241-257 (read introduction as well).

M. Craton, "The Baptist War: The Jamaican Rebellion of 1831-1832," in Testing the Chains, 291-334.

T. C. Holt, The Problem of Freedom. Race, Labour, and Politics in Jamaica and Britain, 1832-1938, 3-51, 381-402.

K. McC. Brown, "Systematic Remembering, Systematic Forgetting: Ogou in Haiti," in S. Barnes, ed., Africa's Ogun, 65-89.

J. Peterson, Province of Freedom, 27-44, 45-48, 81-85, 189-226.

P. Lovejoy, "Fugitive Slaves: Resistance to Slavery in the Sokoto Caliphate," in G. Y. Okihiro, In Resistance, 71-95.

V. Bickford-Smith, "Meanings of Freedom. Social Position and Identity among Ex-slaves and Their Descendants in Cape Town," in Worden and Crais, ed., Breaking the Chains, 289-312.

R. Roberts, "The End of Slavery in the French Soudan, 1905-1914," in S. Miers and R. Roberts, eds., The End of Slavery in Africa, 282-307. The introduction is a fine overview.

L. M. Heywood, "Slavery and Forced Labor in the Changing Political Economy of Central Angola, 1850-1949," in Miers and Roberts, End of Slavery, 415-436.

For the study of resistance and revolt, each course member should select a case study that matches an area in Africa in order to address questions about the carry over to the Americas of patterns of leadership, institutions, etc. Among the works available are:

J. J. Reis, Slave Rebellion in Brazil: The Muslim Uprising of 1835 in Bahia, 73-136.

S. Schwartz, "Rethinking Palmares: Slave Resistance in Colonial Brazil" in Schwartz, Slaves, Peasants, and Rebels. Reconsidering Brazilian Slavery, 103-136.

R. Thornton, "I Am the Subject of the King of Congo': African Political Ideology and the Haitian Revolution," Journal of World History 4:2 (Fall, 1993), 181-214. (read with Geggus)

Discussion leaders may wish to review the thesis of E. Genovese in From Rebellion to Revolution.

Mar. 25   FROM   MERCANTILE   CAPITAL   TO   INDUSTRIAL   CAPITAL: "ARTICULATION" QUESTIONS 1700-1850

Review L. Benton article listed for Jan. 21.

A. K. Smith, "Where was the Periphery?: The Wider World and the Core of the World-Economy," Radical History Review 39 (1987), 28-48.

P. Lovejoy, Transformations in Slavery, 135-183, 246-282.

E. Williams, Capitalism and Slavery, 51-84, 98-107, 135-153, 169-212.

P. K. O'Brien, "European Economic Development: The Contribution of the Periphery," The Economic History Review 35 (1982) 1-18.

B. Solow, Capitalism and Slavery in the Exceedingly Long Run," in B. L. Solow and S. L. Engerman, British Capitalism and Caribbean Slavery, The Legacy of Eric Williams, 1-77 and other chs.

D, Eltis, Economic Growth and the Ending of the Transatlantic Slave Trade, 3-28.

S. Mintz, Sweetness and Power, 151-186.

P. K. O'Brien, "Intercontinental Trade and the Development of the Third World since the Industrial Revolution," Journal of World History, 75-133.

R. Barnet and J. Cavanaugh, "A Globalizing Economy," in B. Mazlish and R. Buultjens, Conceptualizing Global History, 153-171

Apr. 1 GENDER, ETHNICITY, RACE, CLASS AND NATION IN THE IMPERIAL ERA AND TODAY

M. Adas, "'High' Imperialism and the 'New' History," in Adas, Expansion, 311-344.

P. Wolfe, "History and Imperialism: A Century of Theory, from Marx to Postcolonialism," American Historical Review 102:2 (1997), 388-420. (read for historiographic overview)

M. Strobel, "Gender, Sex, and Empire," in Adas, Expansion, 345-375;
skim J. Tucker, "Gender and Islamic History," in Adas, 37-73
Also select articles from N. Chaudhuri and M. Strobel, eds., Western Women and Imperialism.

B. S. Cohen, Colonialism and Its Forms of Knowledge, 3-15.

S. Thorne, "'The Conversion of Englishmen and the Conversion of the World Inseparable,' Missionary Imperialism and the Language of Class in Early Industrial Britain," in F. Cooper and A. L. Stoler, eds. Tensions of Empire. Colonial Cultures in a Bourgeois World, 238-262.

A. Stoler, "Making Empire Respectable: The Politics of Race and Sexual Morality in 20th-Century Colonial Cultures," American Ethnologist (1989), 634-660.

A. Stoler, Race and the Education of Desire, 95-136.

M. Adler, "Skirting the Edges of Civilization': Two Victorian Women Travellers and 'Colonial Spaces' in South Africa," in K. Darian-Smith, et al., eds. Text, Theory, Space. Land, Literature and History in South Africa and Australia, 83-98.

John L. Comaroff, "Images of Empire, Contests of Conscience. Models of Colonial Domination in South Africa," in F. Cooper and A. L. Stoler, eds. Tensions of Empire, 163-197.

I. Hofmeyer, "Building a Nation from Words: Afrikaans Language, Literature, and Ethnic Identity, 1902-1924," in S. Marks and S. Trapido, eds., The Politics of Race, Class and Nationalism in 20th Century South Africa, 95-123.

I. Goldin, "The Reconstitution of Coloured Identity in the Western Cape," in S. Marks and S. Trapido, eds., The Politics of Race, Class and Nationalism in 20th Century South Africa, 156-187.

G. Mare, Ethnicity and Politics in South Africa, 52-95.

R. Nixon, "Of Balkans and Bantustans: Ethnic Cleansing and the Crisis in National Legitimation," in Transition 60: 4-32.

A. Howard and D. E. Skinner, "Ethnic Leadership and Class Formation in Freetown, Sierra Leone," in N. W. and N. Z. Keith, eds., New Perspectives on Social Class and Socioeconomic Development in the Periphery, 83-118.

K. R. Haraksingh, "Structure and Process and Indian Culture in Trinidad," in H. Johnson, ed., After the Crossing. Immigrants and Minorities in Caribbean and Creole Society, 113-122.

E. N. Wilmsen, "Premises of Power in Ethnic Politics," E. N. Wilmsen and P. McAllister, eds. The Politics of Difference. Ethnic Premises in a World of Power, 1-24, 189-205.

N. Ignatiev, How the Irish Became White, 34-59, 148-188.

J. Nash, "The Revindication of Indigenous Identity: Mayan Responses to State Intervention in Mexico." unpubl. paper.

E.Z.L.N. Manifesto, 2 March, 1994.

A. Gupta and J. Ferguson, "Beyond 'Culture': Space, Identity, and the Politics of Difference," Cultural Anthropology 7:1 (1992), 6-23.

The course was planned to include L. Spitzer, Lives in Between. Assimilation and Marginality in Austria, Brazil, West Africa 1780-1945. The book is out of print, but is highly recommended.

Apr. 8 "DEVELOPMENT," SPACE, AND POLITICAL ECOLOGY IN ATLANTIC HISTORY

T. Silver, A New Face on the Countryside. Indians, Colonists, and Slaves in the South Atlantic Forests, 1500-1800, 104-138, 186-198. (or read D. Watts)

D. Watts, The West Indies. Patterns of Development, Culture and Environmental Change since 1492, 382-405, 484-539.

K. Reilly, "Energy and Environment," in The West and the World. A History of Civilization, 145-161.

E. R. Wolf, "The Movement of Commodities," in Europe and the People without History, 310-353.

D. Harvey, The Condition of Post Modernity, 240-283.

D. Worster, Dust Bowl. The Southern Plains in the 1930s, 80-117, 210-243.

R. A. Austen, African Economic History, 122-147.

M. Cowen and R. Shenton, "The Invention of Development," in J. Crush, ed., Power of Development, 27-43.

M. J. Watts, "Living Under Contract: Work, Production Politics, and the Manufacture of Discontent in a Peasant Society," in A. Pred and M. J. Watts, Reworking Modernity: Capitalisms and Symbolic Discontent, 64-105.

R. A. Schroeder, "Shady Practice: Gender and the Political Ecology of Resource Stabilization in Gambian Garden/Orchards," Economic Geography 69:4 (1993), 349-365.

Graduate and Professional Courses

K. Manzo, "Black Consciousness and the Quest for a Counter-Modernist Development," in Crush, Power, 228-252.

J. Agnew and S. Corbridge, Mastering Space, 211-227.

J. O'Connor, "Is Sustainable Capitalism Possible," in M. O'Connor, ed. Is Capitalism Sustainable. Political Economy and the Politics of Ecology, 152-175.

Apr. 15   LABOR SEGMENTATION, GENDER, RACE, AND CLASS CONSCIOUSNESS

P. Stearns, "Interpreting the Industrial Revolution," in Adas, Expansion, 199-242.

L. Tilly, "Industrialization and Gender Inequality," in Adas, Expansion, 243-310.

Smith, "Class, skill and sectarianism in Glasgow and Liverpool, 1880-1914," in R. J. Morris, ed, Class, Power and Social Structure in British Nineteenth Century Towns, 158-215.

L. Tabili, "Labour Migration, Racial Formation and Class Identity. Some Reflections on the British Case," North West Labour History 20 (1995-96), 16-35.

D. Northrup, Indentured Labor in the Age of Imperialism, 1834-1922, 1-42.

E. R. Wolf, "The New Laborers," in Europe and the People Without History, 254-283.

C. A. Brown, "Testing the Boundaries of Marginality: Twentieth-Century Slavery and Emancipation Struggles in Nkanu, Northern Igboland, 1920-1929," JAH 37:1 (1996), 51-80.

K. E. Atkins, "'Kafir Time': Preindustrial Temporal Concepts and Labour Discipline in Nineteenth-Century Colonial Natal," JAH 29 (1988), 229-244.

T. Maloka, "The Struggle for Sunday: All-Male Christianity in the Gold Mine Compounds," in R. Elphick and R. Davenport, eds. Christianity in South Africa. A Political, Social, and Cultural History, 242-252.

I. Berger, "Sources of Class Consciousness: South African Women in Recent Labor Struggles," International Journal of Africa Historical Studies 16:1 (1983), 49-66.

V. A. Shepherd, "Indian Women in Jamaica, 1845-1945," in F. Birbalsingh, ed., Indenture and Exile. The Indo-Caribbean Experience, 100-107.

Graduate and Professional Courses

P. Mohammed, "Writing Gender into History. The Negotiation of Gender Relations among Indian Men and Women in Post-Indenture Trinidad Society," in V. Shepherd, et al., Engendering History. Caribbean Women in Historical Perspective, 20-47.

J. Nash, "The Impact of the Changing International Division of Labor...," in J. Nash and M. P. Fernandez-Kelly, ed., Women, Men and the International Division of Labor, 3-38.

H. I. Safa, "Women and Industrialisation in the Caribbean," in S. Stichter and J. L. Parpart, eds., Women, Employment and the Family in the International Division of Labour, 72-97.

Watts and I. Boal, "Working Class Heroes. E. P. Thompson and Sebatiao Salgado," Transition 68 (1995), 90-115.

Apr. 22   USING AUTOBIOGRAPHIES, BIOGRAPHIES, AND NOVELS TO TEACH WORLD HISTORY

During this week, course members will read an autobiography, biography (or collective biography), or novel that relates to one or more of the themes in this course and prepare a paper on how to use that work in teaching a survey in world history.

A. M. Howard, "Teaching about Gender, Ethnicity, Race, and Class: Using African Biography and Autobiography," in E. G. Friedman, et al., Creating an Inclusive College Curriculum, 82-89.

In addition, there are many newly published works, such as:
L. Denzer, Constance Agatha Cummings-John. Memoirs of a Krio Leader.
C. Johnson-Odim and N. E. Mba, For Women and the Nation. Funmilayo Ransome-Kuti of Nigeria.

Apr. 29   RACE, ETHNIC, CLASS, AND GENDER IDENTITIES AND POLITICS IN THE METROPOLE; CULTURE AND THE CHALLENGES TO RACISM AND WESTERN HEGEMONY; DIASPORAS AND NEW REVERBERATIONS

P. Gilroy, There Ain't No Black in the Union Jack.

A. McClintock, "No Longer in a Future Heaven. Nationalism, Gender, and Race," in Imperial Leather. Race, Gender and Sexuality in the Colonial Contest, 353-389.

G. W. Johnson, "The Impact of the Senegalese Elite on the French, 1900-1940," in G. W. Johnson, Double Impact, 155-178.

Graduate and Professional Courses

D. Frost, "Ethnic Identity, Transience and Settlement: The Kru in Liverpool since the Late Nineteenth Century," in D. Killingray, ed., Blacks in Britain, 88-106.

S. Hall, "Cultural Identity and Diaspora," in J. Rutherford, ed., Identity, 222-237.

P. Gilroy, The Black Atlantic, 1-40, 187-223 (and some critiques)

J. Clifford, "Diasporas" Cultural Anthropology 9:3 (1994), 302-338.

H. Campbell, "Rastafari: Culture of Resistance," Race and Class XXII:1 (1980), 1-22.

Beriss, D. "Scarves, Schools and Segregation: The Foulard Affair," French Politics and Society 8 (1990), 1-13.

D. J. Cosentino, "Repossession: Ogun in Folklore and Literature," in Barnes, Ogun, 290-314.

P. Scher, "Unveiling the Orisha," in Barnes, Ogun, 315-331.

D. A. Hollinger, "How Wide the Circle of 'We'? American Intellectuals and the Problem of the Ethnos since World War II," AHR 98:2 (1993), 317-337.

Exam period May 6:   TEACHING ABOUT THE ATLANTIC: We will organize around final paper topics and:

a) discuss broad interpretive writings on world history (please review those already read and select from those listed below).

b) assess the use major texts--Bulliet et al.; Reilly; Strayer et al.; Stearns, Adas, and Schwartz; and Wolf--for teaching undergraduate World History courses.

c) examine syllabi for World/Atlantic History courses. This will include the syllabi published in the Marcus Weiner series, syllabi and articles in Radical History Review, and syllabi developed by graduate students and faculty at Rutgers University and elsewhere.

d) critique contemporary "travel writing" by "experts" who manufacture stereotypical images of the "Third World" for "western" readers. (See N. Farah, "Highway to Hell. The Travel-Writing of Disaster," Transition 70 (1996), 60-70.)

For this week select from the following:

Graduate and Professional Courses

M. Adas, "Bringing Ideas and Agency Back In: Representation and the Comparative Approach to World History," unpub.

C. Bright and M. Geyer, "For a Unified History of the World in the Twentieth Century," Radical History Review 39 (1987), 69-91.

F. Cooper, "Conflict and Connection: Rethinking Colonial African History," American Historical Review 99:5 (1994), 1516-1545.

W. A. Green, "Periodization in European and World History," Journal of World History, 3:1 (1992), 13-53.

B. K. Gills, "Hegemonic Transitions in the World System," in Frank and Gills, eds., The World System, 115-140.

B. Mazlish, "Global History in a Postmodernist Era?," in Mazlish and Buultjens, Conceptualizing, 113-127.

H. Rebel, "Cultural Hegemony and Class Experience: A Critical Reading of Recent Ethnological-Historical Approaches," American Ethnologist (1989), 117-136, 350-365.

I. Wallerstein, "World System vs. World-Systems," in Frank & Gills

II.

Surveys

Survey Courses: Full

George E. Brooks
University of Indiana, Bloomington
Themes in World History

B391
Themes in World History

Mr. Brooks   **Fall 1996**

Brooks, G.E., Getting Along Together: World History Perspectives for the Twenty-First
  Century (1994)
McNeill, W., A World History (C.U.P., 2nd ed. with maps, 1971 is preferable to 3rd ed.,
  (1979) D21 M175
World Map, National Geographic Magazine (December 1988) Try your family garage and
  second-hand bookstores.
_____ Hammond Comparative World Atlas
  _____ The Economist is recommended reading for the course. Current (via air mail) issues are
    available at the Periodical Room of the Library and the School of Business Library. (Note
    that student and faculty subscriptions are half-price.)
  The Aspen World History Handbook (1994) includes lesson plans, book reviews, and other
    materials prepared by teachers. D16.2 .A86 1994

There will be a practice map quiz on _____, a mini-exam on _____ 10% of grade, a midterm
examination on _____ 35%, a second mini-exam on _____ 10%, and a final examination on
_____ 45%. Undergraduates are responsible for a short paper analyzing a "less-developed" country.
Graduate students have the option of a term paper or preparing a lesson plan incorporating a World History
topic.

World outline maps (Denoyer-Geppert 24099 or 25099 or Rand McNally Robinson Projection) are available
at the bookstore. Bring a map to class for the practice map quiz on _____, and for each examination.
You will be tested from the following list. Not all the following are on the map handout, which is intended
only as a guide. Use large scale maps in atlases in the Library Reference Room to ensure precise locations.
You are also responsible for knowing the world's principal ecological areas depicted in the Physical
Environment Map at the back of McNeill, A World History (1st and 2nd editions only).

OCEANS AND SEAS

Black	Persian Gulf	Arabian	Caspian
Adriatic	South China	Red	Yellow
Baltic	Aegean	Indian	

Survey Courses: Full

RIVERS

Amazon	Yellow/Hwang Ho	Zambezi	Senegal
Ganges	Niger	Rhine	Jaxartes/Syr-Darya
Nile	Congo/Zaire	Danube	
Indus	Yangtze		

COLD OCEAN CURRENTS

Labrador	Canary	Benguela	Humboldt (Peru)

ARCHIPELAGOS AND ISLANDS

Ceylon (Sri Lanka)	Sicily	Sumatra	Balearic
Moçambique	Singapore	Canary	Taiwan/Formosa
Crete	Philippines	Socotra	Cape Verde
Arguim (Cape Blanco)	Kilwa (Tanzania)	Madeira	Comoro
Cyprus	Madagascar	Zanzibar	Molluca
São Tomé	Fiji	Hong Kong	Macao
			Hormuz

CITIES

London	Kano (Nigeria)	Ceuta	Cadiz
Benin	Nagasaki	Delhi	Larache/Lixus
Goa	Hamburg	Malindi (Kenya)	Mecca
Florence	Guangzhou/Canton	Baghdad	Sofala
Elmina (Ghana)	Alexandria	Venice	Marseille
Rome	Tokyo	Damascus	Acapulco
Calcutta	Paris	Timbuctu	Rio de Janeiro
Vienna	Genoa	Istanbul/Constantinopl	Mexico City
Nara	Meroe (Sudan)	Jerusalem	Manila
Axum (Ethiopia)	Athens	Moscow	Malacca
Carthage	Singapore	Kiev	Beijing/Peking
Los Angeles	New York	Boston	Bangkok
Montreal	San Francisco	Cape Town	

PLACE NAMES

Pyrennes Mountains	Cape Horn	Mongolia
Macedonia	Straits of Malacca	Caucasus
Mayan Territory	Benin Empire (West Africa)	Kush (Nile Valley)
Gibraltar	Aztec Empire	Great Zimbabwe
Balkans	Hong Kong	Bering Strait
Inca Empire	Aragon	Akjoujt (Mauritania)
Fertile Crescent	Phoenicia	Kongo Empire (West-Central
Sahara	Castile	Africa)
Cape of Good Hope	Peru	Ghana, Mali, & Songhai Empires
Ethiopia	Lake Turkana (NE Africa)	(West Africa)

Lectures and Assignments

It is imperative that you read the assignments before class to understand fully the lectures and participate intelligently in the discussion periods. If you are not prepared to comply with this prerequisite you should withdraw from the course.

The National Geographic, Scientific American, and Atlantic Monthly are held in the Undergraduate Library on the same floor as the Reserve Room. See File A (four file cabinets) and File B (ask at desk) for other journal articles. * items are recommended for browsing; the illustrations will considerably enhance your understanding of assigned readings. Most assignments are relatively short to allow time for research and writing the very important term paper. Likewise, plan ahead to complete the insightful and interesting novels listed in the "Era of Imperialism" and "World Since 1900" assignments.

Assignments

Introduction to the course

The Contemporary--and Future--World

Brooks, Introduction and Chapter 1.

Linton, R., "One Hundred Per Cent American," The American Mercury, Vol.40 (1937), 427-429. File A.

Fuller, R.B., "Remapping our World," Today's Education (Nov.-Dec. 1974),40-44; 107-110.   L13 N165 U, File Aand Filee B

Caiden, N. and Wildavsky, A., Planning and Budgeting in Poor Countries, "Prologue" Ii-iv).   HC 59.7 C28

Garreau, J., The Nine Nations of North America, 1-13, and maps following p. 204. E38 C37

Survey Courses: Full

Paleolithic Times to the Neolithic `Evolution'
Brooks, Chapter 2.
McNeill, World History, Chapter 1
Leadey, M.,"The Dawn of Humans," National Geographic G1N2(V)188, 3 (September 1995), 38-51
*Schick, K.D. and N. Toth, Making Silent Stones Speak GN799.T6 S35, 1993

The `Secondary' Neolithic: Euphrates, Nile, Indus, & Yellow River Valleys
Brooks, Chapter 3.
McNeill, Chapter 2.
Davidson, B., African Kingdoms (Time-Life), 33-57. 960 DAV (shelved after Z)
*Casson, L., Ancient Egypt, (Time-Life) DT60 .C34

Indo-European and Austronesian Migrations
Brooks, Chapter 4.
McNeill, chapters 3, 4.
Emory, K.P. "The Coming of the Polynesians, "National Geographic. G1 N2 (U) 146,
(December 1974), 73-746; alsoo 756-781 passim,, File B
*Howe, K.R., Where the Waves Fall: A New South Sea Islands History from First Settlement to
Colonial Rule DU28.3.H68 1984

The Americas to 1492
Brooks, Chapter 5.
McNeill, Chapter 17, "The Americas."
Miner, H., "Body Ritual among the Nacirema," American Anthropologist (1956), 503-507.
GN1 A5 58, File A and File B.
Hall, E.T., The Silent Language, Introduction, chapters 1 and 10. HM258 .H17
*Leonard, J.N., Ancient America E61 L57
*"A Word in Your Ear: A Study in Language." Tape Lab, BH 108, catalogue
number: Linguistics E09.01
*Stuart, G.S. & G.E., Lost Kingdoms of the Maya. F1435 .S88 1993

Ancient Religious Beliefs and Cultural Heritages
Brooks, Chapter 6.
McNeill, chapters 6, 10.
*India (Time-Life) Chapter 2.

Four Mediterranean Trade Diasporas: Phoenician, Greek, Roman, and Jewish
Brooks, Chapter 7.
McNeill, chapters 5, 8, & 9.
*Bowra, C.M., Classical Greece (Time-Life) DF78 .B78
*Hadas, M., Imperial Rome (Time-Life) DG272 .H12
*McEvedy, C., The Penguin Atlas of Ancient History G1033 .M142

The 'Southernization' of Eurasia
Brooks, Chapter 8.
McNeill, chapters 11, 12.
*Wolpert, S., India, 35-46, DS436 .W86
*Shaffer, L. "Southernization," Journal of World History, 5,1 (1994), 1-21. D1.J62

Eurasia During The Era of Muslim and Chinese Ascendancy
Brooks, Chapter 9.
McNeill, chapters 13, 14.
*Abdul-Rauf, M, "Pilgrimage to Mecca", National Geographic (November 1978) 573-607.   G1
  N2 (U)
*Simons, G., Barbarian Europe (Time-Life) D117.S612
*Sherrard, P., Byzantium (Time-Life) DF521 .S55
*Stewart, D., Early Islam (Time-Life) D199.3 .S85

Eurasia during the Era of Uralic-Altaic Conquests
Brooks, Chapter 10.
McNeill, chapters 15, 16.
*Jordan, R.P., "Viking Trail East," National Geographic (March 1985), 278-317. G1 N2 (U)
*Edwards, M., "When the Moguls Ruled India," National Geographic (April 1985),
  462-493. G1 N2 (U)
*Abercrombie, T.J., Ibn Battuta, "Prince of Travelers," National Geographic (December 1991),
  2-49.

East Africa and the Indian Ocean Trading Complex
Brooks, Chapter 12.
Davidson, B., African Kingdoms (Time-Life), 87-95; 129-141; 178-181. 960 DAV (Shelved after
  Z)
*Davidson, B., The Story of Africa DT20 .D32 1984
*Garlake, P., The Kingdoms of Africa DT14 .G38 1990

Survey Courses: Full

West Africa and trans-Saharan Trade
Brooks, Chapter 13
Davidson, B., African Kingdoms (Time-Life), 43-57 ("The Oldest Africans"). 79-99 ("Merchant Empires"); 10-119 ("Forest Kingdoms") 960 DAV (Shelved after Z).
McIntosh, S. & R., "Finding Jenne-jeno," National Geographic (September 1982), 396-418. G1 N2 (U)

The Transmutation of Europe... and the World
Brooks, Chapter 11.
McNeill, Chapter 19.
Riesman, D., et alii, The Lonely Crowd, 11-36. BF755 .A5 R5
*Hale, John R., The Renaissance (Time-Life) DG533.H16
*Simon, E., The Reformation (Time-Life) BR305.2 .S58

The Era of European Reconnaissance
Brooks, Chapter 14.
McNeill, chapters 18, 22.
Crosby, A.W., The Columbian Exchange, Chapter 2; chapters 3 and 4 passim. E98 .D6 C94
*Hale J.R., Age of Exploration (Time-Life), G80 .H18

Interlocking World Economies: The South Atlantic System
Brooks, Chapter 15.
Curtin, P.D., "The Atlantic Slave Trade, 1600-1800" in J.F.A. Ajayi, and M. Crowder, History of W. Africa, Vol. I, Chapter 7. DT 475 .A312
Haley, A., Roots, chapters 33-35 and 118-120. E185.97 .H24 A33
Opala, J.A., The Gullah E185 .S7063 1987.
*"Family Across the Sea" videotape E185 S7 F35 1990.

The Era of Imperialism
Brooks, Chapter 16.
Brooks, G., "Africa and European Relations to 1870" and Gellar, S., "The Colonial Era," in Martin and O'Meara, Africa. DT3 .A23 1986
Ellis, J., The Social History of the Machine Gun, 9, 79-91, 135-145 passim. UF620 A2 E47
Achebe, C., Things Fall Apart. PR9387.9 .A2 T4 1969
Orwell, G., Burmese Days, chapters I-V. PR6029 .B8 B9 1950

The World since 1905
Brooks, Chapter 17.
McNeill, chapters 29, 30.
Brooks, G., "Tropical Africa: The Colonial Heritage," in Themes in African and World History. DT20 .B873 1982
Markandaya, K., Nectar in a Sieve (PR6063 .A68N3 1971), chapters 1-9. Read "The Reincarnation of Caste," The Economist, June 8, 1991, 21-23. H1 E22

The Transformation of World Demographic, Social, and Cultural Patterns
Brooks, Chapter 18.
McNeill, Chapter 23.
Crosby, The Columbian Exchange, chapters 5 & 6 passim. E98 .D6 C94
McDowell, B. and S. Maze, "Mexico City: An Alarming Giant," National Geographic (August 1984), 138-177. G1 .N2
Fox, R.W., "The World's Urban Explosion," Ibid., 178-185.
Keyfitz, N., "The Growing Human Population," Scientific American (September 1989), 119-126. Q1.S45

Sharing the Same Planet: The Impoverished 80% and the Affluent 20%
Brooks, Chapter 19.
Stryker, R., "Development Choices," in Martin and O'Meara, Africa. DT3 .A23 1986
Hancock, G., Lords of Poverty, xiii - xvi, photographs after p. 48; check the Index for the "ldc" you are studying. HC60.H278 1989B
Gellar, S., "The Ratched-McMurphy Model Revisited," Issue, XIV (1985), 25-28. File A.
Jesus, C.M. de, Child of the Dark, passim. HN290 S33 J52

Contemporary World Relationships: Towards the 21st Century
Brooks, Chapter 20.
Kaplan, R.D., "The Coming Anarchy," The Atlantic Monthly (February, 1994), 44-76. AP48
Daly, H.E., "The Perils of Free Trade, Scientific American (November 1993), 50-57. Q1.S45
Lewis, B., "The Roots of Muslim Rage," The Atlantic Monthly (September 1990), 47-60. AP48
Barber, B.R., "Jihad Vs McWorld," The Atlantic Monthly (March 1992) ,53-63. AP48
*Reich, R.B., "The Real Economy," The Atlantic Monthly (February 1991), 35-52. AP48
*Stavrianos, L.S., Lifelines in Our Past:A New World History 139-172 passim. DT20.S83 1989
Connelly, M. and P. Kennedy, "Must it be the Rest against the West?", The Atlantic Monthly (Decembe 1994), 61-91. AP48

FINAL EXAMINATION

Survey Courses: Full

Undergraduate Student Papers

Undergraduates are responsible for a three (only!) page double-spaced paper describing a "less-developed" country. Answer as many of the following questions as you can; if information is not available explain why. Obtain the latest data possible, and cite your sources in social science style, e.g., consult the American Anthropologist (GN1 .A5) and xerox several pages for reference. List references cited on page 4 of your paper (with the library call numbers). Include a xeroxed map as page 5. Papers that do not adhere to instructions will be returned for revisions.

When did the country become independent?
What form of government did it have at independence? Now?
Who/what ethnic group, social groups, economic interests, control the government, armed forces, religious and educational institutions?
What are the country's principal exports and imports? With which countries? Total amounts ($) and %'s.
Who owns the principal business enterprises: mines, plantations, industries, commercial firms, etc.?
Does the country belong to a marketing arrangement for its primary product(s)?
What were the consequences of the "Green Revolution"?
What were the consequences of the OPEC price increases? of decreases?
What are the principal goals of the current economic plan? What of the successes or failures of the current and previous plans?
What are the environmental circumstances and prospects: water, soils, forests, fishing?
How has the 1993-1994 GATT/WTO Agreement affected the economy?
Role in the North-South dialogue?
What is the amount of indebtedness and to whom is it owed? $ and % of nation's annual budget?
Foreign Aid: from which countries? How much ($)? % of government budget?
Population and rate of population increase? % living in which urban centers of over 100,000 population?

Selection of countries will be made following discussion of the project on _____.

Begin your research by reading the "Sharing the Same Planet" assignment, encyclopedia articles on your country, and reports in The Economist H1 E22 (U) for the past twelve months. Current issues of The Economist are kept behind the counter in the Periodicals Reading Room; ask the librarian on duty. Facts on File AG5 F159 (U), The Statesman's Yearbook AY754 S7 (U), World Almanac and Book of Facts AY67 N5W9 (U),; Author S. Banks, Political Handbook of the World (annual) JF37 .P7 Ref., and U.S. Department of State Background Notes are useful for statistics and specific facts. Consult InfoTrac data base for assistance regarding journals and magazines and the Subject Index files in the Graduate side of the Library. Look for recently published general studies. The Economist Intelligence Unit, Country Profiles (Business/SPEA Library) and USFI Reports (Universities Field Staff International) are excellent sources for many countries.

Survey Courses: Full

A preliminary bibliography (one page) including at least two citations from reference works, two books on the country or region, all reports in The Economist during the past twelve months, and the "Country Profile" from The Economist Intelligence Unit is due on _____. Papers are due _ _____; late papers will be penalized. Make two copies of your paper, keeping one for reference. When I return the first copy, give me your second copy. Keep your xerox and notes to help prepare for a final exam question on "ldcs."

Graduate Student Papers

Graduate students have three options on papers, depending on goals and interests.

(1) Graduate students intending to teach World History at the college or high school level are encouraged to prepare a lecture outline on a subject of special interest. The topic must incorporate a large geographical area and/or time period, or a world trend or theme, such as the lectures for this course. Papers should be five double-spaced pages maximum and include the following: an outline of the main points of the lecture on the first page; discussion of the main points on the following three pages citing the sources for your statements (use social science style, e.g., consult the American Anthropologist and xerox several pages for reference) (GN1 .A5); and page five should list references cited--no more than five sources, the most valuable sources you found. The objective of the paper is to identify the most important statements you can make about the topic you have chosen: statements that organize, describe, and highlight the significance of your topic. Include no more than five xerox pages of maps, charts, graphs, films, videos, etc., you would use in a lecture presentation. Include the sources and page numbers for the xerox pages you submit.

(2) Graduate students may prepare ten page double-spaced term papers on topics cited in (1) or on major groupings of "less-developed" countries in Africa, Asia, and Latin America, describing their inter-relationships, e.g., the ACP (African, Caribbean, and Pacific) countries associated with the European Economic Community, the Andean Pact countries in Latin America, and the ASEAN countries.

(3) Combine (1) and (2), following instructions for (1).

Consult with the instructor concerning your interests and preferences. Topics should be approved by the instructor by _____. Prepare a preliminary outline and bibliography by _____ . Papers are due _____; late papers will be penalized. Submit two copies; the original will be returned to you.

Note: Graduate Students are also responsible for learning about a selected "less-developed country" (the Undergraduate project), but not for submitting the 3-page paper.

Peter Stearns
Carnegie Mellon University
Introduction to World History

INTRODUCTION TO WORLD HISTORY (79-104)
SPRING 1997

Monday and Wednesday-Lecture, Friday-Section meeting with individual instructors.

CONTENTS:
Course Purposes
Books to be Purchased
Course Requirements
Class Schedule & Assignments
Questions for Discussion

COURSE PURPOSES:
This course surveys major features of the principal existing civilizations of the world, as they were originally formed and as they have been altered during the past two to four centuries by the "forces of modernity." We will try to define what the major traditional features of each civilization were, and particularly how cultures persisted and changed, and what the "forces of modernity" have been. Obviously, a survey of this sort in one semester involves some challenges for all participants. Here are some advance clues on what to look for in developing an analytical approach to a world history overview.

We will be dealing with three main approaches to world history. These are outlined in the next paragraph, and then spelled out more fully (you may wish to save this fuller statement for later).

APPROACH #1: Involves asking about the role of culture in individual and social behavior.

APPROACH #2: Involves comparison among the major civilizations, as wholes and in key features such as government or economic institutions as well as cultures.

APPROACH #3: Involves discussing how the major civilizations changed, particularly as traditional features encountered new forces during the past few centuries; emphasis here will be on long time periods in world history, whereby major "new forces" can be defined, in terms of new kinds of international contacts and connections .

APPROACH # 1:
Culture refers to a system of ideas about the nature of the world and how people should behave in it that is shared, and shared uniquely, by members of a community. Many issues in our society involve questions about how much behavior a culture causes, but also what factors can cause a culture to change. A world history course must discuss how cultures form -- particularly, large regional cultures like those of China or Islam; how much history these cultures explain; and how and

to what extent cultures change. World history is not the only framework for cultural analysis, but it highlights some major features. In dealing with leading civilizations over time, one analytical issue focuses on culture squarely: the extent to which a society holds to particular values from its early history to the present, and so responds to common challenges in distinctive ways.

APPROACH #2:
The comparative approach is vital in analysis of world history. Each civilization can be compared, at major stages, to others. We suggest breaking down each civilization into political, cultural, economic, and social categories--i.e., how it is governed, how it explains and represents the world, how it supports itself, and how it structures social groups and families. Each of these categories, and also their interrelationships in forming a whole civilization, can be compared across space--with the other major civilizations. You can even keep an informal chart of each civilization, in its four aspects, for comparative purposes. We will be dealing with seven civilizations: East Asia, India and southern Asia, the Middle East, Eastern Europe, Western civilization, sub-Saharan Africa and Latin America.

APPROACH #3:
The course will introduce the factor of change over time. We will be dealing with four major time periods (after brief discussion of the earliest civilization phase): a classical period, from about 1000 B.C. to about 500 A.D., in which large civilizations formed in China, India and around the Mediterranean. A "spread of civilizations" period, 500-1400 A.D. in which changes occurred in the classical civilizations and new civilizations arose, to the total of seven ongoing cases mentioned above, but in which new connections among civilizations also developed. Next, the "rise of the West" or "creation of world economy" period, 1400-1900, in which new contacts and various ideological and economic developments brought some degree of change to each of the seven civilizations we¢re dealing with. And finally, the 20th century as a new period in world history, in which changes building in the previous period turn into a full-fledged confrontation with the forces of modernity, in each major civilization.

The three main approaches in world history, combined, produce two related analytical tensions. The fundamental issue in current world history scholarship involves the balance between the separate cultural traditions and the steadily-expanding contacts among major civilizations, in causing major developments. How many of the features of China, or the United States, around 1800, can be explained by distinctive patterns in each nation, including distinctive cultural traditions, and how many by involvement with some larger international experiences and contacts? This is the kind of question that can fruitfully be applied to earlier as well as later time periods, and to all areas of the world.

This basic tension in interpreting world history, between distinctive cultures and interconnections, generates a more specifically modern variant: as international contacts spread in recent centuries, leading to more extensive technological, commercial, cultural, even biological connections among societies, how have different traditional cultures reacted? Are present-day societies shaped primarily by common forces, like a desire for economic growth, or by the heritage of older cultures? Here is the central analytical focus for the second half of this course, after the major cultural traditions and earlier kinds of interconnections have been explored.

Survey Courses: Full

One other point about the purpose of the course. We will be relying on an essay-format textbook for general coverage, with particular issues and comparisons highlighted in lectures. We will also discuss some more specific readings, to deal with types of historical evidence and problems of conflicting interpretation--two skills areas that the study of history inevitably entails when it goes beyond straight memorization, as we intend to do.

BOOKS TO BE PURCHASED:
Hammond World Map
Stearns, *World History: Patterns of Change and Continuity*
Cipolla, *Guns, Sails, and Empires: Technological Innovation & the Early Phases of European Expansion 1400-1700*
Stearns, et al, eds., *Documents in World History*, 2 Volumes

TESTS AND PAPERS:
Quiz 1 (Map Test) - Session 1, January 17.
Quiz 2 - Session 3, January 31.
Paper 1 (One Page) - Due Lecture 9, February 10.
Mid-Term Examination - Lecture 12 - February 19.
Paper 2 (Three Pages) - Lecture 17, March 12.
Quiz 3 - Session 11, April 4.
Paper 3 (Three to Five Pages) - Lecture 26, April 21.
Homeworks - Sessions 3, 4, 7, 8, 10, and 13.
Final Examination (2 hours in examination period)
Assignments described at due date in syllabus or in later handouts

COMPONENTS OF GRADE: The final grade of the course will be determined in the following manner:
10% for Homeworks
10% each for Papers 1, 2 and 3
10% for Mid-Term Examination
25% for Final Examination
25% for class participation, attendance and quizzes

World History World Wide Web Page
http://cil.andrew.cmu.edu/projects/World_History
The World Wide Web Page can be used to: get information on your section and your instructor; get course materials you may have missed; tell you where you can go for help; and link to historical sites to get more information in areas that interest you. Please check in often for course news, updates and information.

CLASS SCHEDULE AND ASSIGNMENTS
NOTE: It is assumed that assigned reading will be done before the class for which it is designated.

Jan. 13: (M)   Lecture 1   Introduction: Why World History
        Assignment   Hammond Map

Jan. 15: (W)   Lecture 2   The Nature of Agricultural Societies: What is Civilization
        Assignment   Stearns (World History text), pp. 1-32

Jan. 17: (F)   Session 1   The Organization of Human Societies
        Assignment   Documents I, Selection 2, pp. 16-20

    1. What is an historical source? How does it differ from secondary work and   textbooks?

    2. How can we determine that the Code is a product of a civilization?

    3. What is the social and family structure of Babylonian civilization, as suggested by the Code?

    4. Why did agricultural civilizations tend to have such harsh penalties for crimes?

    5. Judging by the Code, how would you describe major advantages and drawbacks in a civilization compared to other forms of social organization?

    Quiz 1 - MAP TEST

Jan. 20: (M)   Lecture 3   Classical Civilizations: China and India
        Assignment   Stearns, pp. 33-82

Jan. 22: (W)   Lecture 4   Understanding Cultures: Definitions & the Problems of
                                Change
        Assignment   Stearns, pp. 83-106, Documents I, Selection 13 & 14, pp. 77-86

Jan. 24: (F)   Session 2   Indian and Chinese Philosophy: Concepts & Concerns
        Assignment   Documents I, Selections 5, 6, 9, 10 & 11, pp. 35-46, 57-72

    1. How was Confucianism different from a religion? Whose interests did it serve? How did it substitute for religion? Why did it place so much emphasis on ceremony?

    2. Compare Chinese Legalism and the political ideas of Kautilya. How do you account for the similarities? What was the impact of each on the actual political system (of China and India respectively)?

3. How did Buddhist values differ from Confucian values?

4. What was the Hindu concept of dharma, and how did it differ from the Confucian ethic?

5. What implications did Hinduism and Confucianism have for patterns of social and political behavior? How did each deal with cultural relations between elite and masses? Which belief system would an ordinary peasant prefer?

Jan. 27 : (M) Lecture 5   Social History & the Classical World
    Assignment   Stearns, pp. 83-106 (Review), Documents I, Selection 15, pp. 87-90

Jan. 29 : (W)   Lecture 6   Theories on the Rise & Fall of World Civilization
    Assignment   Stearns, pp. 107-131

Jan 31: (F)   Session 3   Women in Classical India & China, including the
                       Tang/Sung Period
    Assignment   Documents I, Selections 8, 12 & 22, pp. 51-56, 73-76, 128-134

1. What was the "ideal woman" in classical China? How did the Chinese ideal mesh with Confucianism?

2. What was the role of women in classical India? How did this role differ from that of women in China?

3. What are the problems with the evidence available about womenþs roles-- how good is cultural evidence as an overall index? What are the problems of social class in the evidence from the classical period?

4. Was the Mediterranean tradition concerning women, as suggested by Aristotle, different from the Indian and Chinese?

5. Why were women socially subordinate to men in classical civilizations? How could women adjust to patriarchal conditions?

QUIZ 2:   On the classical civilizations, readings covered to this point
Homework Due.

Feb. 3 : (M)   Lecture 7   The Issue of Heritage: Change, Continuity and the Spread   of World
                            Religion
    Assignment   Stearns, pp. 133-176, 188-199

Feb. 5: (W)   Lecture 8   The World Network: New Exchanges
    Assignment   Stearns, pp. 255-263

Feb. 7 : (F)   Session 4   Islamic Philosophy & Change
Assignment   Documents I, Selections 17, 18, 19, 20 & 26, pp. 97-120, 150-154

1. What were the main religious duties and rewards for a faithful Muslim?

2. Why was Islam such a successful religion?

3. What were the main similarities and differences between Islam and Buddhism? Between Islam and Christianity?

4. How did Islam define religious and political organization?

5. What changes did the Koran make in Arab family law? How could Muhammed argue that Islam improved the conditions of women?

Homework Due.

Feb. 10: (M)   Lecture 9   Expanding Civilization and the World Network: Japan and Europe
Assignment   Stearns, pp. 199-243

PAPER 1 DUE One page-topic to be assigned, comparing religions

Feb. 12: (W) Lecture 10   Civilizations in Africa
Assignment   Stearns, pp. 177-187

Feb. 14: (F)   Session 5   Feudalism and Religion: the Struggle for Power
Assignment   Stearns, pp. 223-243: Documents 1, Selections 24, 28 & 29, pp. 140-144, 159-168

1. What is feudalism? In what circumstances did it develop? Whatþs the difference between feudalism and other decentralized systems of government? How does it differ from manorialism?

2. How does the Magna Carta illustrate the impact of feudalism? Of Christianity and the power of the church?

3. How did European feudalism compare to Japanese feudalism, in values and in political structure?

4. How did Church-state relations in Russia differ from those in Western Europe?

5. Which proved more important for later Western political development: the Greco-Roman political tradition or the feudal political tradition?

6. Compared to other political systems at the time, was feudalism an advantage or a disadvantage for European development? How would a Muslim or Confucian evaluate the Magna Carta?

Feb. 17: (M) Lecture 11   Civilization in the Americas
       Assignment   Cipolla, Epilogue and chapter 1; Stearns, pp. 177-187, 244-   254

Feb. 19: (W) Lecture 12   MID-SEMESTER EXAMINATION

Feb. 21: (F) Session 6   Arms & Expansion
       Assignment   Cipolla, Chapter 2 and Epilogue

1. How did the military balance between Europe and Asia change between the Middle Ages and 1500?

2. The military superiority Europe attained by the seventeenth century made European expansion in the East possible. What were the motives behind this expansion? In what ways was European dominance still limited, and why?

3. Why did the people of the East fail to assimilate Western military innovations? Did they make a mistake in their policy?

4. How does Cipolla explain change? Is he a technological determinist? What other factors can explain European expansion after the 15th century?

5. How might a Confucian Chinese or Muslim historian judge Cipollaþs account?

Feb. 24: (M) Lecture 13   Periodization & World Trends, 1450 Onward: Comparing the 15th and the 20th Centuries
       Assignment   Stearns, pp. 259-280, 304-330

Feb. 26: (W) Lecture 14   The Transformation of Popular Mentalities in the West: The "Big Changes"
       Assignment   Documents II, Selection 2, pp. 17-24; Stearns, pp. 280-303

Feb. 28: (F) Session 7   Colonies & World Economy
       Assignment   "The Development of a World Economic System"
                    (handout)

1. Define the key terms: core, periphery, semi-periphery, external. Illustrate each from one society in the early modern period.

2. Can each type be illustrated with a society in the world today?

3. How did political systems and labor systems differ among the four types of economies in the early modern centuries? How does or might culture fit in the world economy, as cause or effect?

4. What major criticisms might be raised against the world economy interpretation?

5. Is the world economy interpretation optimistic or pessimistic about the prospects for general economic progress? How does it compare to a technological-determinist approach to modern world history?

Homework Due.

Mar. 3: (M)   MID-SEMESTER BREAK

Mar. 5: (W)   Lecture 15   The Rise of Russia: Change & Continuity
Assignment   Stearns, pp. 331-347

Mar. 7: (F)   Session 8   Aspects of Change in Russia
Assignment   Documents II, Sections 4, 5 & 6, pp. 31-48

1. What did Peter the Great Westernize, and why? Why did he not try to have Russia achieve core status?

2. Compare the views of Radishchev and Karamzin on serfdom. How do they disagree? Why do they disagree?

3. Why and in what ways did an ambivalence toward the West develop in Russia? What kinds of criticism of the West surfaced in Russia?

4. What are the main continuities between late 18th-century Russia and the Soviet Union?

Homework Due.

Mar. 10: (M)   Lecture 16   Categorizing Early Modern Reactions: Asia, Africa and the Americas
Assignment   Stearns, pp. 348-381 (Review pp. 304-330)

Mar. 12:(W)   Lecture 17   The Industrial Revolution: The West and the World
Assignment   Stearns, pp. 382-385, 426-444, Environmental History (handout)

PAPER 2 DUE Three-Page Essay on the Early Modern World Economy

Mar. 14: (F)   Session 9   Modernization Theory & Social Change
Assignment   Stearns, "Modernization Theory" (handout)

1. Explain the concept of modernization. What does it refer to when applied (respectively) to politics, economics, intellectual attitudes, family life?

2. Is there a definable cultural modernization?

3. Why is the term modernization regarded by some as ethnocentric? What may it conceal and distort in the study of past societies?

4. When is participation in the world economy modernization? Was Peter the Great a modernizer?

Mar. 17: (M)   Lecture 18   Industrialization; Work, Family and Progress
Assignment   Documents II, Selection 3, pp. 25-30; Stearns, pp. 392-419

Mar. 19: (W)   Lecture 19   Nationalism and Traditional Cultures
Assignment Stearns, pp. 426-444 (Review), 445-460

Mar. 21: (F)   Session 10   The Problem of Latin American Civilization and the "New Nations" Issue
Assignment   Stearns, pp. 461-480; Documents II, Selections 14, 15 &   16, pp. 82-94

1. Why did the wars for independence occur in Latin America? (Were they revolutionary?) What were the goals of leaders like Bolivar?

2. What were the political results of "new nation" formation? What political styles developed, and why? (Compare to new nations since 1945.)

3. Did independence change Latin Americaþs position in the world economy during the 19th century? Did it affect systems of labor?

4. In what ways did Latin America, by the 19th century, seem part of Western civilization? In what ways did it differ?

5. Which helps more in understanding 19th century Latin America: modernization theory or world economy theory?

Homework Due.

March 31: (M)Lecture 20   Latecomer Modernizers: Russia & Japan
Assignment   Stearns, pp. 481-500

Survey Courses: Full

April 2 : (W)   Lecture 21   The United States and World History
         Assignment   Stearns, pp. 420-425

April 4: (F)   Session 11   Tradition & Change in Japan
         Assignment   Stearns, pp. 491-498 (Review); Documents II
                      Selections 9 & 27, pp. 59-62, 147-151

   1. What problems did the Japanese have in figuring out what the West was like?

   2. What did the Japanese "Westernize?" Why was there so much stress on education?

   3. What have the Japanese not Westernized, and why?

   4. Will Japan, as part of ongoing modernization, become increasingly like the West in such
       areas as the condition of women?

   5. Do you think Japan has been particularly successful in modernizing, compared even to
       the West? What explains its dynamism?

   6. What are the limitations of explaining modern Japanþs success in terms of successful
       imitation alone?

   QUIZ 3   On Problems of Industrialization and Colonialism
            Coverage: Readings since hour exam

April 7: (M) Lecture 22   The Problem of the 20th Century
         Assignment   Stearns, pp. 501-547

April 9: (W)   Lecture 23   The Third World, the World Economy, and Economic
                           Development

April 11: SPRING CARNIVAL   NO CLASSES

April 14: (M) Lecture 24   Patterns of Revolution
         Assignment   Stearns, pp. 548-570, 577-582, 588-592

April 16: (W) Lecture 25   Comparative Issues for Non-Western Civilizations
         Assignment   Stearns, pp. 571-671

April 18 (F)   Session 12   Comparing Revolutions
         Assignment   Stearns pp. 633-642; Documents II Selections 22, 23, 25
                      & 34, pp. 122-130, 136-141, 180-186

   1. In what ways is Marxism a particularly useful ideology for modern revolution?

2. How do Lenin and Mao compare as revolutionary leaders? How did each adapt Marxism? How did each react to modern forces and ideas?

3. How do revolutionaries "change their tune" as they move from protest to consolidation of a new government?

4. How did the Mexican revolution compare, in cause and result, with the Russian Revolution of 1917? How does each relate to the theory of modernization?

5. Why have there been revolutions in so many different societies outside the West in the 20th century? Can Wallersteinps world systems approach explain this phenomenon? Have the conditions for social revolution ended in the 1990s?

April 21 (M)   Lecture 26   Comparative Issues: Modernization and Education

PAPER 3 DUE Three to five pages; topic to be assigned

April 23 (W)   Lecture 27   Patterns of Belief in the Contemporary World
        Assignment   Documents II, Selections 28, 31 & 32, pp. 152-156, 165-174

April 25: (F) Session 13   Directions of 20th Century Africa
        Assignment   Documents I, Selection 33, pp. 184-186; Documents II, Selections 18, 19, 37
                        & 38, pp. 100-108, 194-204

1. What factors prompted some Africans to oppose missionary Christianity, and others to accept it?

2. What is nationalism? What are the distinctive features of African nationalism?

3. What problems have African nationalists had in defining and spreading their beliefs?

4. Has "Westernization," to the extent it has occurred, hurt or helped Africa in the 20th century? Compare Western cultural influence in Africa and in Japan over the past 100 years.

5. To what extent have African values modernized? (and how does one measure?)

Homework Due.

April 28 : (M) Lecture 27   Issues of Democracy and Women: Updating Modernization

April 30: (W) Lecture 28   Post Industrial Society & World Societies, Present and Future
            Assignment   Stearns, pp. 672-684

May 2: (F)   Session 14   Modernization and Women: Comparative Studies
            Assignment   Documents II, Selections 21, 24, 27, 30 & 38, pp. 117-121,   131-135,
                    147-151,161-164, 200-204

1. What has the "modernization" of women involved in Western history? How does Western feminism fit this pattern of change? Is modern Western history a case of steady progress for women?

2. Are conditions improving for African women? For women in India? What are the main differences in womenþs conditions from one society to the next today?

3. What factors account for differences in womenþs roles and status in the later 20th century? Is diversity or modernization the better description of 20th-century international patterns for women?

4. How can you set up a comparison between women conditions in India and those in Japan? How do you explain the main differences?

5. Are trends in the conditions of women a good measurement of overall social change in the modern world? Why have conditions changed in so many societies in the 20th century?

6. What has happened to "patriarchy" as a framework for understanding women's roles?

Survey Courses: Pre-Modern

A. J. Andrea
University of Vermont
Global History to 1500

HISTORY 9
GLOBAL HISTORY to 1500
Spring 1996

Course Instructor: Prof. A. J. Andrea
Teaching Assistant: Diane Dolbashian
203 Torrey Hall
MWF 1:25-2:25

Professor Andrea's office hours are: MTWThF 11:00-12:00 *and by appointment.*
office: 302 WHEELER HOUSE
e-mail: AANDREA@ZOO.UVM.EDU
private office phone and voice mail: 656-4488
Please do not call Professor Andrea at home

REQUIRED TEXTS:
William H. McNeill, *A History of the Human Community*, 5th ed., Vol. I: Prehistory to 1500
Andrea and Overfield, *The Human Record*, 2nd. ed., Vol. I: to 1700

Course Objectives:
History 9 provides an overview of world history from about 8000 B.C.E. (Before the Common Era) to the late fifteenth century C.E. (the Common Era). Its objectives are to provide you with: (1) a knowledge of the overall patterns of early global history; (2) an awareness of the distinguishing characteristics of the world's major premodern civilizations; (3) an understanding of the significant relationships and points of cultural exchange among these societies; (4) insight into the historical roots of many of the world's major cultural traditions; (5) an introduction to the art of historical inquiry and elementary practice in the methods of historical analysis.

Course Philosophy:
A course in history at any level must transcend the simple dissemination of information. In this course we will practice history rather than simply memorize historical facts that, in and of themselves, have little or no relevance to our lives. History itself is terribly relevant, but its relevance depends on our active engagement with the past. In this course you will be expected to understand the past and, by understanding it, to make it your own. This can never be accomplished by memorization alone. Rather, it requires your full involvement in the learning process, whereby you analyze historical data, look for patterns and relationships, ask probing questions and, in short, discover for yourself the meaning of the past. Such historical inquiry will serve you well in your drive to become an educated person. I trust you will also find it fun.

The Special Perspectives of Global History:

Survey Courses: Pre-Modern

Global history is **not** the cumulative histories of a number of separate cultures. Rather, it is the systematic study of the major **patterns** of global historical development that connect and influence the histories of many different cultures. For this reason, rather than attempting the impossible--a detailed history of all the major cultures and events that were part of the historical fabric of the world from roughly 8000 B.C.E. to 1500 C.E.--we will look selectively at the big picture and focus our attention on those events and traditions that had profound impact on the course of human history. As we do this, we shall be asking two major questions of the past. First, what can we learn from a comparative analysis of the different historical cultures that we are studying? Global history is, at least partially, comparative history. Second, how have these different cultures influenced one another and, thereby, the general course of global history? Societies change often as a result of coming into contact with other cultures. We are going to pay particular attention to the complex processes of cultural exchange and conflict. As a consequence, we will focus on particular eras, such as the period 200 B.C.E.--200 C.E., that proved to be major watersheds in the history of the human community. We will also adopt a wide-angle geographic vision, looking at vast regions, such as Inner Eurasia, as historically coherent areas.

Course Requirements:

I. Discussion:
Beginning Friday, 24 January, *and every Friday thereafter, except for 14 March*, we will hold a general discussion in which you will be expected to discuss thoughtfully the week's assigned sources and writing exercise. Your participation in discussion will weigh heavily in your course grade; so it is in your best interest to let us know who you are by your active participation.

II. Attendance:

III. **Weekly Essays**:
One of the best methods for mastering any subject is to write about it, and the best way to learn history is to read and analyze evidence from the past and then to write on one's insights. Consequently, this course emphasizes out-of-class writing, and every writing assignment will involve your intellectual interchange with a specific source or group of sources. Each Friday you will bring to class a *typed, formal essay of at least two full pages (double spaced, one-inch margins)*, in which you have written a thoughtful and full answer to the Question of the Week. This essay must conform to all of the accepted standards of university-level English prose. Grammatical errors, lapses in correct prose structure and punctuation, and misspellings are not acceptable. In evaluating these essays, we will consider both form and content. Of the two, content will count twice as much as form, and content essentially means how seriously and fully you have responded to the question you have been asked to address. Additional explanations of what is required of you so far as content and form are considered appear below under the headings HISTORICAL ESSAYS and SOME SIMPLE PROSE RULES.

 Anyone who has difficulty with writing should visit the Writing Lab at the Learning Coop in Living/Learning Commons. We urge you to do so immediately and to make provision for as many visits to a writing tutor as you need. It would be foolish and irresponsible to fail to take advantage of this help if you need it.

Survey Courses: Pre-Modern

Essay Grades: Each essay will receive two preliminary grades: one for content and one for style. The content grade will be double weighted. To arrive at any essay's final grade, we will add the content and style grades and divide by three. For example, suppose an essay receives an A- (92) for content and a C (75) for style: 2x92=184 + 75 = 259. Divided by three, the result is 86, or B. Is this clear?

IV. **Examinations**

We will have *two* examinations. Each should take you about an hour to complete, but you will be allowed three hours for each. Some of you might do better knowing that you can take the examination at a leisurely pace. The mid-term examination will take place on 12 March and the final examination will be held on 2 May. Each examination will consist of twelve terms or names, and you will be required to compose mini-essays (about a paragraph each) on ten (10) of them. Each term or person will be what I often flippantly call "a big ticket item." That is, it will be a major person or phenomenon (for example, Confucius or the Silk Road). All items for which you are responsible will appear on a list of about sixty terms that will be handed out about two weeks prior to each examination. The second examination is *not* comprehensive and only contains material covered from 24 March onward.

Course Grades:

Your course grade will be **roughly*** computed according to the following formula:

March Examination		20%
May Examination		20%
Weekly Essays	45%	
Class Discussion		15%

* We reserve the right to reward consistent effort and improvement. We also will penalize persons who consistently skip class. As noted above, excessive unexcused absences will result in an automatic failure. We consider more than four unexcused absences to be excessive.

Anyone who wishes to receive early word of his/her course grade should hand in a stamped, self-addressed envelope at the final examination. Do not call the History Office; our staff is instructed not to give out grades over the phone. In fact, it is illegal and unethical to do so.

Academic Honesty:

You are on your honor at all times, and our presumption is that each of you is honest. However, we are required to remind you that the university does not tolerate academic dishonesty of any sort, and everyone is responsible for knowing the university's definition of what constitutes academic dishonesty. In case you do not know, it is contained in the Fall 1996 schedule of courses under the heading "University Policies." In a sentence, it boils down to the fact that absolutely all **written** work that you hand in--essays and examinations--must be exclusively your work. At the same time, we encourage you to study together and to read and analyze the sources in *The Human Record* in small groups as you prepare for weekly class discussions. The weekly essays, however, must be composed individually. If you are not clear on this point, ask Professor Andrea for additional clarification.

Survey Courses: Pre-Modern

COURSE SCHEDULE AND ASSIGNMENTS

Discussion sections will be devoted to our analysis of sources contained in *The Human Record.*

Please note that I ask you to jump around a bit when reading McNeill's text because my way of seeing and presenting early global history differs in some ways from his. You will also note that at times I will disagree with some of his interpretations and even (gasp!) some of the dates and supposed facts that he presents. Do not be unduly alarmed by this. Historians often differ in their interpretation of the data, and our evidence is at times so fragmentary and ambiguous as to cause historians to disagree about such basic items as the actual dates of events. Take heart in the knowledge that the study of history is not the mindless process of memorizing cut-and-dried, immutable facts.

Please also note that when it comes to Romanizing Chinese words, McNeill uses the older Wade-Giles convention (e.g. Chou and Tao), whereas *The Human Record* uses the newer Pinyin convention (e.g. Zhou and Dao). I will try to point out the differences and clarify them in class.

Notwithstanding my disagreements with McNeill, I have chosen his text because I believe it to be student friendly. I hope you find it so.

I. AN INTRODUCTION TO THE ART OF HISTORY; THE RISE OF AGRICULTURE AROUND THE WORLD AND ITS CONSEQUENCES (14-24 JAN)
McNeill, Preface and pp. 1-26; *The Human Record*, Prologue, pp. P-1 to P-16 (note: P-1 through P-16 are the specially numbered pages of the Prologue), and Chapter 1, pp. 30-31 and 37-39.

20 JANUARY Martin Luther King, Jr. Holiday

24 JAN DISCUSSION: 1. What is History?; 2. Reading Written and Artifactual Evidence
ESSAY TOPIC OF THE WEEK: Question 8 on page P-7 (the Prologue) of *The Human Record.* Be prepared to discuss the following: The entire Prologue, especially the letter by Columbus and the woodcut (pages P-6--P-15); question 5 on page P-7; questions 1-4 on page 31; and questions 1-7 on page 39.

II. THE FIRST RIVERINE CIVILIZATIONS: MESOPOTAMIA, EGYPT, INDIA, AND CHINA (27-31 JAN)
McNeill, pp. 24-46, 71-74, and 142-150; *The Human Record*, Chap. 1, pp. 1-24 and 32-37.
31 JAN DISCUSSION: 1. The Transit of Cultural Influences; 2. Egypt and Mesopotamia: A Comparative Analysis
ESSAY TOPIC OF THE WEEK: **Syncretism** is a term that refers to the *adoption and adaptation* of the traits of one culture by another (for example, the infusion of Buddhism, which originated in India, into the cultures of Central and East Asia). Study all of the images in sources 9 and 10 on pages 32-37. What evidence do you find of syncretic borrowing? Be specific. What was borrowed? Who was the source, and who was the borrower? Were these elements adopted without change or were they adapted to meet the preexisting environment of the host culture? What do you conclude from your answers to these questions?

We will also discuss in class questions 4 and 5 on page 18, question 6 on page 13, and possibly questions 5 and 6 on page 22.

III. THE CHARIOT AND IRON AGES: INVADERS AND STATES (3-7 FEB)

McNeill, pp. 48-70 and 150-154; *The Human Record*, Chapter 1, pp. 24-29, and Chapter 2, entire

7 FEB DISCUSSION: The Worldviews of the Aryans, the Zhou (Chou), the Early Hellenes, and the Israelites: A Comparative Analysis

ESSAY TOPIC OF THE WEEK: Question 5 on page 58. Your essay must show that you understand fully the Mandate of Heaven and the Covenant, which means understanding their similarities and differences.

We will also discuss in class questions 6 and 8, on page 26, questions 5 and 6 on page 47, question 1 on page 55, and questions 1-2 on page 58.

IV. THE RISE OF ETHICAL MONOTHEISM AND THE QUEST FOR NIRVANA (11-14 FEB)

McNeill, pp. 79-98 and 121-139; *The Human Record*, Chapter 3.

14 FEB DISCUSSION: The Search for God in Southwest Asia and India

ESSAY TOPIC OF THE WEEK: "In India religion became the vehicle for negating the world, whereas in the Middle East religion became the means of transforming the world." Whatever does this anonymous author mean? Do you agree or disagree with this assessment? In constructing your answer, you must deal, in detail, with Brahminical Hinduism, Buddhism, Jainism, Zoroastrianism (Zarathustrianism), and Judaism.

We will also discuss in class question 8 on page 64, question 7 on page 67, question 5 on page 73, question 4 on page 75, and question 8 on page 83.

17 FEB Presidents' Day Holiday

V. TWO SECULAR SOCIETIES: CHINA AND HELLAS (19-28 FEB)

McNeill. pp. 154-161, 169-184, and 99-121; *The Human Record*, Chapter 4.

21 FEB DISCUSSION: China's Three Ways of Thought

ESSAY TOPIC OF THE WEEK: Consider the policies of Qin Shi Huangdi (Ch'in Shih Huang Ti) as delineated in source 27. Compose a three-way discourse on those policies in which a Legalist, a Daoist (Taoist), and a Confucian debate their merits. As always, be specific. In doing this exercise, allow free range to your creativity and have fun, but be sure to give each philosopher arguments and critiques that correctly reflect his particular philosophical school's world view. Are there any points on which they would agree?

28 FEB DISCUSSION: The Search for the Good Life in China and Hellas

ESSAY TOPIC OF THE WEEK: Compose an essay that compares in detail the ideals and realities of Hellenic and Chinese societies in the period ca. 500-200 B.C.E. As always, be specific and draw your evidence and data primarily from the sources in *The Human Record*. At the same time, do not overlook material provided by McNeill and in lecture.

VI. THE FIRST AFRO-EURASIAN ECUMENE (3-10 MARCH)

McNeill, pp. 163-168 and 185-202; *The Human Record*, Chap. 5 (except source 41).

7 MARCH DISCUSSION: Regional Empires and Afro-Eurasian Linkage: 300 B.C.E.--500 C.E.
ESSAY TOPIC OF THE WEEK: Compose an essay answer to question 8 on page 141 of *The Human Record*. Again, feel free to use your imagination, but be sure that whatever words you put into Asoka's and Caesar Augustus's mouths are based on historical evidence, primarily the evidence of sources 33, 37, 42, and whatever other sources you deem relevant.
   We will also discuss in class, as time allows, questions 5 and 6 on page 122, question 5 on page 129, questions 3 and 7 on page 132, questions 7 and 8 on page 150, and question 8 on page 154.
10 MARCH Continue to *discuss* issues and questions relating to Chapter 5 of *The Human Record*.

12 MARCH MID-TERM EXAMINATION

14 MARCH Spring Recess Begins. No Class Today. Enjoy the holiday.

VII. FOUR ECUMENICAL RELIGIONS OF SALVATION: BHAKTI, MAHAYANA, THE CULT OF ISIS, AND CHRISTIANITY (24-28 MARCH)
McNeill, pp. 203-212; *The Human Record*, pp. 157--160, 162-176, 184-187, and 193-207.
28 MARCH DISCUSSION: Different Avenues to Salvation
   ESSAY TOPIC OF THE WEEK: The Cult of Isis, Bhakti, Mahayana Buddhism, and Christianity: In what ways are they similar? In what ways are they different? Which are more significant, the similarities or the differences? What do you conclude from your answers to these three questions?

VIII. THE RISE OF ISLAM (31 MARCH--4 APRIL)
McNeill, pp. 226-248; *The Human Record*, Chapter 8, entire, Chapter 6, pages 177-180, and Chapter 9, pages 276-280 and 284-288, Chapter 11, pages 320--323.
4 APRIL DISCUSSION: Islam and Unbelievers
   ESSAY TOPIC OF THE WEEK: Read sources 48, 61, 62, 75, 77, and 85 carefully. How does Islam view the Unbeliever? What were the varieties of historical reality regarding Muslim-Infidel relations? What do you conclude from your answers to these two questions?

IX. CHINA AND THE WORLD: THE AGE OF CHINESE HEGEMONY (7-11 APRIL)
McNeill, pp. 250-267; *The Human Record*, Chapter 9, pp. 243-269.
11 APRIL DISCUSSION: China and Japan: Teacher and Pupil?
   ESSAY TOPIC OF THE WEEK: Read sources 67-70 carefully. China, especially in the Tang Era, had a profound influence on Japan. Notwithstanding that influence, Japan evolved its own distinctive civilization. What light do sources 67-70 shed on both the influences of Chinese culture on Japanese society and ways in which Japanese civilization differed from that of China?

X. BYZANTIUM AND WESTERN EUROPE: THE CHRISTIAN STATES OF WESTERN EURASIA, 500-1500 (14-18 APRIL)
McNeill, pp. 213--219, 273-299, and 330-351; *The Human Record*, Chapter 7, pp. 207-219, and Chapter 10.
18 APRIL DISCUSSION: Different Visions of World?

ESSAY TOPIC OF THE WEEK: Compose an essay on question 5, page 304.

We will also discuss in class, as time allows, question 1 on page 209, question 5 on page 212, questions 1-5 on page 219, question 7 on page 294, question 4 on page 301, question 8 on page 307, and question 7, page 310.

XI. THE MONGOLS AND A NEW AFRO-EURASIAN ECUMENE (21-25 APRIL)

McNeill, pp. 304-312; *The Human Record*, pp. 342-361.

25 APRIL DISCUSSION: The Pax Mongolica

ESSAY TOPIC OF THE WEEK: Compose an essay on question 4, page 360.

We will also discuss in class, as time allows, question 6 on page 346, question 4 on page 349, and questions 1-6 on pages 353.

XII. THE WORLD ON THE THRESHOLD OF GLOBAL INTERCHANGE (28-30 APRIL)

McNeill, pp. 312-327; *The Human Record*, review Columbus's letter in the Prologue and read pp. 367-382.

FINAL EXAMINATION 2 MAY, 4:00-6:00 P.M.

If you wish to receive your blue book(s) back (along with your grade), please provide a stamped (four first-class stamps should suffice), self-addressed manila envelope. The department cannot pay for postage.

Survey Courses: Pre-Modern

John A. Mears
Southern Methodist University
World Cultures and Civilizations

History 1301
WORLD CULTURES AND CIVILIZATIONS
Syllabus of Lectures and Discussions

Instructor: John A. Mears   Office Hours: 11-12 MWF
Office: 58D Dallas Hall   Telephone: 768-2974

Textbooks

Brian M. Fagan, World Prehistory: A Brief Introduction
Brian M. Fagan, The Great Journey: Peopling of Ancient America
Kevin Reilly, Readings in World Civilizations, Vol. One
Dennis Sherman et. al. (eds.), World Civilizations, Vol. I
J. Kelly Sowards, Makers of World History, Vol. I

Session Topics and Reading Assignments

I.   Setting the Context: Nature, Biology, and Culture

   Aug. 26   Introduction: Approaches to World History

   Aug. 28   Overview: Structures of World History

   Aug. 30   Origins of the Universe: Cosmic Connections

   Sep. 2   UNIVERSITY HOLIDAY

   Sep. 4   Anomalous Blue Planet: Our Cosmic Niche

   Sep. 6   Nature's Miracles: The Appearance of Life

   Sep. 9   Life's Diversity Unfolding

   Sep. 11   The Importance of Being a Primate

          Readings: Fagan, World Prehistory, Chaps. 1-4
                        Fagan, The Great Journey, Chaps. 1-3

Survey Courses: Pre-Modern

II. The Upper Paleolithic Cultural Release: The First Great Milestone

Sep. 13   In Search of Human Origins

Sep. 16   The Development of Hominid Patterns

Sep. 18   The Emergence of Our Kind

Sep. 20   Gathering and Hunting Adaptations

Sep. 23   Technological Consequences of Human Development

Sep. 25   Art and Ritual in the Upper Paleolithic

Sep. 27   Population and Human History

Sep. 30   The Peopling of Our World

Oct. 2   HOUR EXAMINATION

          Readings: Fagan, World Prehistory, Chap. 5
                        Fagan, The Great Journey, Chaps. 4-9

III. Origins of Complex Societies: The Second Great Milestone

Oct. 4   Domestication, Food Production, and Sedentary Communities

Oct. 7   Evolution of Cultural Complexity

Oct. 9   Advent of Civilization in Mesopotamia

Oct. 11   Coalescence of Egyptian Civilization

Oct. 14   Rise of Civilization in the Indus River Valley

Oct. 16   From Tribe to Empire in Northern China

Oct. 18   The Persistence of Nomadic and Hunting-Gathering Societies

          Readings: Fagan, World Prehistory, Chaps. 6-8
                        Fagan, The Great Journey, Chaps. 10-12
                        Reilly, Chaps. One and Two
                        Sherman, pp. 1-5, 14-23

Survey Courses: Pre-Modern

IV. The Development of Early Civilizations (2500 BPE-500 BPE)

Oct. 21   The Primacy of a Cosmopolitan Middle East

Oct. 23   The Collapse of Harappan Civilization

Oct. 25   Toward Alternative Styles of Civilization in India and Greece

Oct. 28   The Belated Definition of Chinese Civilization

Oct. 30   Origins of Complex Cultures in the Americas

Nov. 1   Changes on the Peripheries of the Eastern Hemisphere

Nov. 4   The Role of Nomads in Eurasian Civilizational Change
               ANALYTICAL ESSAY DUE

        Readings: Fagan, World Prehistory, Chaps. 9-10, pp. 223-227,
                         244-251
                      Reilly, Chap. Three, pp. 61-65, 67-73
                      Sherman, pp. 1-8, 14-23, 25-31, 73-78
                      Sowards, pp. 1-53

V. The Classic Age (500 BPE-500 PE)

Nov. 6   The Concept of the Axial Age

Nov. 8   Maturation of Regional Empires

Nov. 11   Civilizational Contact and Interaction

Nov. 13   Cultural Creativity: Greece and the Middle East

Nov. 15   Cultural Creativity: India and China

Nov. 18   World-Historical Religious Developments

Nov. 20   Disruption of Classical Civilizations

        Readings: Fagan, pp. 227-30, 250-53
                      Sherman, pp. 35-72, 90-92, 110-118
                      Sowards, pp. 55-174
                      Reilly, pp. 86-93, 116-161

Survey Courses: Pre-Modern

VI. Post-Classic Recovery (500-1000 PE)

Nov. 22   The Making of Byzantium

Nov. 25   Islam and the Reintegration of the Middle East

Nov. 27   Latin Christendom: The Crucible of Europe

Nov. 28-29   THANKSGIVING HOLIDAY

Dec. 2   The Ironies of Indian History

Dec. 4   The Regeneration of China

Dec. 6   Developments in the Americas: The Mayan Achievement

Readings: Reilly, pp. 163-86, 200-34, 243-49
Sherman, pp. 128-37, 150-52, 177-80, 217-31
Sowards, pp. 177-212
Fagan, World Prehistory, pp 230-37, 254-55

Dec. 10   FINAL EXAMINATION   Tuesday, 8:00 a.m. - 11:00 a.m.

Formal Requirements

In addition to an hour examination (25% of the course grade) and a final (50%), students
will write an analytical essay (25%) which must be submitted by Monday, November 4. Students
will lose one-third of a letter grade for each day that the paper is **late**.

Students will be expected to attend class fully prepared on a regular basis. A sign-in sheet
will be passed around during each class hour. Those who miss a total of six classes (the
equivalent of two full weeks) will be administratively dropped from the course.

Survey Courses: Pre-Modern

Analytical Essay

Historians generally agree that most agricultural civilizations have tended to downgrade the status and potential of women. Although conditions have varied from one society or period of time to another, agricultural civilizations, in the words of Peter Stearns, "were characteristically patriarchal; that is, they were run by men and based on the assumption that men directed political, economic, and cultural life." Drawing on the documents from our reading assignments that are listed below, explore the validity of this thesis in a 5-7 page analytical essay. Indicate how the thesis should be qualified as well as the various ways you find it to be true. Please remember that your purpose is to develop an interpretation rather than to summarize information. You may find it helpful to consult additional library materials. You should footnote your paper to express indebtedness and append a bibliography to indicate your use of additional sources.

Reilly, pp. 21-25, 46-48, 86-93, 186-92
Sherman, pp. 5-8, 25-26, 31-34, 52-54, 77-79, 114-15,
       179-80, 227-28, 272-73
Sowards, pp. 25-53, 145-75, 199-214

Survey Courses: Pre-Modern

Kevin Reilly
Raritan Valley Community College
World Civilization I

RARITAN VALLEY COMMUNITY COLLEGE

Kevin Reilly, World Civilization I, Fall, 1997
Tuesdays and Thursdays

TEXTS:
Kevin Reilly, The West and the World: A History of Civilization from the Ancient World to
    1700, (Marcus Wiener, 1997).

Kevin Reilly, Readings in World Civilizations, (St. Martin's Press, 1995) third edition, vol. I.

SCHEDULE OF CLASSES AND ASSIGNMENTS:
Assignments are due on the day indicated. (WW=The West and the World; RWC=Readings in
World Civilizations). In general, readings for WW will be for Tuesday classes and those for
RWC will be for Thursday classes, but there will be exceptions.

COURSE GOALS:
The course has the following three goals:

1. To teach you "history" in the conventional sense. You should learn something about the past
ten thousand years of human behavior. You should be able to discuss some of the major changes
in human history, understand the more important human societies and cultures, and see the way
in which the past has become the present.
2. To teach you to think more historically about particular issues of current concern in our own
society. These issues are a) Men and Women, b) Cities and Civilization, c) Religion and Society,
and d) War and Peace. Ultimately my goal is that by learning to think more historically about
these issues, you will be able to think more historically about other issues that you might face in
the future.
3. To teach certain skills in critical thinking, especially as they relate to your understanding of
the past and its relationship to the present. These thinking skills will be pursued specifically as
you read the selections in the book of readings (RWC above) and handouts (marked HO) that I
will give you. Normally this will be the main activity on Thursdays. These skills can be
summarized as follows:
a) careful reading and use of primary and secondary sources (esp. Aug. 28, Sept. 4, and Sept. 18);
b) ability to plot and understand historical processes, trends and changes (esp. Sept. 4, Sept. 18,
and Oct. 9);
c) ability to draw and evaluate comparisons of different societies, cultures, or civilizations (esp.
Sept. 25 and Oct. 28);
d) ability to compare different responses to a cross-cultural encounters (esp. Oct. 16, Nov. 25,
and Dec. 4);

e) ability to understand a theme (like gender or war) across different cultures (esp. Oct. 23, Nov. 4, and Dec. 2).

CLASS FORMAT AND EVALUATION:

While there will be occasional slides, films, and lectures, the class format will be mainly discussion. It is my belief that we discover what we think not only by reading and reflecting, but also by writing and speaking. To facilitate this process, there will be a 10 minute essay quiz at the beginning of every class. Each time I will ask you to write a few paragraphs about what you learned. The questions listed after each assignment can serve as a guide to those quizzes as well as to class discussions. You will also be asked to keep a journal/notebook in which you take notes and answer questions on the reading you do for each class. I will ask to see your notebooks on each exam day, including the day of the final.

Your grade will be based on all of these in approximately the following proportions: the two exams (15% each), journal/notebooks (20%), the quizzes (20%), class participation (10%), and the final exam (20%).

UNIT I MEN AND WOMEN

AUGUST 26 INTRODUCTION

Film: "The Hunters" on the Koisan people of the Kalahari desert in southern Africa.
While you watch the film take notes that help you remember material (images and narration) that
    help you answer the following questions:
1. What was the life of these hunting and gathering people like?
2. How were the lives of men different from those of women?

AUGUST 28: HUNTERS AND GATHERERS

Continuation of film.
RWC:
1. Amazon Hunters and Gatherers
Read the article carefully and write answers to the questions in the introduction.

SEPTEMBER 2: MEN AND WOMEN

WW: CH 1
Write a summary of each part of the chapter in your notebook. Be prepared to answer the following questions: What is "natural" and what is "historical" in being a man or woman? Did men always rule? Did anyone? How were the lives of men and women in hunting/gathering society different from our lives today?

SEPTEMBER 4: HUNTERS AND GATHERERS TO FARMERS: THE GREATEST CHANGE
RWC:
2. Memories of a !Kung Girlhood
3. Hunter Religion: An Eskimo Shaman
4. Women and the Agricultural Revolution
HO. The Journey from Eden, Brian Fagan
Write a summary of each article in your notebook. In class we will again stress accurate reading.
We will also ask about long-term changes in human history.

SEPTEMBER 9: AGRICULTURAL AND URBAN REVOLUTIONS
WW: CH 2
How did the agricultural revolution change the lives of men and women? What is the evidence
for women's status in the early "garden" stage of agriculture? How was later plow agriculture
different from early agriculture?

SEPTEMBER 11: Films: Agricultural and Urban Revolutions
Take notes that help you remember some of the information and images of each of the films.
After viewing the films write a page on how the presentation of these films is similar to, and
different from, the presentation of the same subject in your chapter.

UNIT II: CITY AND CIVILIZATION

SEPTEMBER 16: CITY AND CIVILIZATION
WW: ch. 3
How did cities come about? What were some of the achievements and drawbacks of city life?
What is the relationship between cities and civilization? On balance were people better off in
cities?
In which of the cities that you studied would you rather live? Why?

SEPTEMBER 18: URBAN REVOLUTION: Change: Primary and Secondary Sources
RWC: Numbers 7, 8, 9, and 10
7. The Epic of Gilgamesh
8. Hammurabi's Code
9. Indus Civilization and the Aryan Invasion
10. The Vedas
    10.1. The Rig-Veda: Sacrifice as Creation
    10.2. The Upanishads: Brahman and Atman
    10.3. The Upanishads: Karma and Reincarnation
In these readings we will deal with the issue of long-term change and the differences between
primary and secondary sources. In your notebook, write a brief summary of each of the readings.
Consider how each of the readings reveals elements typical of early "civilization" or urban life.
Also consider how the ancient civilization of the Middle-East was different from that of India.

SEPTEMBER 23: CITY AND STATE
WW Ch. 6
Summarize each section of the chapter in your notebook. When you are finished, write a few paragraphs on the differences between the cities you have studied. In class you will also be asked which of these cities you prefer. This raises the larger theoretical question about the relationship between our tastes and our understanding.

SEPTEMBER 25: ANCIENT GREECE AND INDIA: COMPARISON OF CIVILIZATIONS
RWC
12. The Definition of Greek Civilization
10.1 The Rig-Veda: Sacrifice as Creation
13. The Constitution of Athens
14. The Funeral Oration of Pericles
22. The Bhagavad-Gita
15. The Republic
This is your fist exercise in comparative analysis. Read these documents in the order above. The first (a secondary study) develops an argument about the difference between Greek and Indian civilization. What is that argument? Show how each of the other documents offers supporting evidence for that argument.

SEPTEMBER 30: CITIES, CITIZENS, AND SUBJECTS
WW CH 11
What was Max Weber's thesis about the Medieval European city? How were Chinese cities different from European ones? In what ways were Chinese cities important? In what ways were cities important to Islamic civilization? In what ways were European cities different from those in other parts of the world? What was the significance of this difference? How did the cities of Europe change the political culture of Europe? How did European cities change again in the seventeenth and eighteenth centuries? What have we gained, or lost?

OCTOBER 2: EXAM ON UNIT I & II

UNIT III RELIGION AND SOCIETY

OCTOBER 7: AGE AND FAMILY: RELIGION AND CULTURAL CHANGE
WW CH 4
Take notes on each section of the chapter. After finishing the chapter write two pages summarizing the major points of the chapter. How is this history of religion similar to, or different from, what you might have expected?

OCTOBER 9: JUDE0-CHRISTIAN TRADITION: CHANGE OVER TIME
RWC
19. The Bible
This is an exercise in understanding how things change over time. As you read the selections from the Bible, try to understand in what order they were written and how they reflect changes in the history of Judaism and early Christianity. Hint: the chapter in WW and the intros to each selection from the Bible provide guidance.

OCTOBER 14: CHRISTIANITY, HINDUISM, AND THE SELF
WW CH 5
Take notes on each section of the chapter. When you are finished write two pages summarizing the argument of the chapter. Be prepared to tell the class why you agree or disagree with this argument.

OCTOBER 16: BUDDHISTS AND CONFUCIANS: A GREAT ENCOUNTER
RWC
Buddha
  23.1 Gotama's Discovery
  23.2 The Buddha's First Sermon
Confucius
  24. The Analects of Confucius
The Encounter
  28. Buddhism in China: The Disposition of Error
  29. The Introduction of Buddhism into Japan
Take notes on each of these primary documents. What do these documents tell you about the world's of Buddhists and Confucius. How were their worlds similar? How were they different? How did Buddhists and Confucians perceive each other?

OCTOBER 21: ECOLOGY AND THEOLOGY
WW CH 12
What, according to Toynbee and White, does ecology have to do with theology? Have the religious traditions of Asia been more "environmentally friendly" than the Judaeo-Christian tradition?

OCTOBER 23: TECHNOLOGY AND SCIENCE: ACROSS CULTURES
RWC
49. The Emperor's Giraffe / Samuel M. Wilson
33. China, Technology, and Change
HO. Muslim on Frankish Medicine/Usamah ibn-Munquidh
HO. Religion and Ecology
    Life of Boniface: Converting the Hessians
    Popular religion: charms
What do these readings tell you about the comparative scientific and technological traditions of each culture? In what ways do these sources support or challenge Toynbee and White?

OCTOBER 28: CHRISTIANITY AND ISLAM: TWO OR THREE WAYS
HO. Kings and Priests: the two powers
     Pope Gelasius, Two Swords
     Justinian, Civil Law
  Koran
HO. Icons and Iconoclasm
     John of Damascus, On the Divine Images
     Koran
42. Feudalism and Manorialism
     1. A Feudal Oath of Homage
     2. Duties of a Villein
36. Civilization of Medieval Islam
48. The Great Islamic Empires
Take notes on each of these readings. For each of the three topics compare the approaches of
Orthodox Christianity, Roman Christianity and Islam. In what ways was Orthodox Christianity
more like Islam than it was like Roman Christianity?

OCTOBER 30: EXAM ON UNIT III

UNIT IV: LOVE AND SEX

NOVEMBER 4: LOVE AND SEX IN GREECE, ROME, AND INDIA
WW: CH 7
What did the Athenians think of love and sex? How were their ideas different from those of
other societies that you have read about? What accounts for those differences? How were
Roman ideas of love and sex different from those of the Greeks? In what ways were Christian
ideas of love and sex a response to Greek and Roman ideas or behavior? How were Indian ideas
of love and sex different from Greek, Roman, and Christian?

NOVEMBER 6: COURTLY LOVE
WW CH 10
What sounds foreign, and what sounds familiar, in Ulrich von Lichtenstein? Was courtly love a
patriarchal trick or a recognition of women? How much of these ideas do we still share in
Western society? In what ways did Indian and Japanese society have different ideas of love,
religion, and sexuality?

NOVEMBER 11: SEX AND GENDER: ACROSS CULTURES
RWC
31. A Wife's Collection / Li Ch'ing-chao
34. Japan: The Tale of Genji
HO. The Koran
38. The Rubaiyat
43. The Art of Courtly Love / Andreas Capellanus
What ideas of love are expressed in each selection? How do these reflect cultural differences described the in WW Ch. 10?

UNIT V WAR AND PEACE

NOVEMBER 13: Film: The Roman Arena
Take notes that enable you to write a brief essay on Roman attitudes towards violence. Write two pages on the subject after viewing the film.

NOVEMBER 18: WAR AND SOCIETY
WW CH 8
Take notes on the chapter, section by section. Then write two pages comparing Roman and Chinese empires and the role of soldiers in each.

NOVEMBER 20: RELIGION AND WAR
WW CH 9: Violence and Vengeance
Take notes on each section of the chapter. Then write a two page essay on the causes of war and violence in the Middle Ages.

NOVEMBER 25: CRUSADES AND MONGOLS: ARMED ENCOUNTERS
RWC
HO. Ideas of Holy War
    Blessing swords
    Koran
    Summa Theologica: Just War
46. The Impact of the Turkish and Mongol Conquests
47. Marco Polo Travels to Kublai Khan
Compare Christian and Islamic ideas of holy war. How were the crusades different from the encounter with the Mongols?

DECEMBER 2: SPORT AND COMBAT: ACROSS CULTURES
Handouts:
The Medieval Tournament / Richard Barber
America's Ball Game / Stephan F. Borhegyi
Take notes on each of the articles. Then write a brief essay on the relationship between sport and combat.

DECEMBER 4: ATLANTIC ENCOUNTER AND CONQUEST
Spanish Conquest of Aztec Mexico
    55. A Spanish Description / Bernal Diaz
    HO. Aztec account of the Conquest
HO. Beyond Blame: Two modern interpretations
    1. Ecological Impact, Alfred Crosby
    2. Continuity of past,
How was the Spanish account of the encounter with the Aztecs different from the Aztec account?
How are modern interpretations of the conquest different from those of the time? What would
you say is the real meaning of the encounter?

Survey Courses: Modern

Kenneth J. Andrien
The Ohio State University
World History, 1500-Present

Professor Kenneth J. Andrien
Office: 210 Dulles Hall
Office Telephone: 292-0324
Department Telephone: 292-2674 (for messages)
Office Hours: Monday, Wednesday, 10:30-11:15; Tuesday, 3:30-4:30; and by appointment.

History 200.02: World History, 1500-Present

Course Objectives

This course examines the major issues that have shaped the human experience from 1500 to the present. The major theme of the course is the gradual integration of the various regions of the world into a single interconnected world system, beginning with the expansion of Europe in the sixteenth century. It will also attempt to examine the internal dynamics for change in the various parts of this growing world system. Each week we will study one major set of issues, examining questions of particular importance to analyze their **global significance**. Our goal is to convey factual knowledge about the human experience over the past five hundred years, and to provide an interpretative framework for understanding these historical changes.

Assigned Readings

Geoffrey Baraclough, The Times Concise Atlas of World History
Mark A. Kishlansky, Sources of World History
Carlo Levi, Christ Stopped at Eboli
Peter Stearns, Michael Adas, and Stuart Schwartz, World Civilizations: The Global Experience

Course Requirements

I. Class attendance and participation in the weekly discussion sections are an integral part of the course and will count **15%** towards the determination of the final grade.

II. There will be a midterm examination scheduled for **April 28, 1995**. The examination will be primarily essay in character and include material from the readings and the class sessions. The instructor will only approve make-up examinations after receiving a valid written excuse. It is the student's responsibility to take such a make-up examination at the time and place specified by the instructors. The midterm will count **25% of the final grade**.

II. The will be a short paper of approximately five pages (1,250 words) which will count **25% of the final grade**. The paper assignment will be based on Carlo Levi's *Christ Stopped at Eboli*; it is due on **May 22, 1995**.

III. The final examination is scheduled for **Tuesday, June 6, 1995, between 7:30 and 9:18 AM**, in our normal classroom. It will be primarily essay in nature and will count **35% of the final grade**.

<u>Schedule of Class Assignments and Class Topics</u>

Part I: The World Shrinks, 1450-1750

Week I: The Beginnings of Global Integration, 1500-1650

> **Reading:** Stearns, chs. 21-23; Atlas, 64-71.

March 27: Introduction: The World in 1500

March 29: Regional Civilizations: Islam, Asia and Africa

March 31: Europe and the Invasion of America

Week II: The Growth and Consolidation of the World System

> **Reading:** Stearns, chs. 24-26; Atlas, 72-81; Kishlansky, **vol. 1**, dcts. 65, 68, 69, 72, 77.

April 3: Spanish America and Silver

April 5: The Fur Trade in North America

April 7: The Russian Expansion

Week III: The Rise of a Global Economy, 1650-1750

> **Reading:** Stearns, chs. 27-28; Atlas, 82-87; Kishlansky, **vol. 2**. dcts. 83, 92, 107, 109.

April 10: The Struggle in the European Core

April 12: The Limits of European Power: Africa

April 16: The Limits of European Power: Japan

Survey Courses: Modern

Part II: Industrialization and the Rise of Western Global Hegemony, 1750-1914

Week IV: The Age of Revolutions, 1750-1850

> **Reading:** Stearns, ch. 29; Atlas, 88-95; Kishlansky, dcts. 87, 100, 102, 113.

April 17: The Age of "Atlantic Revolutions"

April 19: Political Upheavals in the Peripheries

April 21: The Industrial Revolution and Socioeconomic Ferment

Week V: The Renewal of European Imperialism, 1750-1850

> **Reading:** Stearns, ch. 30; Atlas, 98-99; Kishlansky, dcts. 119, 126, 128, 136.

April 24: The Era of Free Trade Imperialism

April 26: European Imperialism in Asia

April 28: **Midterm Examination**

Part III: The Twentieth-Century World

Week VI: The World and the New Industrial Order, 1850-1930

> **Reading:** Stearns, chs. 31-32; Atlas, 96-97; 104-7; Kishlansky, dcts. 118, 123, 124, 130.

May   1: Transportation, Communication, Migration, and Global Unity

May   3: Dependent Peripheries: Latin America

May   5: The Crisis of the Ottoman Empire

Week VII: New Crises in the World System, 1850-1930

> **Readings:** Stearns, chs. 33-34; Atlas, 102-03; 108-15; Kishlansky, dcts. 133, 135, 138, 141.

May   8: Industrialization in Japan

May   10: Global War and Revolution

May   12: The War in the Peripheries

Week VIII: The World System in Depression, 1930-1945

Reading: Stearns, ch. 35; Atlas, 116-25; 130-31; Levi, entire; Kishlansky, dct. 149.

May   15: Global Depression in the Core

May   17: Global Depression in the Peripheries

May   19: The Second Global War

Week IX: The Rise and Decline of the Bipolar World, 1945-1995

Reading: Stearns, chs. 36, 38, 39, 41; Atlas, 126-29; 132-43; Kishlansky, dcts. 143, 152, 154, 158.

May   22: The Rise of Bipolarity. **LEVI PAPERS DUE**

May   24: Decolonization

May   26: The Epic of the Chinese Revolution

Week X: The Search for a New World Order

Reading: Stearns, 37, 40, 42; Atlas, 144-51; Kishlansky, dcts. 142, 147, 162, 165, 164.

May   29: No Class

May   31: The Rise of the Pacific Rim

June   2: The Collapse of the Soviet Union and the Rise of a Multipolar World

* * * * *

Survey Courses: Modern

Paper Assignment on *Christ Stopped at Eboli*

Write a paper of approximately five pages (1,250 words) on Carlo Levi's book, *Christ Stopped at Eboli*. Please type the paper and double space. If it is impossible to submit a typed paper, you must double space, write legibly, and try to keep the length at approximately 1,250 words. Papers that do not follow these directions will be returned to the student. **Late papers will be penalized five points per day up to a maximum penalty of thirty points!**

Each paper must address the issues raised in the following questions. In what ways are the large-scale political, economic, and social forces of world history shaping the lives of the Italian villagers described by Levi? How are these people unaffected by such global forces? In formulating your answer consider the following issues: village social stratification, attitudes about religion and the natural world; the role of the state; and the place of brigandage and rebellion.

Use specific examples from Levi, the text, and the class sessions wherever necessary to support your argument. This is an exercise in exploring the relationship between the large-scale forces of global change and the lives of individuals.

Remember that every good paper has an introduction that describes the basic issues covered in the paper, a body that uses specific information to formulate a coherent argument, and a conclusion that pulls together your argument and indicates clearly its significance. Be sure to check spelling, grammar, and correct all typographical errors before submitting your paper.

* * * * *

Culture, Civilization, and World Economies:
Definitions and Terms

CULTURE: (1) **High Culture:** artistic, literary, or religious-sacred traditions in any society

(2) **Popular Culture:** the sum total not just of high culture but all the ideas and artifacts that tie a society together: everything from commonplace items like pottery to folk art

CIVILIZATION: When one culture expands its influence over others (particularly by using war or economic power) in a long-lasting way, such as the Mongols in Central Asia or Rome in the Mediterranean, it becomes a **macroculture** or **civilization**.

Civilizations are defined by a number of characteristics:

1. They produce an economic surplus of regional produce and/or luxury goods;

2. They have economically specialized roles, with considerable social stratification--into priests, bureaucrats, farmers, and merchants, etc.;

3. They have defined urban centers that serve as an integrative force in matters of trade, culture, and politics;

4. They are often characterized by a widely accepted religious tradition, with a well-defined social role for the clergy;

5. They have a government with military and administrative powers.

WORLD SYSTEM: a single geopolitical unit (or macro civilization), which controls many different cultures or civilizations across the globe through its economic and military power.

1. The first civilization or zone to achieve this status was centered in **Europe** and began its period of expansion after 1492.

2. By the twentieth century this single world system, emanating from Europe, had incorporated or controlled much of the globe, vastly increasing the degree of global political, social, and especially economic interrelatedness.

3. The world system was linked fundamentally by **economic** connections (especially through world trade), and it included many different cultures.

What is the "Hierarchy of Zones" in the World System?

1. The **Core or center zones** are the dominant regions in the world system, and they were centered in Europe until the end or World War II. They are the most economically advanced zones, with diverse economies (usually characterized by considerable industrial strength) advanced technologies, and greater accumulations of wealth.

2. **Intermediate or semiperipheral zones** are less dominant regions; they may be termed the "backyard" of the core zones. Often semiperipheries act as "conveyer belts" transferring resources from the regions producing raw materials to the more advanced core zones. They are often regions or nation states that are rising to core status or falling from that position. This often happens to second rank powers in periods of decline, such as Great Britain after World War II.

3. **Peripheries or satellites** are part of the world system, but they are much less prominent. They are usually the colonies of the core powers or dependencies (those regions or nations that are politically independent but are economically subordinate, such as many Latin American or African nations).

4. **External arenas** are those parts of the world outside the sway of the world system. They can be (1) powerful international actors, such as the former Communist states, (2) relatively isolated or underdeveloped regions, such as the poorest nations in Africa, or (3) frontier zones that are largely unsettled and undeveloped. These last two types of external arenas decreased rapidly in number during the second half of the twentieth century.

What are the general rules that define the World System?

1. It has vaguely defined **boundaries** that change, but usually slowly over time.

2. A key **city or cluster of cities** (by the twentieth century) are the important centers of exchange and contact.

3. A **strong state** operates at the core zones, although the type of political structure varies over time, from a monarchy or elite-controlled system to pluralistic democracies.

4. It has a **multicultural** union of different peoples.

5. There is an **uneven distribution of wealth** through the hierarchy of zones (i.e. rich and poor nations) depending on how they were incorporated into the world system.

6. There is also a markedly **uneven distribution of wealth within the various zones** of the world system (i.e. socioeconomic stratification within nations).

7. **Trade and war** are the most important factors in the expansion of the world system, but trade is by far the most important of these two factors.

8. It tends to have a **single dominant core power**, but there are times when more than one core power exists.

9. All of these rules apply **only at the macro level**--at the level of international trade, politics, and diplomacy. Many rural peasants, in particular, at the bottom of their socioeconomic strata are quite removed from these trends. They eke out a living much as before being incorporated into the world system, whether they live in a core or a peripheral zone. Over time, the world system does penetrate more deeply into societies, affecting even this subsistence sector. This is a slow process, however, that is barely perceptible except over relatively long time periods.

Survey Courses: Modern

Lynn Hollen Lees
Sumathi Ramaswamy
Lee Cassanelli
University of Pennsylvania
The World: History and Modernity

History 11   **Profs. Lees/Ramaswamy/Cassanelli**
Spring 1998   **lhlees@history.upenn.edu**
M/W/F 10-11   **ramaswam@sas.upenn.edu**
Stiteler B-21   **lcassane@sas.upenn.edu**

THE WORLD: HISTORY AND MODERNITY

Books for purchase:

Adas, Michael, Islamic and European Expansion (Temple)
Cesaire, Aime, Discourse on Colonialism (Monthly Review Press)
Dunn, Ross, Ibn Battuta (U Cal)
Gandhi, M.K., Hind Swarj (Navjian)
Northrup, David, ed. The Atlantic Slave Trade (Heath)
Solzhenitsyn, Alexander, One Day in the Life of Ivan Denisovitch (Bantam)
Times Concise Atlas of World History (Hammond)

Written work:

1 in-class Mid-term (map quiz plus essay)
Final Take-home exam
2 essays (3-5 pages) on assigned readings

Lectures and Assignments

Part I. THE WORLD AROUND 1400

1.   Jan. 12.   Introduction: themes, problems; rethinking conceptual categories

     Jan. 14.   Space and boundaries. Maps in 1400

     Jan. 16.   MAPS
                   Limitations imbedded in maps;
                   How is the world divided today? Are civilizations the major units
                       primed for conflict?

2.   Jan. 19.   Ways of life and culture: City centered civilizations

        Jan. 21.   Raiders and Traders

        Jan 23.   Discussion of Ibn Battuta

            reading: Ross Dunn, Ibn Battuta, pp. 1-105, 116-128, 290-310
            maps: Times Concise Atlas, 40-1, 46-49
            issues: structures of social life and exchange; Islam as a world civilization;
                travel and encounters on the eve of modernity;

3.   Jan. 26:   World religions - I Hinduism & Buddhism

        Jan. 28   World religions II: Islam
                Guest Lecturer : Barbara von Schlegell

        Jan. 30.   Discussion of week's readings

            reading:
                Dunn, Ibn Battuta, pp. 183-240, 310-318
                R. Eaton, "Islamic History as Global History," in M. Adas, Islamic &
                    European Expansion, 1-36.
                J. Tucker, " Gender and Islamic History," in Adas, 37-74.
            documents: "Four Ends of Man," "Basic Doctrines of Theravada Buddhism,"
                "Therigatha;" texts on Islam: The Qur'an.
            maps: Times Atlas, 26-9, 38-9, 58-59
            issues: cultural meaning of religion; comparisons of Islam, Buddhism,
                Hinduism as "world" religions

4.   Feb. 2.   The Periphery: Europe around 1490

        Feb. 4.   The Periphery: Central America and the Maya, c. 1490
            (Class Trip: Meet at side entrance of University Museum Guided tour of
            Mayan exhibits.)

Feb. 6.   Discussion of documents and readings

     reading:
          J. Abu-Lughod, "The World System in the Thirteenth Century: Dead
             End or Precursor?" in Adas, 75-103;
          W.H. McNeill, "The Age of Gunpowder Empires, 1450-1800," in
             Adas, 103-140.
      documents: H. Cortes, "Description of Mexico city in 1520" and Bernal
          Diaz, the Entrance into Mexico."
      maps: 56-57, 62-63
      issues: different types of sources; material culture; What and how do we
          know about the Maya? How can you explain European expansion
          into the Americas?

II. TURNING POINT: 1492, 1498, AND THEIR CONSEQUENCES

5.   Feb. 9:   1492 and Christopher Columbus

       Feb. 11:   1498 and Vasco da Gama

       Feb. 13:   discussion

     reading:
          A. Crosby, "The Columbian Voyages, The Columbian Exchange and
             their Historians, in Adas, 141-164;
      documents:
          C. Columbus, excerpts from "Journal of the First Voyage to
             the Americas;"
          "R. Eaton, "Multiple Lenses: Differing Perspectives of
             Fifteenth-Century Calicut;" "Edward Terry" in Foster,
             ed., Early Travels in India.
      maps: 62-67
      issues: disease pools and ecology; culture conflict; understanding
          "the Other"; the lure of trade

III. THE WORLD AROUND 1700: APPROACHING THE MODERN?

6. Feb. 16. The Impact of the Slave Trade in Africa
            Guest: Lee Cassanelli

    Feb. 18. Migrations: Voluntary and Involuntary

    Feb. 20   Debate on the Slave Trade

        reading:
                P. Curtin, "The Tropical Atlantic in the Age of the Slave Trade," 165-
                    198 in Adas, Islamic & European Expansion;
                David Northrup, The Atlantic Slave Trade..
        maps: 60-61
        issues: quantitative vs qualitative sources; slavery and racism; links of slave
                trade to Afr. militarism, domestic production, and state building;
                global flows of people

7. Feb. 23. Japan in 1700
            Guest lecturer: Prof. Cameron Hurst

        reading:
                Conrad Shirokauer, A Brief History of Japanese Civilization, chaps.
                    6 & 7;
                David Lu, Sources of Japanese History, excerpts era on merchants in
                    Tokogawa.
        maps: 50-51, 106-107.

    Feb. 25. discussion and review

    Feb. 27. HOUR EXAM IN CLASS

        issues: merchant capitalism in Japan; how different was Japan c. 1700 from
                the rest of Asia?

114

8. March 2:   Enlightenment in Europe

    March 4.   Expecting the Enlightenment

    March 6:   Discussion of documents F. Bacon, "New Organon;"

        reading: documents:
            I. Kant, "What is Enlightenment;" Condorcet, "Sketch of the Progress
                of the Human Mind,"
            Sugita Gempaku "The Beginning of Dutch Studies in Japan;" Rokeya
                Hossain, "Sultana's Dream,"
            Macaulay, "Decision to Introduce English Education into India."
        maps: 68-69, 84-87
        issues: Global intellectual transformations: "Europeanization" of the world?

SPRING BREAK!!

IV. TURNING POINT: 1789 AND ITS CONSEQUENCES

9. March 16.   Revolution In France

    March 18.   Revolutions in Latin America
                 Guest lecture: Prof. Franks

    March 20.   discussion of readings

        reading:
            L.S. Stavrianos, "Europe's Political Revolutions," 457-78;
        documents:
            "Declaration of the Rights of Man and of the Citizen,"
            "Declaration of the Rights of Woman";
            P. Curtin, "Revolution in the French Antilles;" "The Vision of
                Bolivar."
        maps: 88-91
        issues: what is a revolution? How to explain its outbreak? What does
            revolution do to racial, gender hierarchies?

V. THE INDUSTRIAL AGE: NATIONALISM, EMPIRE, AND TECHNOLOGY

10.   March 23:   The Industrial Revolution in Europe

       March 25:   Industrialization in Asia and Africa

       March 27:   Debate

           reading:
           F. Engels, "Conditions of the Working Class in Manchester,"
           P. Tsurumi, "Factory Girls;"
           maps: 82-83, 98-99, 108-109
           issues: impact of industrialization on social relations, capitalism in the
               underdeveloped world

11.   March 30:   Ideologies of Imperialism

       April 1   Gender, Sexuality and empire

       April 3   discussion of readings

           reading:
           M. Adas, "High Imperialism and the 'New' History," in Adas, 311-
               344;
           M. Strobel, "Gender, Sex and Empire, in Adas, 345-375;
           documents:
           G. Orwell, "Shooting the Elephant;"
           R. Kipling, "The White Man's Burden,"
           V. Lenin, "Imperialism is the Monopoly State of Capitalism"
           maps: 100-105
           issues: Contradictions and fragilities in imperial rule; does gender matter in
               imperial rule?

12.   April 6.   Nationalism and Decolonization

        April 8.   video: "From the Barrel of a Gun"

        April 10.   Discussion of Gandhi and Cesaire

            reading:
                Aime Cesaire, <u>Discourse on Colonialism</u>;
                M. K. Gandhi, <u>Hind Swaraj</u>
            maps: 114-119, 122-3, 126-7, 132-139
            issues: What is a nation? Nationalism in the colonial world - a derivative
            discourse?

VI. TURNING POINT: THE COLD WAR ENDS, 1989.

13.   April 13.   Lenin and Stalin in Russia

        April 15.   The Cold War

        April 17:   discussion of Solzhenitsyn

            reading:
                A. Solzhenitsyn, <u>One Day in the Life of Ivan Denisovitch</u>
            documents:
                W. Churchill, "Iron Curtain" speech;
                J. Stalin, "Pravda Interview"
            maps: 136-137, 140-141, 146-149
            issues: Why did the Cold War develop? Why did communism collapse?

Survey Courses: Modern

14. April 20.   Global Capitalism and Global Consumerism
                   Guest Lecture: Prof. Ludden

     April 22   Global Linkages in 1997: the Past in the Present

     April 24:   review and questions Map Quiz

          reading: documents:
               F. Fukuyama, excerpt from The End of History and the Lost Man;
               S.P. Huntington, "the Clash of Civilizations" Foreign Affairs,
                   (Summer 1993)
               Ali Shariati, "Reflections on Humanity."
          maps: 150-151
          issues: global capitalism and homogenization; clashes of civilizations;
               ethnicity in late 20th Century

Survey Courses: Modern

John A. Mears
Southern Methodist University
World Cultures and Civilizations

History 1302
WORLD CULTURES AND CIVILIZATIONS
Syllabus of Lectures and Discussions

Instructor: John A. Mears   Office Hours: 11-12 MWF
Office: 58D Dallas Hall   Telephone: 768-2974

Textbooks

Michael Adas, Islamic and European Expansion
Arnold Pacey, Technology in World Civilization
Kevin Reilly, Readings in World Civilizations, Vol. Two
Dennis Sherman et. al., World Civilizations, Vol. II
J. Kelley Sowards, Makers of World History, Vol. 2

Session topics and Reading Assignments

I.   Setting the Stage: The world in the Year 1000

        Jan. 13   Introduction: Approaches to World History

        Jan. 15   Great Milestones in the Human Experience

        Jan 17   Varieties of Cultural Complexity

        Jan. 20   UNIVERSITY HOLIDAY

        Jan 22   The Civilizations of Eurasia: China and India

        Jan 24   The Civilizations of Eurasia: Islam and Europe

        Jan. 27   Cultural Contours of the Western Hemisphere

        Jan. 29   Sub-Saharan Africa, Australia, and Polynesia

                Readings: Adas, pp. vii-36
                              Pacey, Chap. 1

II. The Era of Nomadic Empires (1000-1500)

Jan. 31   The Turco-Mongol Invasions

Feb. 3   The Predominance of China

Feb. 5   China's East Asian Outliers

Feb. 7   Ottoman, Safavid, and Mogul Empires

Feb. 10   The Rise of Latin Christendom

Feb. 12   Empires, Kingdoms, and Tribes in Africa

Feb. 14   The Amerindian Civilizations

Feb. 17   HOUR EXAMINATION

  Readings: Adas, pp. 37-102
                  Pacey, Chaps. 2-3

III. The Onset of Globalization (1500-1750)

Feb. 19   The Self-Transformation of Europe

Feb. 21   European Expansion: Causes and Consequences

Feb. 24   The Americas in the 16th and 17th Century

Feb. 26   Continuity and Disruption in the Moslem World

Feb. 28   Hindu India and Buddhist Southeast Asia

Mar. 3   China from Ming to Manchu

Mar. 5   Japan: The Tokugawa Shogunate

  Readings: Adas, pp. 103-64
                  Pacey, Chaps. 4-6
                  Reilly, pp. 22-57, 72-86
                  Sherman, pp. 1-28, 51-68
                  Sowards, Chaps. 1, 3-4

IV. European Assertion and Its Repercussions (1750-1850)

    Mar. 7   Europe's Continuing Expansion

    Mar. 8-16   SPRING BREAK

    Mar. 17   The Reenergizing of Europe: Political Revolutions

    Mar. 19   The Reenergizing of Europe: Industrialism

    Mar. 21   The Americas: Contrasts and Common Denominators

    Mar. 24   Sub-Saharan Africa and the Wider World

    Mar. 26   Disjuncture in the Moslem Heartlands

    Mar. 28   UNIVERSITY HOLIDAY

    Mar. 31   India and China: Crisis in the Traditional Order
              ANALYTICAL ESSAY DUE

           Readings: Adas, pp. 165-310
                         Pacey, Chaps. 7-8
                         Reilly, pp. 92-110, 117-49
                         Sherman, pp. 74-5, 77-8, 108-15, 139-47, 153-9
                         Sowards, Chaps. 7, 9-10

V. The West and the World in the Era of European Primacy (1850-1900)

    Apr. 2   Western Cultural Creativity

    Apr. 4   The German/American Phase of Industrialism

    Apr. 7   The European State-System at the Culmination of Western
                        Imperialism

    Apr. 9   The Modernization of Japan

    Apr. 11   India and China: Interaction with the West

    Apr. 14   Africa and the Middle East at the Turn of the Century

Survey Courses: Modern

Apr. 16   The Nineteenth-Century Americas in their Global Context

   Readings: Adas. pp. 311-75
        Pacey, chaps. 9-10
        Reilly, pp. 154-87, 198-202
        Sherman, pp. 176-221, 235-42

VI. The Contemporary World: Humankind in a Global Age

  Apr. 18   The Crisis of European Dominance

  Apr. 21   War on a Global Scale (1900-1950)

  Apr. 23   Superpower Bipolarity and Global Conflict in the "Cold War" (1950-2000)

  Apr. 25   Culture, Technology, and the Global Economy

  Apr. 28   Regional Responses to Global Integration

  Apr. 30   Disrupted Expectations at Century's Close

  May 2   Conclusion: Perspectives on Our Times

   Readings: Pacey, chap. 11
        Reilly. pp. 229-36, 255-7, 269-328, 354-8
        Sherman, pp. 276-302, 317-25, 327-62
        Sowards, chaps. 11-14

  May 7   FINAL EXAMINATION 11:30 a.m. - 2:30 p.m.

Formal Requirements

In addition to an hour examination (25% of the course grade) and a final (50%), students will write an analytical essay (25%) which must be submitted by Monday, March 31. Students will lose one-third of a letter grade for each day that the paper is **late**.

Students will be expected to attend class fully prepared on a regular basis. A sign-in sheet will be passed around during each class hour. Those who miss a total of six classes (the equivalent of two full weeks) will be administratively dropped from the course.

Survey Courses: Modern

Analytical Essay

In his essay featured in the Adas volume, Richard M. Eaton argues that Islam was "history's first truly global civilization," while Peter N. Stearns discusses "the global perspective on industrialization." Drawing as necessary from the bibliographical references provided by these authors, write a 5-7 page essay exploring the meaning and significance of one of these phrases. How does your author use the word "global?" How does his theme relate to "the forging of a global order?" If you chose Islam's "global character," explain in particular how the careers of Suleiman and Akbar (Sowards, pp. 1-22, 47-66) can be related to Eaton's theme. If you chose the idea that "industrialization was an international process," be sure to draw upon the material contained in Pacey, chaps. 7-8. Please remember that your purpose is to develop an interpretation rather than to summarize information. You may find it helpful to utilize ideas presented in class discussion. You should footnote your paper to express indebtedness and append a bibliography to indicate your use of additional sources.

Survey Courses: Modern

Kevin Reilly
Raritan Valley Community College
World Civilization II

RARITAN VALLEY COMMUNITY COLLEGE

World Civilization II, Spring, 1998, Honors Section
Professor Kevin Reilly

TEXTS
Kevin Reilly, The West and the World, 2nd ed., vol. II (HarperCollins, 1989). Indicated below
   as "WW."
Kevin Reilly, Readings in World Civilizations, 3rd ed., vol. II (Bedford/St. Martin's Press, 1995).
   Indicated below as "RWC."
Handouts when appropriate.

SCHEDULE OF CLASSES AND ASSIGNMENTS:
Assignments are due on the day indicated. (WW=The West and the World; RWC=Readings in
World Civilizations). In general, readings for WW will be for Tuesday classes and those for
RWC will be for Thursday classes, but there will be exceptions.

COURSE GOALS:
The course has the following three goals:

1. To teach "history" in the conventional sense. You should learn something about the past five
hundred years of human behavior. You should be able to discuss some of the major changes in
this period of human history, understand something about the more important societies and
cultures, and see the way in which the past has become the present.

2. To help you think more historically about particular issues of current concern in our own
society. These issues are a) Individual and Society. b) Race and Racism, c) Politics and Culture,
and d) Economics and Ecology. Ultimately my goal is that by learning to think more historically
about these issues, you will be able to think more historically about other issues that you might
face in the future.

3. To teach certain skills in critical thinking, especially as they relate to your understanding of
the past and its relationship to the present. These thinking skills will be pursued specifically as
you read the selections in the book of readings (RWC above).
a) careful reading and use of primary and secondary sources;
b) ability to plot and understand historical processes, trends and changes;
c) ability to draw and evaluate comparisons of different societies, cultures, or civilizations;
d) ability to compare different responses to cross-cultural encounters;
e) ability to understand a theme across different cultures.

Survey Courses: Modern

HONORS SECTION:
This honors section will be different from other sections in the following three respects.
1. Additional readings will be handed out periodically (see unnumbered readings under "handouts" below).
2. There will be a class trip to Ellis Island and the Museum of Modern Art with an additional related paper assignment.
3. There will be another paper which will require additional reading (see under week 1).

CLASS FORMAT AND EVALUATION:
While there will be occasional slides, films, and lectures, the class format will be mainly discussion. It is my belief that we discover what we think not only by reading and reflecting, but also by writing and speaking. To facilitate this process, there will be a 10 minute essay quiz at the beginning of every class. Each time I will ask you to write a few paragraphs about what you learned. I also ask you to keep a journal/notebook in which you take notes on the reading you do for each class. I will ask to see your notebooks on each exam day, including the day of the final. Your grade will be based on all of these in approximately the following proportions: the two exams (10% each), the two papers (10% each), journal/notebooks (15%), the quizzes (15%), class participation (10%), and the final exam (20%).

WEEK 1: INTRODUCTION
Social and Individual Identity in 16th Century Europe
Film: "The Return of Martin Guerre"
Questions to consider in watching film:
How has individuality changed in the last five hundred years? Are people more or less individualistic today than they were in the sixteenth century? In what ways was life more "public" or "private" then? How did people understand their own or someone else's identity then? Did people know each other any better in the sixteenth century than we know each other today? What made a person an individual? What does today?

*Assignment of paper on Individuality for week 3; Extra readings from The Return of Martin Guerre by Natalie Zemon Davis, The Cheese and the Worms by Carlo Ginzburg, or Montaillou by Emmanuel Le Roy Ladurie.

WEEK 2: Comparative 16th Century Individuality
Conclusion of film. Also following reading:
WW CH 1
RWC Ch 1 AND HANDOUTS:
1. The Prince
3. City Women and Religious Change
Neo-Confucianism
Appeal to the German Nobility / Martin Luther
Anti-Luther and Anti-Catholic printed tracts
Safavi culture: Sufis and painting
Mogul toleration

WEEK. 3: The Columbian Exchange or Conquest
WW ch. 2
RWC and Handouts: Atlantic Contacts and the Slave Trade: Uneven Encounters
Columbus Letter
6. A Dutch Massacre of the Algonquins
The Slave Trade
    Nzinga Mbemba, Appeal to the King of Portugal, 1526
    William Bosman, Slave Trader, 1700
    7. Olaudah Equiano, Enslaved Captive, 1756
    John Newton, Slave Trader, ca. 1754
    Osei Bonsu, Asante King, 1820

WEEK. 4: GENDER AND EMPIRE IN 17TH CENTURY ASIA
RWC AND HANDOUTS
A. Gender and Family: Across Cultures
11. Commerce and Gender in Southeast Asia / Anthony Reid
Death of Woman Wang, Jonathan Spence
Family Instructions for the Miu Lineange, late 16th cent.
Letters from Constantinople / Lady Mary Wortley Montague

B. Asian Continental Empires: Comparative Empires
12. The Late Ming Empire / Jonathan Spence
13. The Ottoman Empire under Sulayman / Busbecq
14. The Russian Empire: Two Law Codes
    1. Peasants Reduced to Serfdom, 1649
    2. Westernizing by Peter the Great, 1701-1714

WEEK. 5: POLITICS, MORALITY, AND SCIENCE IN 17TH CENTURY EUROPE
WW: Ch. 3
RWC AND HANDOUTS
A. The Scientific Revolution: Changes in Thinking
15. The Scientific Revolution in the West
16. Women and Science / Anderson and Zinsser
17. China, Technology and Change
18. A Dutch Anatomy Lesson in Japan
Galileo dialogue

B. Enlightenment and Revolution: Windows on an Age
19. On Miracles
20. What is Enlightenment?
21. Two Revolutionary Declarations
     1. The American Declaration of Independence
     2. The French Declaration of the Rights of Man and Citizen
22. The U.S. Bill of Rights
Simon Bolivar, Letter to Jamaica

WEEK. 6: EXAM

WEEK 7: CAPITALISM AND THE INDUSTRIAL REVOLUTION
WW CH 4
RWC AND HANDOUTS: Capitalism and the Industrial Revolution: The Modern Change
24. Asia and the Industrial Revolution / Pacey
25. The Wealth of Nations
26. The Factory System of Production
The Sadler Report of the House of Commons
27. The Communist Manifesto
The Industrial Revolution outside the West / Peter Stearns

WEEK 8: INDUSTRIALIZATION AND SOCIALISM
WW: Ch. 5 and Ch. 6

WEEK 9: Nationalism and Colonialism
WW ch. 8
RWC AND HANDOUTS: Western Economic Expansion: Encounters with Power
30. The Letter of Commissoner Lin to Queen Victoria
29. Nehru, British Rule in India
31. American Expansion from the Indian Perspective

WEEK 10: IMPERIALISM AND RACISM
WW ch. 7
RWC AND HANDOUTS: Migrations and Imperialism: Colonial Encounters
Lord Lugard, The Scramble for Africa
Rudyard Kipling, "The White Man's Burden"
35. The Tools of Empire

*TRIP TO ELLIS ISLAND AND MUSEUM OF MODERN ART
Paper Assignment on Imperialism, Racism, Migration, or Modern Culture announced.

WEEK 11: MODERN CULTURE
WW Ch. 9
RWC AND HANDOUTS: Culture and Change: Change in Thinking
36. The Origin of Species
Sigmund Freud, An Interpretation of Dreams

WEEK 12: NATIONALISM, COMMUNISM AND WAR
WW Ch. 10
RWC AND HANDOUTS: World War and its Consequences: Windows on War and Peace
War
Wilfred Owen, "Dulce et decorum est"
Kande Kamara, Africans on the front in France
Private William Davis, Oral Testimony
National Self Determination
42. Woodrow Wilson's Fourteen Points
43. The League of Nations Covenant, 1919
Syrian Congress at Damascus, 1919

WEEK 13: THE INDIVIDUAL AND TOTALITARIANISM
WW Ch. 11
RWC AND HANDOUTS: Fascism, World War II, and the Holocaust: Window on Horror
Fascism / Benito Mussolini
45. The Rise of Hitler
47. The Holocaust
    1. Himmler Speaks to the SS
    2. Treblinka
    3. A Village in Vichy France
Japanese in China and Korea
Mandelstam, Hope against hope

WEEK 14: ECONOMICS AND ECOLOGY SINCE 1945
WW HANDOUT AND Ch. 12

WEEK 15: GLOBALIZATION AND POST-MODERN CULTURE
WW HANDOUT
RWC AND HANDOUTS: Globalization: Encountering Each Other
Japanese Industrialization
    1. Mitsubishi Letter to Employees, 1876
    2. The Useful War, John Dower
The Multi-national corporation
    Jihad vs. McWorld / Benjamin R. Barber
The Clash of Cultures
    Huntingdon, Foreign Affairs, Nov/Dec '96

Philip F. Riley
James Madison University
World History Since 1500

James Madison University
Department of History
History 102
World History Since 1500

Philip F. Riley, X-6172 JA 207, E-mail rileypf MWF 1000-1100 T/Th 9:30-10:30

Readings

>   John Isbister, *Promises Not Kept: The Betrayal of Social Change in the Third World* 3rd
>   edition. (Kumarian)
>
>   Jonathan D. Spence, *Emperor of China: Self Portrait of K'ang-hsi* (Vintage)
>
>   Sawako Ariyoshi, *The Doctor's Wife* (Kodansha)
>
>   A. Adu Boahen, *African Perspectives on Colonialism* (Johns Hopkins)
>
>   Philip F. Riley, et al., *The Global Experience: Readings in World History Since 1500* 2/E
>   ,   Vol 2 (Prentice-Hall)
>
>   Hammond, *Hammond Historical Atlas of the World* revised expanded edition.
>   (Hammond)
>
>   Map sets are: 1) World(Africa), 2) Soviet Union (East Asia), 3)Middle East (Europe).
>   Use one set for practice, bring the other to the exams.

Requirements

There will be two scheduled examinations, a comprehensive Final Examination, two short
papers, and frequent class discussions based upon the readings. Read the daily assignments
before coming to class and be prepared to discuss them. On days specifically designated
"discussion" be prepared to discuss the current assignments and previous lectures.* Examinations
will be essay in form, have a map section, and a take-home component. The daily topics on the
syllabus are the general themes from which examination questions will be drawn. Class
contribution is expected and will be considered. Grading scale is roughly as follows: 60-70--D,
71-80--C, 81-90--B, 91--A. Please purchase four examination booklets.

Ground Rules

Survey Courses: Modern

Attendance is expected (Woody Allen's rule applies). If you cannot come to class on time, remain for the entire class, or must eat, sleep, or read Danielle Steele, *et al.*, do not distract the class(or the old Professor) by coming. Generally make-up examinations will consist in having your Final Examination (with added questions) weighted double. If you miss an examination you must apply for a make-up examination during my office hour. Violation of the ground rules will affect your grade.

Discussions

For discussions you will be asked to personally submit, at the beginning of class, a typed paragraph (minimum) *critique*(not a summary) of the document(s) addressing the question: How does this reading inform me of this particular aspect of World History? Along with your critique also include two or three discussible questions based upon the reading. A discussible questions is one for which there is no absolutely correct answer. Occasionally critiques may be done in class. Film reviews and critiques will be graded (e.g.,5--10 pts.) and included in your final grade. Late (or absentee) critiques will not be accepted. Honor code applies.

Papers

**Papers must be titled, typed, double-spaced, four (minimum) to five pages in length (1200 words minimum), and written in standard English. Please type your name on your paper. When you quote please cite the page. Late papers will be penalized. All out-of-class writing is to be done individually: *these papers are not group efforts, secondary sources may not be used.* Diana Hacker, *A Writer's Reference* is the arbiter for all matters of citation and style. Keep a copy of each paper written for this class.

Honor Code

A full commitment to the James Madison University Honor Code is expected in all work in this class. Take-home examinations and papers are not group efforts. Secondary, critical sources are not to be used. Absentee critiques violate the Honor Code.

Bonus Points

You may earn up to 20 bonus points by reading two chapters from volumes in the Carrier Library. Bonus report is due February 16. If you are interested in this option please see me during my office hour.

Syllabus

Jan 10 Introduction: Global Perspectives

Survey Courses: Modern

Jan 12 Patterns of Global Reach
            Riley, Documents numbered l,4,9,24
            Zheng-He
            Hammond, 2,3,33,37

Jan 15 The European Miracle
            Hammond,23,42
            Isbister, intro 1,2; pp 71-6

Jan 17 The Columbian Exchange
            Riley, 2,3
            Columbian Exchange

Jan 19 African Slavery and the Middle Passage
            Riley, 7
            reader, 7a
            Hammond, 40,

Jan 22 Adam Smith and the Enlightenment
            Riley, 8,10,13,14,15,21

Jan 24 Ideas and Revolution
            Riley, 16,17,18,19,20
            reader, 19a,19b
            Hammond, 29

Jan 26 Sans-culottes and Napoleon
            Riley, 28,29
            reader, 20, US &VA Declarations..., "Rye map"
            Hammond, 30,31

Jan 29 Reactions to Revolution
            Riley, 27,30,31

Jan 31 Peter the Great and Imperial Russia
            Riley, 12,22,23
            reader, 23 a
            Hammond, 38

Feb 2 Russia's Road to Bloody Sunday
            Riley, 39,52,53
            Hammond, 39

Feb 5 Why Karl Marx?
        Riley, 35,36,99,104
        Hammond, 36

Feb 7 Critics of Marx
        Isbister, 3
        reader, 38a, 106C
        Hammond, 60,61,62,63

Feb 9 Empires and Upheavals
        Riley, 43,44,90
        Isbister, 4
        A. Adu Boahen, 1,2

Feb 12 Africa: The Imperial Scramble
        Riley, 84,85,86,87
        Hammond, 40,41,57,61,62
        A. Adu Boahen, complete
        Map quiz. Please bring the World Map.

Feb 14 First Examination

Please bring a blue book and the out of class paper. Write a paper analyzing the arguments and the evidence of Anonymous, *Sophia, Woman Not Inferior to Man* (Reading 21) and J-J Rousseau's *Sophie* (Reading 22). Which of the readings is more compelling? Why? The paper must be typed, titled, double-spaced, four (minimum) to five pages in length, and written in standard English. Please type your name on your paper. When you quote please cite the page.** Part 3: will be an identification section. In this section I will ask you to identify terms, names, or titles.(e.g.,Cheng Ho, The Federalist, Number 10, Vasco da Gama, engrafting,"The Columbian Exchange," Mercantilism, John Locke, *The Social Contract,* Shahhat, J-J Rousseau, Montesquieu, Walt Rostow, "Dependency Theory," Olympe de Gouges, Rigoberta Menchu, etc.,) In each case you must write a complete paragraph in standard English, in ink, answering the questions WHO, WHAT, WHEN, WHERE, WHY, and comment briefly on the significance of the item in relation to its historical epoch. Part 4. will be an essay question framed around one of the themes on the syllabus or an explication of a text we have read.

Feb 16 India: Jewel of the Crown
        Riley, 41,45
        Hammond, 39,47
        Isbister 4,5
        Bonus paper due

Feb 19 The Empire Strikes Back: M. Gandhi and M. Jinnah
          Riley, 45,88
          Isbister, 105-13

Feb 21 China and the Imperial Scramble
          Riley, 17,24,25,42
          "Tea"
          Hammond 39,41,50
          Spence, all

As a foreign ambassador to the court of the Emperor of China you have been asked by your government to write a "portrait" of K'ang-Hsi and his China. Drawing upon Spence what type of ruler is he? What kind of country does he rule? What should your government know about him? ** Paper is due February 28.

Feb 23 China: the long revolution
          Riley, 37,51
          Hammond, 61,62,63
          Isbister, 113-17

Feb 26 Mao Zedong and the CCP
          Riley, 80

Feb 28 The legacy of Imperialism
          Isbister, 4,5
          Spence paper due

Mar 1 Meiji Japan
          Riley, 5,6,26,46,47,48
          Japan
          Hammond 18,39,50
          Ariyoshi, complete (Choose 1)

1) Sawako Ariyoshi's novel ends with the words "If you stand directly in front of Seishu's tomb, the two behind him, those of Kae and Otsugi, are completely obscured." Is this the proper epitaph for these two women? What do these two women tell us about Tokugawa Japan?**

2) Although Tokugawa Japan is quite often depicted as very much a world dominated by men, this novel underscores the role and importance of women in early modern Japanese society. How does the novel inform you of the place of women, the Japanese social structure at the village level, the state of medicine, and the contours of culture of Tokugawa Japan? ** Paper is due March 15.

Survey Courses: Modern

Mar 11 Japan's Emergence as a Modern State
Riley, 65

Mar 13 The Great Pacific War
Riley, 72,73,106
Hammond, 50

Mar 15 Imperial America
Riley, 31,32,33,34,49,50
US Intervention, 48a
Ariyoshi paper due

Mar 18 United States and Central America
Riley, 89,101,102,103,104,105
Isbister, 134-41; 215-20
Hammond, 33,58

Mar 20 Second Examination

Please bring the Asian Map and a blue book. For the take-home question write a paper based upon A. Adu Boahen, *African Perspectives on Colonialism,* the classes, and the readings (e.g.,Riley documents 7,36,43,84,85,86,87, etc.,; e.g., 8,9,10,77,90,117, etc.,; and Isbister chapters 4,5) evaluating the role and function of colonialism upon Africa. Focus the paper upon Boahen and the documents; use Isbister sparingly. The paper must be typed, titled, double-spaced, four (minimum) to five pages in length, and written in standard English. Please type your name on your paper. When you quote material. Please cite the page. ** (Paper may be turned in on March 22)**

Mar 22 Nationalism, the Balkans and the coming of World War I
Balkans, 40b, 40c, 70b
Hammond, 45

Mar 25 World War I Battle
Riley, 55,56
Hammond, 45

Mar 27 Peacemaking: Lawrence, Lies and the Middle East
Riley, 57,58,59,60,61
Hammond, 46, 47, 54

Mar 29 Russia in Revolution
Riley, 52
Hammond, 48

Survey Courses: Modern

Apr 1 Stalin and the Gulag State
    Riley, 62,63,64,68,82,98

Apr 3 Mussolini and Hitler: The Triumph of Unreason
    Riley, 65,66,67,69,71
    Fascism,

Apr 5 *Endl`sung*
    racial policies

Apr 8 Hitler's European War
    WW II, 71a

Apr 10 World War II and the shattered peace
    Riley, 72,73,74,75,76,77,78
    Hammond, 50,51,52

Apr 12 The Cold War: an armed truce
    Riley, 79,80,81,82,83
    Isbister, 6,7

Apr 15 Decolonization
    Riley, 44
    Indochina War
    Isbister, 117-25

Apr 17 The Second Indochina War and detente
    Riley, 70, 95,96,97,98,99,100

Apr 19 The Arab Israeli conflict
    Riley, 91,92,93,94
    Isbister, 122-31
    Hammond, 54

Apr 22 Towards the 21st century
    Riley, 98,99,100,106
    Isbister, complete

Apr 24 Final Thoughts

Survey Courses: Modern

Please bring blue books, a map of Europe, and the take-home paper. For the take-home examination write a paper answering the following questions. What is Isbister's thesis? How compelling an argument does he present? Do you agree or disagree with his thesis? Why? Why not?**
The above schedule of assignments, requirements, and evaluations is subject to change.

Study Guide for Map

On Feb. 12, you will be asked to locate on a world outline map 20 of the items listed below. Most of the items can be found in the *Hammond: Historical Atlas of the World*, or in the atlases in the reference section of the Carrier Library (first floor).

Oceans and Seas	Rivers	Urals	Inchon
Caribbean Sea	Ganges	Himalayas	Berlin
Indian Ocean	Danube	Atlas	St. Petersburg
Persian Gulf	Indus	Cities	Other Places
Red Sea	Niger	Baghdad	Cape of Good Hope
Gulf of Aqaba	Amur	Cairo	Sahara
Islands	Volga	Damascus	Kampuchea(Cambodia)
Barbados	Tigris-Euphrates	Kiev	Kazakhstan
Japan	Rhine	Beijing	Bight of Biafra
Philippines	Mekong	Jidda	Shantung
Cuba	Straits and Passes	Phnom Penh	Yenan
Grenada	Tsushima Straits	Tehran	Bosnia-Herzegovina
Sakhalin	Dardanelles	Minsk	Georgia
Singapore	Straits of Gibraltar	Managua	Kosovo
Hong Kong	Khyber Pass	Vladivostok	Croatia
Zanzibar	Malacca Straits	Murmansk	Ukraine
Madagascar	Mountains	Beirut	Hormuz
Kuril	Alps	Amritsar	Rwanda
Sri Lanka	Caucasus	Islamabad	Somalia
Canaries	Balkans	New Delhi	

Survey Courses: Modern

Judith P. Zinsser
Miami University
World History Since 1500

TOPICS IN WORLD HISTORY SINCE 1500: AN EXPLANATORY NOTE ON GENDER

For those of you unused to the vastness of world history, I want to explain a few of its unique challenges. Because there is so much material, any course in world history will involve choices--very subjective choices--determined by practical realities like instructor interest and training, college requirements, department needs, and so on. The hardest choices are more theoretical. How best to introduce students to new cultures? to give them a coherent picture of the major changes in those cultures from a world-wide perspective? how to engage them in the excitement of being an historian?

I balance all of these demands by formulating just <u>one</u> open-ended historical question and focusing all of the materials and activities around that question. In this syllabus, it is "What causes order in societies? What causes disorder?"

Broad questions like this free me from my old patterns of analysis, give the students the opportunity to formulate their own opinions about events, and make it possible to "gender" the survey. As you look at the syllabus, the topics should appear relatively traditional. There are only a few specific mentions of women. That is because I have gone beyond the "add women and stir" approach. Instead, I work to have my whole course reflect actions, interactions, reactions, by women <u>and</u> men, between women <u>and</u> men, by women <u>and</u> by men.

To do this, I have set three requirements for myself, rules that I follow in writing my lectures, planning discussions, choosing readings and films, formulating oral and written assignments. My course must illustrate: 1) joint actions by women and men in familiar events (as in the three movies I show); 2) interactions between women and men (see the Spence <u>Death of Woman Wang</u> and Kramer's <u>Unsettling Europe</u>); 3) reactions by women and by men as separate experiences reflecting different perceptions (see the <u>Mary Prince</u> account, the Biko trial transcript, and Enloe's feminist analysis of international relations).

The second prepared essay is the most obvious example of how the rules work. I ask students to read an autobiography of a contemporary woman political activist. (See the list of "Optional Books.") They must then analyze the roles of women and men in causing order and disorder. The events are familiar, the account is from a woman's perspective, but the focus is on women <u>and</u> men. Most rewarding has been the way in which this assignment has given the students a richer, more nuanced understanding of recent history. They "gender" their answer without any prompting on my part and demonstrate their ability to imagine and think about events as joint and separate endeavors by women and men.

The syllabus that follows has been used for large lecture classes (with discussion sections) and for those of 40-50. It is, of course, but one of many ways to structure "World History Since 1500." Please use whatever meets your needs.

Judith P. Zinsser (Miami University of Ohio)

HISTORY 298: TOPICS IN WORLD HISTORY SINCE 1500
Judith P. Zinsser - Spring 1998

GOALS
          This course will seem very different from others you have taken because it is not making any claims at inclusion. Quite the reverse. It is only a small piece, a selection of topics, from all that could be included under the title "World History". This course will seem very different in another way from studies of the US or Western Civ. Because there is so much history, it is impossible to give a clear narrative. There are not enough semesters in our lives to describe what everyone was doing every decade. Therefore, I have organized this course around a single theme, or question. Out of all the infinite possibilities, I have chosen just one historical question to explore, and just a few examples of how the experiences of different peoples answer it. This is why we call this course, "Topics in World History."
          1. The question for the course is: **What causes order in a society? in the world? What causes disorder?** This will be the ESSAY QUESTION OF THE EXAM.

          2. Aspects of the question will be explored according to traditional historian's categories, such as political, economic, social and cultural.

_____3. The course is chronological going from the 16th to the 20th century.

_____4. The major reading and discussion will be about whole books and documents, not a textbook. You will read different kinds of sources including: memoirs, official biographies, constitutions, speeches and political position papers. And you will see movies from different cultures. All of these different materials are meant to give you a sense of the variety of sources historians use to write the history you read when you pick up a textbook.

TO SUMMARIZE: the course is organized thematically, regionally and chronologically with a single focus. By the end of the semester you will have an in-depth knowledge of a few very particular places and events. You will have been asked to use a variety of sources and analytical techniques to give you a sense of what historians really do.

ASSIGNMENTS AND GRADE
          The final grade will be based on a number of different assignments and activities. As so many people in the world value the spoken over the written word, regular informal participation in class, and formal participation in a group oral activity will constitute a significant part of the mark.

Survey Courses: Modern

In speaking and writing the following criteria will be used to evaluate your work:
1. Is there an argument, a point of view that is being proved?
2. Is the language clear? Is the sequence of points in the argument clear?
3. What evidence is given? How effective was the use of evidence? Is the point proved?

Please note: Facts are important, but most important is what you do with those facts. Lytton Strachey, an English biographer wrote: "Facts relating to the past, when they are collected without art, are compilations; and compilations no doubt may be useful; but they are no more History than butter, eggs, salt and herbs are an omelette."

The assignments are as follows:
JOURNAL PASS/FAIL
In order to pass the course, students must keep a journal of their responses to class lecture/discussion, to the movies, to the readings. To be handed in twice during the semester.

ORAL ACTIVITIES 30% Choose one of these activities.
PRESENTATION OF ONE REQUIRED BOOK
Lead the discussion of one of the required books on the syllabus. Discussion leaders will be evaluated 1) on how well they give the context of the book, in terms of the author's circumstances and the era as a whole; 2) on the number of people who participate in the discussion as a result of the questions posed by the group. The grade received will be a grade for the group as a whole.

    History of Mary Prince **or** Indian Tales of the Raj **or**   Banana's Beaches and Bases

DEBATE
Students debate the following statement:
"Men and women choose order over rights."

TRIAL
Students will prosecute and defend: George Washington, Simon Bolivar, and Toussaint l'Ouverture for treason.

MEET THE PRESS
Kwame Nkrumah (Ghana) and Julius Nyerere (Tanzania) are being interviewed by ABC, CBS, NBC, PBS and CNN on their controversial views.

Survey Courses: Modern

WRITTEN ASSIGNMENTS 40%
Written assignments <u>require</u> a bibliography and footnotes or endnotes when needed. <u>They may</u>
<u>be rewritten to raise the mark.</u>

ORDER AND DISORDER IN CHINA (5 pp. maximum) Write an essay answering the
following question: To what extent was the central government of China perceived as a source of
order? Consider two time periods, during the early Qing Dynasty (1661-1722) and during the
Chinese Republic of the 1930s? See details in unit on China.

ROLES OF WOMEN AND MEN IN ORDER AND DISORDER (5 pp. maximum)
Write an essay, using **one** of the optional books, in which you compare the roles **and** activities of
men and women in creating order or disorder. See list of Optional Books.

EXAMINATION 25%
You have a single question to answer. Be prepared to write on the following question:
    "What causes order in a society? in the world? What causes disorder?"

Note that there are no "tests," and no midterm in the traditional sense. The other 5% represents
attendance and participation.

<u>SCHEDULE OF CLASSES AND ASSIGNMENTS</u> [Sixteen-week semester]

POLITICAL FACTORS IN ORDER AND DISORDER   **I** [Weeks 1-3]
<u>The Example of China under the Qing Dynasty (1600s-1700s) and in the early years of the</u>
<u>Chinese Republic (1920s-1930s)</u>

The whole unit will be devoted to preparation for an essay on the following question: To what
extent was the central government perceived as a source of order in these two time periods,
during the Qing Dynasty and in the Chinese Republic?

   Where to find information for the essay:
   Read on the Qing Dynasty (1661-1722) in Spence, <u>The Emperor of China</u>, and
   Spence, <u>The Death of Woman Wang</u> (the whole book, not just the chapter of that
   title) for information on the way the imperial government worked.

_____On life during the 1920s and 1930s in rural China the movie "Red Sorghum" will
   be shown in class. It was made by a Chinese filmmaker in the 1980s (winner of
   many film prizes in the West).

141

Survey Courses: Modern

In class: General discussion of factors leading to order or disorder with emphasis on political factors. Movie: "Double Vision" [Southwest Communications Services, 1992] offering Native Americans answering the questions: Who was Christopher Columbus? and Who Discovered America?

Lecture on Chinese Administration.

Read the Emperor's Valedictory and the Final Valedictory issued after his death [See Section VI and Appendix of The Emperor of China]. **Write** in your Journal on the differences between the two statements and what each would contribute to order or disorder.

In class: Screening of "Red Sorghum" [Dir. Zhang Ximou, 1987]

POLITICAL FACTORS IN ORDER AND DISORDER II [Weeks 4-6]
The Example of the Americas from 1763-1830

In class: Lecture comparing Hapsburg/Bourbon and Hanover Empires in the Americas as examples of mercantilist enterprises with some participatory government in a colonial context; of the successful revolutions in each empire.

DEBATE ON ORDER AND RIGHTS [Using evidence from this course.]

In class: Lecture and discussion of two revolutionary constitutions in the Americas. **Read** the US Constitution and Bolivar's Constitution for Bolivia. What in the constitutions contributes to the maintenance of order? what could cause disorder? **Write in your journal about one of the following**: 1) the definition of citizen and how he will participate in the government; 2) checks and balances between the branches of government; 3) the nature and role of the executive; 4) specific guarantees of rights. (Note: consider the constitutions as written in 1789 and 1830, omit all amendments. In the Bolivian Constitution amendments appear in *italics*)

TRIAL OF GEORGE WASHINGTON, SIMON BOLIVAR AND TOUSSAINT L'OUVERTURE FOR TREASON After the trial, **write in your journal** on the "nature of treason" in the Americas, when is disorder remembered as positive? when remembered as negative?

SOCIAL AND CULTURAL FACTORS IN ORDER AND DISORDER I [Weeks 7-8]
The Example of the Caribbean Islands in the 18th and 19th centuries: Enslavement and Emancipation

In class: Lecture on the nature of Enslavement and the plantation economy in the Caribbean Islands and the sources of order and disorder.

142

PRESENTATION OF <u>Mary Prince</u>. Read the book. **Write in your journal** about the ways in which Prince contributed to order, created disorder.

In class: Screening of "Sugar Cane Alley" about Martinique in the 1930s [Dir. Euzhan Palcy, 1984]. After watching the movie **write in your journal** on the continuing sources of order and disorder even after emancipation.

SOCIAL AND CULTURAL FACTORS IN ORDER AND DISORDER II [Week 9-10]
<u>The Example of the 19th and 20th century British Empire in South Asia</u>

In class: Lecture on the Moghul Empire of India before the British and of the establishment of the British Empire.

PRESENTATION OF <u>Tales of the Raj</u>. Read the book. **Write in your journal** from the perspective of the colonized in each major section of the book on how the British Imperial system created order? disorder?

In class: Lecture on the independence movements in India and Pakistan

INTERNATIONAL SYSTEMS AND ORDER AND DISORDER SINCE 1945
[Weeks 11-16]
<u>The Example of 20th century Africa, Neo-colonialism, European Integration, the United Nations, and the World Economic System</u>

In class: Lecture on South Africa and the system of apartheid.
[Self-determination taken to its natural conclusion]

In class: Screening of "Maids and Madams" about South Africa before the end of apartheid [Dir. Mira Hamermesh, 1986, Women Make Movies]. After watching the movie, **write in your journal** on apartheid as a source of order or disorder.

In class: Lecture on "industrialization," "modernization" and "neo-colonialism": the circumstances that led to the economic transformation of some parts of the world and not others, the creation of the global economy, and the consequences.

Read Nkrumah's (Ghana) "Neo-Colonialism" [<u>The End of the European Empire: Decolonization after World War II</u> ed. Tony Smith (DC Heath, 1975)] and Nyerere's (Tanzania) "Arusha Declaration" [<u>Ujama: Essays on Socialism</u> (Oxford University Press, 1971)]. **Summarize in your journal** the main ideas in each selection about development and how to achieve change given the world economic order and be prepared to question the two leaders on their explanations of their countries' problems and their solutions. **MEET THE PRESS: NKRUMAH AND NYERERE**

Read Chap. 2 of <u>Development, Crises, and Alternative Visions</u> by Gita Sen and Caren Grown [Monthly Review Press, 1987]. **Write in your journal** a brief precis of the ideas in the chapter and about how development can be a source of order or disorder.

THE SECOND ESSAY ON THE ROLES OF WOMEN AND MEN: Read one of the contemporary women's memoirs listed under "Optional Books." **Write an essay** in which you compare the roles **and** activities of the women and men create order or disorder.

PRESENTATION OF <u>Bananas, Beaches and Bases</u>. Read the book in preparation for the discussion. **Write in your journal** on the different roles of women and men in international affairs and the different contributions they have made to order and disorder in society. **Make** a chapter by chapter list that shows how that particular group of women contributed to international order or disorder.

In class: Screening of "Salaam Bombay" [Dir. Mira Nair, 1988] After seeing the movie, **write in your journal** on the ways in which order was maintained and disorder created.

Read the Preambles to the League of Nations Covenant and the United Nations Charter (distributed in class), and the New International Economic Order (NIEO) document. **Write in your journal** on 1) the different views of the causes of war in the two preambles; 2) on the ways in which the NIEO would contribute to order or disorder in the world.

In class: Lecture on the United Nations as a factor in order and disorder around the world.

In class: Joint preparation for the examination essay. **Bring** your thesis statement and 20 facts to use as evidence to class.

REQUIRED

Enloe, Cynthia
<u>Bananas, Beaches and Bases</u>
University of California Press #06985-4 pbk

Ferguson, Moira ed.
<u>The History of Mary Prince: A West Indian Slave, Related by Herself</u>
University of Michigan Press #472-08410-0 pbk

Kramer, Jane
<u>Unsettling Europe</u>
Viking Penguin #14-012898-0 pbk

Survey Courses: Modern

Masani, Zareer
Indian Tales of the Raj
University of California Press # 07127-1

Spence, Jonathan
Emperor of China: Self-Portrait of K'ang-Hsi
Vintage Books #394-71411-3 74-17106 pbk

Spence, Jonathan
The Death of Woman Wang
Penguin Viking #0-14-005121 pbk

OPTIONAL BOOKS: CHOOSE ONE

Barrios de Chungara, Domitila
Let Me Speak! Testimony of Domitila, a Woman of the Bolivian Mines
Monthly Review Press # 85345-485-x

Hayslip, Le Ly
When Heaven and Earth Changed Places: A Vietnamese Woman's Journey from War to Peace
Plume/Penguin #452-26417-0 pbk

Kuzwayo, Ellen
Call Me Woman
Aunt Lite Books #879960-09-5 pbk

Xuezhao, Chen
Surviving the Storm: A Memoir
ME Sharpe #1-56324-553-1 pbk

III.

Specialized Courses: Chronological

Specialized Courses: Chronological: Ancient World

Stanley M. Burstein
California State University, Los Angeles
World Civilization: Eurasia to 500 CE

SYLLABUS: HISTORY 110A Mr. Burstein

Office Hours: KH B4066 T-1:00-2:10

Phone: 213-343-2020,

History 110A deals with the Ancient Civilizations of Eurasia and Africa from their origins until the end of antiquity. During the period covered by this course all but one of the civilized traditions and major religions of the contemporary world originated. In studying the origins of these civilizations we will be studying the roots of our world as a whole. Ancient History involves the use of many types of sources including archaeological, linguistic, and literary evidence. Examples of each type of source will examined in the lectures and class discussions.

COURSE REQUIREMENTS:

The class will be conducted through a combination of lectures and class discussions. Grading will be based on: class discussion (10%), the mid-term examination (20%), the final examination (50 %), and a 5-6 page term paper (20%). The papers will be based on one of the books chosen from the four assigned literary texts. The mid-term will take place on the last day of the sixth week of the course and will consist of a short answer identification examination drawn from the first half of the course. The final examination will consist of two parts: (1) a set of identifications drawn from the second half of the course and (2) one essay question.

TEXTBOOKS:

Required:
J. Upshur, World History, vol. 1 (West Publishing)
N. K. Sandars, The Epic of Gilgamesh (Penguin).
Homer, The Odyssey (Penguin).
R. K. Narayan, The Ramayana (Penguin).
Virgil, Aeneid (Penguin)

COURSE OUTLINE:

1. Introduction: Prehistoric Background of Civilization. The Primary Civilizations: Mesopotamia, Egypt, and Indus Valley.

Reading: Upshur: Pages, 4-32, 52-60
Epic of Gilgamesh

Specialized Courses: Chronological: Ancient World

2. The Frontiers of Civilization: The Indo-Europeans in Eurasia.

   Reading: Upshur: Pages 36-48

3. The Small Peoples of the West: Jews, Phoenicians and Greeks

   Reading: Upshur: Pages 86--103

4. Greek Civilization: Character and Values

   Reading: Upshur: Pages 103-110
                   Homer, Odyssey

5. West Meets East: Alexander the Great and the Hellenistic World

   Reading: Upshur: Pages 134-146

   MID-TERM

6. Classical Indian Civilization and its Values: Vedism, Jainism and the Origins of
   Buddhism

   Reading: Upshur: Pages 60-67, 111-115, 159-172
                   Ramayana

7. Unification in East Asia: The Civilization of China and its Values: Confucianism, Taoism,
   and Legalism

   Reading: Upshur: Pages 67-86, 172-186

8. Unification in the West I: The Rise of Rome

   Reading: Upshur: Pages 146-153
                   Aeneid, Books 1-2

9. Unification in the West II: The Roman Empire

   Reading: Upshur: Pages 153-159, 194-201
                   Aenid, Books 4 and 6

10. The Crisis of Late Antiquity: Transformation in the West, Renaissance in the East

    Reading: Upshur: Pages 188-190, 201-203, 246-258

Specialized Courses: Chronological: Ancient World

TERM PAPER TOPIC:

Your Speech teacher has told you that you must prepare a talk on one of the major civilizations of the ancient world using original documents. Choose one or more of the four books listed in the Paper Supplement section of the Syllabus --Gilgamesh, The Odyssey, Aeneid, or the Ramayana--and use it as the basis for discussing some aspect of the beliefs and values of the society in which it was created. In doing this, you should focus your discussion on one theme such as: the place of women in society, what makes a good man, the role of war, attitudes toward foreign peoples, the character of the gods and how people relate to them, attitudes toward death, relations between men and women, etc.

Specialized Courses: Chronological: Medieval

A. J. Andrea
University of Vermont
Medieval Global Exchange: 100–1450

HISTORY 209
MEDIEVAL GLOBAL EXCHANGE: 100-1450

Thursday, 5:00-8:00   102 Wheeler

Professor Andrea's office hours are: M&W 3:00-4:30, T 4:00-5:00, TH 3:00-4:00, F 2:30-3:30,
and by appointment in 302 WHEELER HOUSE
e-mail: AANDREA@ZOO.UVM.EDU
private office phone: 656-4488

Required texts:
> Jerry Bentley, *Old World Encounters*
> E. W. Bovill, *The Golden Trade of the Moors*
> Christopher Dawson, *Mission to Asia*
> Ross E. Dunn, *The Adventures of Ibn Battuta*
> *The Itinerary of Benjamin of Tudela*
> John Mandeville, *Travels*
> Marco Polo, *Travels*

Recommended text:
> Andrea and Overfield, *The Human Record*, 2nd. ed., Vol I

Course Focus:
Although Europe's late fifteenth-century explorations inaugurated a new stage of global
interchange, in many respects the events of 1492 and following were a continuation of a process
of long-range cultural exchange that had been gaining momentum throughout Eurasia and Africa
since antiquity. In this seminar we shall study long distance travel and travelers between the years
ca. 100 and 1450. Our perspective will be global, although we will largely concentrate on the
Afro-Eurasian Ecumene.

The purpose of this seminar is to help you become aware of the dynamics of global travel and
exchange during this millennium and a half, especially the ways in which the major cultures of
Eurasia and Africa cross-fertilized one another.

Course Requirements:
I. Participation
        Because this is a seminar, every person is obligated to attend and participate fully in each
class meeting. A seminar only works if each member pulls his/her weight. You will be asked to
lead discussion on occasion and to make periodic reports to the seminar regarding your term
research project. I will expect you to put a good deal of serious effort into every task.

Specialized Courses: Chronological: Medieval

II. Written Work
A. Book Reviews
  Everyone must submit on 3 OCTOBER a polished (and cleanly typed) critical book review of Jerry Bentley's *Old World Encounters*. Along with this syllabus, you have received a detailed essay on how to write a book review. I expect you to read it and to take its guidelines to heart.

B. Bibliographic Essay
  Everyone must submit a typed bibliographic essay that critically evaluates in an integrated manner all of the primary and secondary sources being used for the term research paper. This essay is due on 24 OCTOBER.

C. The Research Paper
  Everyone is required to write a research paper of approximately 15-20 pages on a specific aspect of this seminar subject. The final, polished version of this paper is due absolutely no later than 5:00 P.M. on THURSDAY, 5 DECEMBER.

A Short List of Available Primary Sources and a Few Suggested Research Topics:

Pilgrimages:
  Muslim (the *hajj*) and Christian pilgrimages are very fruitful topics. Start with Linda Kay Davidson and Maryjane Dunn-Wood, *Pilgrimage in the Middle Ages: A Research Guide* (1992). The various pilgrimages made to Mecca by West African sultans from the Niger River trading kingdoms, such as that made by Mansa Musa in 1324/1325 (see Levtzion below), could be compared with Christian pilgrimages to the Holy Land, Rome, Compostela, and elsewhere. On the pilgrimage to Compostela, see Linda Kay Davidson and Maryjane Dunn-Wood, *The Pilgrimage to Santiago de Compostela: A Comprehensive, Annotated Bibliography*. Your chief primary sources are: *The Pilgrim's Guide to Santiago de Compostela*, trans. William Melczer and *The Miracles of St. James*, trans. Thomas F. Coffey, Linda Kay Davidson, and Maryjane Dunn. For Rome, see *The Marvels of Rome* (*Mirabilia Urbis Romae*) of ca. 1143, 2nd ed. So far as pilgrimages to the Holy Land are concerned, the Palestine Pilgrims' Text Society has published a number of medieval accounts of travels in this region. See also, Thomas Wright, *Early Travels in Palestine*. A recent addition to this body of translated literature is John Wilkinson, ed., *Jerusalem Pilgrimage, 1099-1185* (London, 1988). Among the medieval guides to the Holy Land that have been translated into English, there is Theoderic's *Guide to the Holy Land*. F. E. Peters, *Jerusalem and Mecca: The Typology of the Holy City in the Near East* (N.Y., 1986) is worth consulting; see also his *The Hajj* (Princeton, 1994). You should also consult Amikam Elad, *Medieval Jerusalem and Islamic Worship* (1995). Simon Coleman and John Elsner, *Pilgrimage: Past and Present in the World Religions* (Harvard Univ. Press, 1995), is also worth consulting. Lodovico de Varthema, the first known European to describe the *hajj* to Mecca, published his account in 1510. A translation is available in *Travelers in Disguise* by John Winter Jones and Lincoln D. Hammond. Winter's translation of Varthema's adventures has also been published separately by the Hakluyt Society.

Specialized Courses: Chronological: Medieval

If you want to study Chinese Buddhist travelers to India and Southeast Asia, you must begin with the monk Faxian (Fa-hsien), who traveled from China to India, Ceylon, Java, and back home in the period 399-414 in search of sacred sutras. See James Legge, trans., *A Record of Buddhistic Kingdoms* (Oxford, 1886). For the monk Yijing, see *A Record of the Buddhist Religion as Practised in India and the Malay Archipelago (A. D. 671-695)*, trans. J. Takakusu (Delhi, 1966) and *Chinese Monks in India*, trans. L. Lahiri (Delhi, 1986). For the monk Xuanzang, who spent the period from 629 to 645 in India, see *Si-yu-ki: Buddhist Records of the Western World*, trans. S. Beal, 2 vols. (London, 1906). For other accounts, see Yang Xuanshi, *Memories of Loyang: Yang Hsüan-shih and the Lost Capital (493-534)*, trans. W. J. F. Jenner (Oxford, 1981). For a Japanese monk in Tang China, see: Ennin, *Ennin's Diary: The Record of a Pilgrimage to China in Search of the Law*, trans. Edwin O. Reischauer (new York, 1955). Also consult Reischauer's *Ennin's Travels in T'ang China* (New York, 1955).

Ibn Jubayr and Ibn Battuta:

Ibn Jubayr (1145-1217) journeyed from Granada, Spain to Mecca and beyond. His account is available in J.C. Broadhurst, trans., *The Travels of Ibn Jubayr*. F. E. Peters treats Ibn Jubayr in chapter 3, "The Medieval Hajj," of his *The Hajj*. Ibn Battuta is off limits as a research topic, because we will be reading in common Ross Dunn's study of his fourteenth-century travels (unless someone can come up with an ingenious way of incorporating Ibn Battuta's travels into a larger study). However, for your information: H. A. R. Gibbs has translated the bulk of Ibn Battuta's account of his travels in Asia and sub-Saharan Africa between 1325 and 1354. A better translation of his travels in sub-Saharan Africa is available in Levtzion (see below). In 1994 Marcus Weiner Publishers brought out *Ibn Battuta in Black Africa*, the 1975 translation of that portion of Ibn Battuta's account by Said Hamdun and Noël King. Ross Dunn has composed an introduction. Henry Yule, *Cathy and the Way Thither*, Vol. 4, has a less acceptable translation of Ibn Battuta's description of India and China. Mahdi Husain, *The Rehla of Ibn Battuta* contains a translation of his travels in the Indian Ocean.

Muslim Geographers:

Arab and Persian geographers, particularly of the tenth century, reflect the wide-ranging ecumenical vision of *Dar al- Islam*--the Abode of Islam. The tenth-century geographer al-Muqaddasi has been studied by Basil A. Collins in *Al-Muqaddasi: The Man and His Work*. George S.A. Ranking and R.F. Azoo have translated al-Muqaddasi's description of the Middle East. V. Minorsky translated the anonymous *Hudad al-`Alam*. "The Regions of the World," *A Persian Geography 372 A.H.-982 A.D.* in 1937. A more recent (1970) translation is by C.E. Bosworth. William Ouseley has translated Ibn Hawqal's *Kitab Surat al-`Ard* under the title: *The Oriental Geography of Ebn Haukel, an Arabian Traveller of the Tenth Century*. G.R. Tibbetts, *Arab Navigation in the Indian Ocean...* provides a translation of Ibn Majid's late fifteenth-century *Kitab*. S. Maqbul Ahmad has translated portions of the encyclopedic geography of the twelfth-century scholar al-Idrisi in *India and the Neighboring Territories in the Kitab Nuzhat...of...al-Idrisi*. The late thirteenth-early fourteenth- century work of Abu l-Fida appears in translation in S.M. Ahmad and M.M. Andarabi, "Abu l-Fida's Description of India (Hind and Sind)," *Medieval India Quarterly* 2 (1957): 147-170.

Specialized Courses: Chronological: Medieval

Sub-Saharan Africa:
The single best collection of sources on Africa south of the Sahara is N. Levtzion and J. F. P. Hopkins, eds., *Corpus of Early Arabic Sources for West African History*. See especially the sources relating to Mansa Musa's *hajj*. O.G.S. Crawford has edited a series of accounts of travels to Ethiopia in *Ethiopian Itineraries, circa 1400-1524*.

Europeans in Muslim Lands:
Nicolo de Conti and Ludovico de Varthema both passed themselves off as Muslims in their journeys through Islamic lands. J.W. Jones and L.D. Hammond have translated the accounts of their late medieval adventures in *Travellers in Disguise*.

Benjamin of Tudela and Other Jewish Merchants:
This pious merchant from Spain was Judaism's twelfth-century counterpart to Ibn Battuta. Because we are reading his account in class he is, like Ibn Battuta, off limits, unless someone can come up with an ingenious way of incorporating his travels into a larger study. If you want to read something quite a bit removed from his original travelogue but interesting for the information it provides, see Sandra Benjamin's imaginative "fleshing out" of his Benjamin of Tudela's travel notes, which appears under the title *The World of Benjamin of Tudela* (1995). An earlier and better translation of Benjamin of Tudela's account by M. N. Adler appears under the title *The Travels of Rabbi Benjamin of Tudela* (1907). Manuel Komroff, ed., *Contemporaries of Marco Polo*, also contains a translation of Rabbi Benjamin's travels. The *Encyclopaedia Judaica* has a good introductory essay on Benjamin. See also Elkan N. Adler, *Jewish Travellers: A Treasury of Travelogues from Nine Centuries* and J. Voporsanger, "The Travels of Benjamin...," *Bulletin of the Geographic Society of California* 2 (1894): 77-96. Another valuable book of sources is S.D. Goitein, *Letters of Medieval Jewish Traders* (Princeton, 1973). By far, however, the most important set of translated documents relating to Jewish merchants is S. D. Goitein, *A Mediterranean Society: The Jewish Communities of the Arab World as Portrayed in the Documents of the Cairo Geniza*, 6 vols. to date. An interesting *novel*, which uses the Geniza documents and liberally mixes fantasy and fact is Amitov Gosh, *In an Antique Land* (1993). You might also want to consult Martin Gilbert, *The Atlas of Jewish History* (1969, 1992).

The Norse:
The place to begin is Gwyn Jones, ed. and trans., *The Norse Atlantic Saga*, 2nd. ed. If you wish to pursue the issue of the so-called Vinland Map, which some scholars accept as genuine and date to ca 1440, see the new edition of R. A. Skelton, et al., *The Vinland Map and the Tartar Relation* (New Haven: Yale University Press, 1995). The new edition contains essays that bring the controversy forward from 1965, when the map first became the center of a heated controversy.

Specialized Courses: Chronological: Medieval

The First Expansion of Europe:
The secondary work with which you must begin is J. R. S. Phillips, *The Medieval Expansion of Europe*. The crusades are an especially rich area, so far as translated documents and potential topics are concerned. Excellent crusade bibliographies are available in Jonathan Riley-Smith, *The Crusades* and Hans E. Mayer, *The Crusades*, 2nd. ed., as well as Volume VI of *The History of the Crusades*, ed. Kenneth Setton, et al. Consult also Jonathan Riley-Smith, *The Atlas of the Crusades* (1991). An excellent study that places the crusades into a global perspective is Archibald R. Lewis, *Nomads and Crusaders, 1000-1368* (1988). Anyone who has taken or is currently enrolled in a course on the crusades may **not** elect to do a paper on the crusades for this seminar.

In addition to the crusades, Medieval Europe expanded outward in a number of other areas and ways. A good collection of sources relating to this opening up of Europe's frontiers is James M. Muldoon, ed. *The Expansion of Europe: The First Phase*.

The late medieval rediscovery of such islands as the Canaries and the Portuguese exploration of the west coast of Africa deserve study. One excellent source for the explorations patronized by Prince Henry is Gomes Eannes de Azurara, *Chronicle of Guinea*, translated by Charles R. Beazley and Edgar Prestage. See also R. H. Major's translation of *The Canarian*.

An interesting book, well worth your reading, is Valerie I. J. Flint, *The Imaginative Landscape of Christopher Columbus* (Princeton, 1992).

Above all else, consult J.R.S. Phillips's excellent bibliography on pp. 260-284.

Islam Comes to India:
The basic source collection is Henry M. Elliot and John Dowson, eds., *The History of India as Told by its Own Historians*, 8 vols.

European Missions and Travels in India:
Henry Yule has translated *The Wonders of the East* by the fourteenth-century Franciscan friar Jordanus. Accounts of four 15th-century travelers to India--an Afghan, a Russian, and two Italians--have been translated by R. H. Major and deserve a comparative analysis. These accounts probably should also be compared with Ibn Battuta's description of India a century earlier. See also Edward F. Oaten, *Travel and Travellers in India, A.D. 1400-1700*.

The Mongols:
The Mongols certainly have to rate as the most significant group of world travelers in the thirteenth century. Juvaini's Persian classic, *The History of the World Conqueror*, trans. John A. Boyle, covers contemporary Mongol history down to 1260. *The Universal History of Rashid al-Din* is translated in part in Boyle's *The Successors of Genghis Khan*. Bertold Spuler, *History of the Mongols, Based on Eastern and Western Accounts of the Thirteenth and Fourteenth Centuries* is a potpourri of translated snippets. The thirteenth-century *Secret History of the Mongols* is available in several editions. The best is by Paul Kahn. E.V. Bretschneider, *Medieval Researches from Eastern Asiatic Sources*, 2 vols. contains a number of important Chinese and Mongol sources relating to the Chinese and the Mongols in Central and West Asia.

India in the Fifteenth Century:

Specialized Courses: Chronological: Medieval

The Age of the *Pax Mongolica* and Its World System?:
Henry Yule, *Cathy and the Way Thither* contains quite a few important documents, especially Francesco Pegolotti's *Descriptions of Countries*. For a turgid yet valuable secondary account of this era, see Janet L. Abu-Lughod, *Before European Hegemony: The World System, A. D. 1250-1350.*

Timur the Lame:
The early 15th-century account of Ruy Gonzalez de Clavijo's embassy to the court of Timur at Samarkand has been translated by Clements R. Markham. Ahmed ibn Arabshah, *Tamerlane or Timur the Great Amir*, trans. by J. H. Sanders, must also be used. Another source that must be used is *The Bondage and Travels of Johann Schiltberger in Europe, Asia, and Africa, 1396-1427*, trans. by J. Buchan Telfer.

Song China:
Zhau Rugua (Chau Ju-kua)'s *Zhufanji* (*Chu-fan-chi*) (*Descriptions of Foreign Peoples*), translated and edited by Friedrich Hirth and W.W. Rockhill, is the work of a man who functioned as inspector of foreign trade in Fukien. His miscellaneous notes on foreign countries and their products provide evidence of the extent and volume of Song overseas trade in the twelfth century. An even more valuable source is Pu Shougeng (P'u Shou-keng)'s account of Chinese-Arab commerce in the late Song era. This Chinese official, who was of Arab descent, later threw his lot in with the Mongols and served the Yuan dynasty. For his account, see: J. Kuwabara, "P'u Shou-keng...A General Sketch of the Trade of the Arabs in China...," *Memoirs of the Research Department of the Toyo Bunko* II, Part I (1928), 1-79; VII, Part II (1935), 1-104. One Song traveler worthy of study is Changchun (Ch'ang-Ch'un), a Daoist monk who traveled to the court of Chinggis Khan ca. 1220. Jeannette Mirsky's collection of sources, *The Great Chinese Travelers*, will get you started on Changchun. A fuller translation is in E. V. Bretschneider, *Medieval Researches*, 1:3-108.

Yuan China:
Zhou Daguan (Chou Ta-Kuan) traveled to Cambodia in 1297 in the service of the Great Khan. See Jeannette Mirsky's English translation of Paul Pelliot's French translation of the Chinese text in *The Great Chinese Travelers*. It has further been translated under the title *The Customs of Cambodia*, by Paul Pelliot and J.G. Paul (Bangkok, 1987).
Rabban Sauma, a Turkish Nestorian Christian monk, traveled from his home in Khanbalik (Beijing) to Baghdad, Rome, Paris, and Bourdeaux in the late 13th century. His adventures are recorded in *The History of Yaballaha III*, trans. by James A. Montgomery.

Ming China:
Ma Huan's *The Overall Survey of the Ocean's Shores*, trans. by J. V. G. Mills details three of the seven great expeditions which Zheng He (Cheng Ho) led into the Indian Ocean between 1405 and 1433.

Great Travel Hoaxes:

Medieval European history is filled with famous hoaxes. Some were literary exercises whose authors may never have intended them to be taken seriously. Some were simple delusions and mistakes. Some were blatant attempts to deceive. Some of the more important travel and adventure hoaxes include: The letter of Prester John and subsequent reports of him (See J.R.S. Phillips, passim); John Mandeville, whose *Travels* we will read and discuss as a class; *The Book of Knowledge of All the World* (See J.R.S. Phillips, especially chapter 10); and the so-called account of the Zeno brothers, which purports to be a fourteenth-century account of the voyages of the Venetian brothers Nicolo and Antonio Zeno to Greenland and beyond. Richard H. Major is the translator.

A Few Suggested Books:
In addition to all of the atlases and other reference works available in the Bailey-Howe Reference Dept. (Such as Colin Platt's *Atlas of Medieval Man*), be advised that the following books might be of interest to you. Also check the bibliographies in J.R.S. Phillips, Abu-Lughod, and Bentley.

The Search Begins in A History of Discovery and Exploration series.
Charles R. Beazley, *The Dawn of Modern Geography*, vols. 2 and 3
K. N. Chaudhuri, *Trade and Civilisation in the Indian Ocean*
Philip D. Curtin, *Cross-Cultural Trade in World History*
George H. T. Kimble, *Geography in the Middle Ages*
Margaret Wade LaBarge, *Medieval Travellers*
Arthur P. Newton, *Travel and Travellers in the Middle Ages*
Norbert Ohler, *The Medieval Traveller*
Leonardo Olschki, *Marco Polo's Asia*.
Christine Price, *Cities of Gold and Isles of Spice: Travel to the East in the Middle Ages*

Grades:
Seminar grades will be determined according to the formula:

Book review	20%
Bibliographic essay	15%
Research paper	40%
Class participation	25%

Specialized Courses: Chronological: Medieval

Seminar Schedule

All reading assignments and exercises must be completed before the class meeting for which they are scheduled. I will lead the first discussion. After that, you will take turns as discussion leaders.

5 SEPT   Orientation

12 SEPT   Silk Roads and Avenues of Salvation: Ancient and Post-Classical Exchanges
Bentley, *Old World Encounters*, chapters 1-3.
Suggested Reading: *The Human Record*, Vol. I, sources 9-10, 32, 35, 37-38, 41, 42-45, 51, and 55. As well as accompanying introductory material.

19 SEPT   Through Twelfth-Century Jewish Eyes: The Mediterranean and Beyond
Benjamin, *The World of Benjamin of Tudela*, entire
Suggested Reading: *The Human Record*, Vol. I, sources 48-49.

26 SEPT   Nomads and Crusaders
Bentley, chapter 4
Dawson, *Mission to Asia*, entire
Suggested Reading: *The Human Record*, Vol. I, sources 77 and 91-92.
WE WILL DISCUSS THE RESEARCH PAPER AND SELECT RESEARCH TOPICS.

3 OCT   The World of Marco Polo
Marco Polo, *Travels*, entire
Suggested Reading: *The Human Record*, Vol. I, sources 92-93 and 95.
THE BOOK REVIEW IS DUE TODAY

10 OCT   Across the Sahara
Bovill, *The Golden Trade of the Moors*, chapters 1-14
Suggested Reading: *The Human Record*, Vol. I, sources 66, 85, and 96.
DEEPER DISCUSSION OF THE RESEARCH PAPERS
Everyone is to present a research question, a rough outline of the proposed paper, and a working bibliography. All of this work and all subsequent reports and drafts relating to the term paper must be typed. Everyone will also present this material to the seminar in a five minute report.

17 OCT   FALL RECESS

24 OCT   BIBLIOGRAPHIC ESSAYS ARE DUE TODAY
Everyone will offer a 5-10 minute synopsis of her/his essay and present a brief summary of her/his research to date.

Specialized Courses: Chronological: Medieval

31 OCT   Traditional *Dar-al-Islam*
      Dunn, *The Adventures of Ibn Battuta*, chapters 1-6

7 NOV   Expanding *Dar-al-Islam*
      Dunn, *The Adventures of Ibn Battuta*, chapters 7-14
      Suggested Reading: *The Human Record*, Vol. I, sources 75-76.
      A FULL OUTLINE OF YOUR TERM RESEARCH PAPER IS DUE
      TODAY; MINIMALLY THIS SHOULD BE FIVE PAGES. FIRST
      DRAFTS WILL BE ACCEPTED IN PLACE OF THIS OUTLINE.

14 NOV   John Mandeville: Traveler or Fraud?
      Mandeville, *Travels*, entire
      Suggested Reading: *The Human Record*, Vol. I, source 97.

21 NOV   The Fifteenth Century
      Bentley, *Old World Encounters*, chapter 5
      Suggested Reading: *The Human Record*, Vol. I, sources 98-100.
      THE FIRST DRAFT OF YOUR RESEARCH PAPER IS DUE TODAY,
      WITH ALL CRITICAL APPARATUS. IT WILL BE READY FOR PICK-
      UP ON MONDAY, 25 NOV.

5 DEC   POLISHED RESEARCH PAPERS ARE DUE
      Everyone will formally present her/his findings in 10-15 minute
      presentations.

IF YOU HAVE MADE IT THIS FAR IN READING THE SYLLABUS, YOU PROBABLY
FEEL OVERWHELMED, AND THE SEMINAR HAS NOT EVEN BEGUN. FEAR NOT, WE
ARE GOING TO HAVE FUN AS WELL AS LEARN A LOT. THAT'S A PROMISE.

Specialized Courses: Chronological: Age of Expansion

Philip D. Curtin
The Johns Hopkins University
The World and the West: The Shifting Balance

THE JOHNS HOPKINS UNIVERSITY
Department of History

THE WORLD AND THE WEST; THE SHIFTING BALANCE

History 110.495
Fall Semester, 1996
Mr. Curtin
Monday and Tuesday at 10:00 am
Four Credits

This course departs somewhat from the usual pattern in history courses. As a study of the ways peoples' cultures or ways of life change through time, it has elements of historical and anthropological studies. It also differs from both disciplines. The scope is too broad to leave room for an intimate picture of any culture or society, so that many anthropologists may feel unsatisfied. Nor will the course follow a sequence of events in any place through a substantial period of time, so that many historians may be equally unsatisfied. The course is episodic of necessity, being a series of case studies illustrating general patterns. This implies a strong comparative element in approach and presentation.

The course also departs from the usual pattern in that most lectures are not delivered in the classroom but are available on tape at the audio-visual desk, A level, Eisenhower Memorial Library. Audio-visual department also lends cassette recorders, if you do not have your own. Outlines and illustrative material for each recorded lecture will be distributed early in the semester.

Some of these taped lectures, as used in the past, have been converted into essays in a book called The Rise and Fall of the Plantation Complex: Essays in Atlantic History. Rather than asking people to hear those lectures, they are part of the reading assignment.

The two class hours each week are used for discussion. As a way of giving structure to those discussions, each session will be opened by student presentation of a "discussion-opener." This is an informal paper, about six typed pages, double-spaced---or equivalent in handwriting if typing is not possible. Discussion-openers for Monday discussions must be available in the container outside the instructor's door by 4 PM on the previous Friday. E-mail distribution as a courtesy may also be possible, but it does not relieve a student of responsibility to make a hard-copy available on time. Please give the instructor's copy for Friday distribution to Shirley Hipley

161

in the history office. Discussion openers for the Tuesday discussion are distributed at the Monday meeting. Suggested discussion-openers are listed each week.

Each student is responsible for at least three discussion-openers during the semester, which may mean that two students may well address the same problem in some weeks. Even if you are not doing a written discussion opener in a particular week, you are responsible for working out an answer to the problem for possible oral presentation in the seminar. Students are urged to look ahead so as to pick dates and topics of their choice. Conflicting choices will be settled by appropriate tosses of the coin. Final grades will be based in equal parts on the quality of discussion openers, the quality of class discussion, and the final examination.

Graduate students normally take the course without credit, but they are expected to read more than the assigned readings. The suggested possible further readings that are listed for some weeks provide a point of departure. Any student should feel free to consult the instructor about further readings on subject matter that strikes his or her interest, and other extensions beyond the normal course. My formal office hours are Office hours 1:00-2:00 PM, but I am in the office most of the time Monday through Wednesday. Students should feel free to drop in or call to make sure that I am in free.

There is no formal text, but a considerable part of the following will be read in the course of the semester. Most will be available for sale in the book center, but not all are available in paperback format; but copies will be on reserve.

C. A. Bayly, *Indian Society and the Making of the British Empire* (71 pages out of Z 21 are assigned)
P. D. Curtin, *Cross-Cultural Trade in World History* (167 of 254 pages are assigned).
P. D. Curtin, *The Rise and Fall of the Plantation Complex*, all assigned.
P. D. Curtin, *Two Jamaicas*, all assigned.
John Thornton, *Africa and Africans in the Making of the Atlantic World, 1400-1680* (107 of 303 pages are assigned).

TOPIC I - THE WORLD AND THE WEST: A SURVEY OF PAST RELATIONS

First Week - The World of the Post-Classical Era

September 9 - Classroom lecture 1: Relations between Societies
September 10 - Classroom lecture 3: The Maritime Revolution

Assigned reading and taped lectures for the second week should be read or heard this week in preparation for discussion on September 18. (Note that lectures are not necessarily assigned in order and that lectures 6, 9, 13, and 16 are not assigned at all this year.)

Further Reading:
Parry, J. H, The Discovery of the Sea, esp. pp. 3-72.

Specialized Courses: Chronological: Age of Expansion

Second Week - Technology and Power in World Perspective

September 16-17 - Discussion based on:
Lecture 2 - Societies beyond Europe: Agriculture and Population
Lecture 4 - Technology and Power in non-Western Societies
Marshall G. S. Hodgson, "Interrelations of Societies in History, in *Rethinking Word History: Essays on Europe, Islam, and World History* (New York: Cambridge University Press, 1993), pp. 3-34.
McNeill, William, *The Pursuit of Power*, pp. 24-62 (Chinese Predominance).
Parker, Geoffrey, "Europe and the Wider World, 1500-1750: The Military Balance," in James E. Tracy (ed.), *Political Economy of Merchant Empires: State Power and World Trade 1350-1750* (New York, Cambridge University Press, 1991), pp. 161-95.
Stephen Morillo, "Guns and Government: A Comparative Study of Europe and Japan," *Journal of World History*, 6:75-106 (1995)
Shaffer, Linda, "Southernization" *JWH*, 5:1-21 (1994).

Possible discussion openers:

1) Was the military revolution a result of gunpowder weapons, or were gunpowder weapons a result of social and political changes?
2) Where was the center of world power between about 1200 and 1500 and why?
3) Can "southernization" be a useful concept in analyzing the comparative technological success of China and Europe, or are other explanations more important?

Further Reading:
Elvin, Mark, *The Pattern of the Chinese Past*, esp. pp. 109-99
Parker, Geoffrey, *The Military Revolution*
Wolf, Eric R., *Europe and the People without History*, pp. 24-72.
Braudel, Fernand, *Civilization and Capitalism 15th-18th Century*, 3 vols., (esp. volume 1 on material life and volume 2, pp. 14-37).
Cippola, Carlo M., *Guns and Sails in the Early Phase of European Expansion, 1 400-1 700*.
Wallerstein, Immanuel, *The Modern World System*, volume 1.

Specialized Courses: Chronological: Age of Expansion

TOPIC II - ASIAN TRADE AND WESTERN SHIPPING

Third Week - Western Thought, Merchant Empires, and the Periodization of World History

September 23-24 - Discussion Based on:
Lecture 5 - Western Thought and the World Overseas

Curtin, *Cross-Cultural Trade in World History*, pp. 1-14, 109-35.
Douglass C. North, "Institutions, Transaction Costs, and the Rise of Merchant Empires," in James D. Tracy (ed.),*The Political Economy of Merchant Empires: State Power and World Trade, 1585-1740* (Cambridge: Cambridge University Press, 1991), pp. 22-40.
Jerry H. Bentley, "Cross-Cultural Interaction and Periodization in World History, *American Historical Review*, 101:749-770 (1996)
Patrick Manning, "The Problem of Interactions in World History," *AHR*, 101:771-782

Possible discussion openers:

1) Is the substantivist position of Polanyi and others still worth discussion, or is it a theory now passed over and worthy of dismissal?
2) What is the most appropriate solution to the problem of dividing history into period like Ancient, Medieval, and Modern?
3) Does the expansion of Europe in the age of the merchant empires really come down to such a petty matter as transaction costs?

Further Reading:
Lach, Donald F., *Asia in the Making of Europe*, esp. vols. 1 and 2.
Steensgard, Niels, *Carracks, Caravans, and Companies*
Elliot, John H., *The Old World and the New*
Pearson, M. N., *The New Cambridge History of India. Volume 1, part 1, The Portuguese in India* (1987).
Stearns, Adas, and Schwartz, *World Civilizations,* 1:257-263 (the post-classic era, 1-87 (the West and the changing balance).

Fourth Week - Missionaries in Asia

September 30 - Slides of maritime Asia - remains of the seventeenth century
October 1 - Discussions based on:
Lecture 7 - Missionary Aims and Achievements
Lecture 8 - Japan's Reception of Christian Missions.
Stearns, Adas, and Schwartz, *World Civilizations*, pp. 593-615 (Muslim Empires); 639-663 (Asia in the fifteenth and sixteenth centuries).

Specialized Courses: Chronological: Age of Expansion

Possible discussion openers:

1) It has been argued that Chinese dynasties rise and fall as a natural process like the individual passage from youth to old age. Could the same be said for the three Muslim empires that flourished in the sixteenth century?
2) Looking at Ethiopia, Timor, and Japan in the sixteenth century, were the missionaries more successful one place rather than another because they were more wise and skillful in their approach, or because local conditions favored their enterprise?
3) Why was Ming China unsuccessful in mastering Indian Ocean trade in the way the Portuguese were to do? Or is the picture of greater Portuguese achievement overdrawn?

Fifth Week - New Entrants and New Technology in Asian Trade

October 7-8 -Discussion based on:
Lecture 10 - Technology and Trade in the seventeenth and eighteenth centuries.
Curtin, *Cross-Cultural Trade*, pp. 158-206.
Steinberg, D. J., and others, *In Search of Southeast Asia*, (Revised edition 1987) pp. 9-20, 49-59.
Bayly, C.A., *Indian Society and the Making of the British Empire*, pp. 7-44.

Possible discussion openers:

1) Africa and Southeast Asia were the last major regions to be brought into consideration as part of world history. Why should that have been the case for Southeast Asia?
2) How would you account for the comparative success of the Bugis and the Armenians as traders in this period? Was it tactics, geography, previous culture, or something else?
3) Was it Mughal weakness or European power that made it possible for the ---India Companies to gain a foothold in India---or neither?
4) Was the impact of Western trade a major theme in Indian history of the eighteenth century, or merely a side-show hinting at the major influence of Europe on India a century later?

Further Reading:
Tracy, James (ed.), *The Rise of Merchant Empires and The Political Economy of Merchant Empires* (1990 and 1991) .
Chaudhuri, Kinti N., *Trade and Civilization in the Indian Ocean: An Economic History from the Rise of Islam to 1750* (1985).
Chaudhuri, Kinti N., *Asia Before Europe: Economy and Civilisation of the Indian Ocean from the Rise of Islam to 1750* (1990)

Specialized Courses: Chronological: Age of Expansion

Sixth Week - Adjustments in Agriculture and Political Structure

October 14 - Fall Break Day - No Class
October 15 - Discussion of:
    Lecture 11 - Asian Agricultural Adjustment
    Lecture 12 - Transition to Territorial Empire: Java and Bengal.
    Steinberg and others, Search for Southeast Asia, pp. 146-59.
    Bayly, Indian Society, pp. 45-78.
    Curtin, Cross-Cultural Trade, pp. 230-54.

Possible discussion openers:

1) Was European trade in Eastern Seas inevitably destabilizing to the Asian political and
    economic order, or was the new instability the result of European political and military
    policies? Or, finally, was the Asian political and economic no more unstable than usual?
2) Why did the Europeans switch from trading-post to territorial empire in Asia?

Further Reading:
Wallerstein, Immanuel, *Modern World System*, vol. 1, Chs. 6-7 (pp. 199-239 in text edition).
Sauer, Carl O., *Agricultural Origins and Dispersals.*
Subrahmanyam, Sanjay, *The Political Economy of Commerce: Southern India, 1500-1800*
    (Cambridge: Cambridge University Press, 1990).

TOPIC III - THE RISE AND FALL OF THE PLANTATION COMPLEX

Seventh Week - Medieval Origins

October 21-22 - Discussion based on:
    Curtin, *Rise and Fall of the Plantation Complex*, pp. 3-28.
    John Thornton, *Africa and Africans in the Making of the Atlantic World 1400-1680*, pp.
    43-97.
    Crosby, Alfred, *The Columbian Voyages, the Columbian Exchanges, and their
    Historians*, pp. 1-25.

Possible discussion openers:

1) Why did the Europeans keep sugar production under their own control, when they were
    content to let others produce tea, coffee, or cloves for sale?
2) Was the origin of the plantation complex an aspect of Linda Shaffer's "Southernization," or the
    beginning of "Westernization" under European control?
3) How important was the role of the state (both African and European)---as opposed to private
    enterprise---in the development of Atlantic commerce?

Further Reading:
Galloway, J. H., *The Sugar Cane Industry: An Historical Geography from its Origins to 1914* (Cambridge, CUP, 1989).
Verlinden, Charles, *The Origins of Modern Colonization.*
Phillips, William D., Jr., *Slavery from Roman Times to the Early Transatlantic Trade* (Minneapolis, 1985).

Eighth Week - Sixteenth-Century Transition

October 28-29 - Discussion based on:
    Curtin, *Plantation Complex*, pp. 29-57.
    Thornton, *Africa and Africans*, pp. 98-125.
    Lockhart, James and Stuart Schwartz, *Early Latin America*, pp. 202-252 (Brazil in the Sugar Age).

Possible discussion openers:
1) What conditions in Africa made that continent a desirable source of slaves, and what conditions in Brazil made African slaves more valuable than European or Indian labor?
2) It is sometimes said that the plantation regime in Brazil was dominated by the nature of sugar as a crop, which left little room for human choice about Brazilian development. Was this the case?
3) Was African slavery and the slave trade forced on Africa by outsiders, or was it an outgrowth of indigenous institutions?

Further Reading:
Russell-Wood, A. J. R., *The Black Man in Slavery and Freedom in Colonial Brazil*, pp. 267-303.
Schwartz, Stuart, *Sugar Plantations in the Formation of Brazilian Society: Bahia 1550-1835.*
Mintz, Sydney, *Sweetness and Power.*

Ninth Week - The Spanish Empire on the American Mainland

November 4-5 - Discussion based on:
    Lecture 19 - Imperial Theory and Demographic Fact.
    Curtin, *Plantation Complex*, pp. 58-70.
    Lockhart and Schwartz, *Early Latin America,* pp. 59-85. (From islands to mainland.)
    Knight, *The Caribbean*, pp. 66-87.

Possible discussion openers:

1) Lockhart introduces a number of process-models to describe Spanish American history in this period. What are his principal process-models? Which are the weakest? Which are the least subject to criticism?

2) Imperial theory may be an interesting intellectual game, but did these theorists really have a serious influence on the course of history?

3) Why did the Spanish establish a territorial empire, while the Portuguese went for the plantation complex? Was it a matter of choice, or determined by demography and environment?

Tenth Week - The Plantation Complex Established

November 11 - Discussion based on:
    Curtin, *Plantation Complex*, pp. 73-110.
    Knight, F. W., *The Caribbean*, pp. 120-158.
    Thornton, *Africa and Africans in the Atlantic World*, pp. 129-151.
November 12- Slides - West Africa and the West Indies.

Possible discussion openers:

1) What caused transfrontier societies to emerge? Environment or human choice?

2) Why did the Caribbean develop such a varied pattern of castes and classes, compared to the two-caste society of the American South? Or were they really more alike than not?

3) Why did slavery move into North and South America beyond the plantation complex proper?

Further Reading:
Dunn, Richard S., *Sugar and Slaves*, p. 46-83, 188-262.

Eleventh Week - Economics and Society in the Caribbean

November 18- 19 - Discussion based on:
    Curtin, *Plantation Complex*, 113-143.
    Brathwaite, Edward, *The Development of Creole Society in Jamaica 1770-1820*, pp. 165-75.
    Curtin, P.D., *Two Jamaicas*, pp. 3-80.

Specialized Courses: Chronological: Age of Expansion

Possible discussion openers:

1) How damaging was the slave trade to the health and well-being of African societies?
2) Why was the Asian process-model of "voyage, factory, fort, colony" not applicable to West
    Africa in the eighteenth century?
3) Aside from the division between master and slave, what were the most serious social
    cleavages in Jamaican society of the late eighteenth and early nineteenth centuries? Did
    they matter?

Further Reading:

Eltis, David, "Free and Coerced Transatlantic Migrations," *American Historical Review*, 88:251-
    80 (1982).
Craton, Michael and James Walvin, *A Jamaican Plantation.*
Paterson, Orlando, *Sociology of Slavery.*
Debien, Gabriel, *Les esclaves aux Antilles francaises.*
Craton, Michael, *In Search of the Invisible Man.*

Twelfth Week - The Democratic Revolution

November 25-26 - Discussion based on:
    Curtin, *Plantation Complex*, pp. 144-69.
    Curtin, *Two Jamaicas*, pp. 81 - 121.

Possible discussion openers:

1) Were the revolutions in the Atlantic basin between the mid-eighteenth and the late nineteenth
    centuries really variants of a "democratic" or "liberal" revolutionary pattern, or did they
    merely use fashionable language for their diverse ends?
2) Slavery in Jamaica and Saint Domingue ended with some level of violence. Why was Jamaica
    so much less violent than Saint Domingue? Could slavery have been ended in either place
    without violence?
3) Were the changes in Jamaican society between 1830 and 1865 mainly imposed from abroad.
    or mainly an outgrowth of local conditions?

Further Reading:

Geggus, David P., *Slavery, War, and Revolution.*
Fick, Carolyn E., *The Making of Haiti: The Saint Domingue Revolution from Below* (Knoxville:
    University of Tennessee Press, 1990).

Thirteenth Week - The End of the Plantation Complex

December 2-3 - Discussion based on:
Curtin, *Plantation Complex*, 173-203.
Curtin, *Two Jamaicas*, pp. 121-209.
Knight, F.W., *The Caribbean*, pp. 121-145.
McNeill, John, "The End of the Old Atlantic World: America, Africa, Europe, 1770-1888, in Karras, Alan L., and John R. McNeill, *Atlantic American Societies: From Columbus through Abolition 1492-1888* (New York: Routledge, 1992), pp. 245-268.

Possible discussion openers:

1) What ended the Atlantic slave trade and what difference did it make to West Africa?
2) What ended the Plantation Complex in the Americas? Was it a single body of causes that were effective everywhere, or different were causes effective in each individual plantation region?

Further Reading:
Higman, Barry, *Slave Population of Jamaica.*
Higman, Barry, *Slave Populations of the British Caribbean.*
Conrad, Robert, *The Destruction of Slavery in Brazil.*
Knight, Franklin, *Slave Society in Cuba during the Nineteenth Century.*
Moreno Fraginals, Manuel, *The Sugarmill.*
Scott, Rebecca, *Slave Emancipation in Cuba.*
Eltis, David, *Economic Growth and the Ending of the Transatlantic Slave Trade.*

Fourteenth Week - Retrospect on the Plantation Complex

December 9 - Discussion - The Atlantic System in Retrospect
Curtin, *Plantation Complex*, pp. 204-26.
Solow, Barbara, "Capitalism and Slavery in the Exceedingly Long Run," *Journal of Interdisciplinary History*, 17:711-37 (1987).
Engerman, Stanley L., "The Atlantic Economy in the Eighteenth Century: Some Speculations on Economic Development in Britain, America, Africa, and Elsewhere," *Journal of European Economic History*, 24:145-175 (1995).

Specialized Courses: Chronological: Age of Expansion

John Gillis
Rutgers University
The Age of European Expansion

506:110 The Age of European Expansion   Fall, 1997

Professor John Gillis
Office   005 Van Dyck Hall
e-mail 75463.217@compuserve.com
Office hours Monday 9-11
Teaching Assistant Patrick McDevitt

Description and the Goals of the Course

Now that we have entered a global era, it is time to turn to our attention to global history. We can no longer afford the illusion that each nation or people has its own unique history. That myth has led to a century of total wars, to mindless and wasteful competitions over irreplaceable resources which have left the planet exhausted and demoralized. Now we must face our interdependence and acknowledge that global cooperation is the only means of ensuring the future of the earth itself.

We are just beginning to understand the history of the earth, of which human history is only a recent moment. And this course deals with only a tiny fraction of human time, focusing on the emergence of an Atlantic World from the 1490s to the present. However, it can be argued that this is precisely the moment which has done more to change the earth, to bring it close to disaster, than any other. Therefore it is an important era to study. And it is particularly appropriate that we explore just five years after the Columbian Quincentenary, when the consequences of the fateful encounters that began in 1492 were so intensely debated.

The title of the course is a little misleading, for it implies that the main actor in the creation of the Atlantic world was Europe. The term "expansion" imputes a consciousness and sense of purpose to Europeans, while denying to Africans and Native Americas a role in Atlantic history. In reality the Atlantic world was the product of all three continents and peoples.

We will begin the course by examining the state of the world in 1997, looking at the vast inequalities of wealth and power that currently exist, not just between world regions but within every society with respect to class, age, and gender. We will also assess the ecological crisis that threatens rich and poor alike. How did this disastrous state of affairs arise? As we will see, before 1492 there was far less discrepancy among the regions bordering the Atlantic; and the environment was relatively stable. The past five centuries have produced the conditions we must cope with today. Therefore, we begin the course by looking at Africa, Europe, and the Western Hemisphere as these existed before contact. We will be looking not just at kings and conquerors but at ordinary people, women as well as men, for in the end it is their biology (diseases as well as diets), their beliefs, and their actions which shape history. Once we have understood the dynamics of the societies of all three areas, then we are ready to understand their fateful interaction over the past five hundred years.

The course is historical but the questions it explores are starkly contemporary. It is through the past that we come to understand ourselves. After this course you will never look everyday things like a cup of coffee or a candy bar in the quite the same way again. You will find that much of what you once thought of as "natural" -- including habits, ideas, even bodily functions -- are the product of history, the result of change and thus subject to further transformation. The purpose of learning is not just to understand the world but to change it, to make it better. That too is the purpose of this course.

You are probably used to thinking of history as an accumulation of facts, for that is the way the subject is usually taught at the secondary level. But, while an educated person must master a certain body of material, history is a way of thinking about the facts not the facts themselves. In this course you will be compelled to be an active creator rather than a passive consumer. In the discussions and writing assignments, you will be asked to think for yourself. The lectures will provide a model of how one goes about understanding the past, but you will be your own historian.

Requirements: Every student will be required to write four short papers and a final exam. The course also fulfills Livingston College's Level III writing requirement. Those taking it for Level III credit will also write a research paper.

The following books are in Livingston bookstore:

> E. Wolf, Europe and the People without History
> W. Schivelbusch, Tastes of Paradise
> P. Kennedy, Preparing for the Twenty First Century
> H. Konig, Columbus: His Enterprise

You are to read all the assignments listed on the syllabus before the Monday lecture. They provide the materials basic to the understanding of the lectures and discussions.

Grading: Each paper will receive extensive comments and grades. Your final grade will be based on the progress that you have made during the course. Remember that learning is an active process and that the measure of an educated person is not just what he or she knows but their ability to communicate that knowledge to others. Knowledge is indeed power, but it must never be treated as private property, but always shared as a public good.

Specialized Courses: Chronological: Age of Expansion

Part I   The World We Have Inherited

Week I   What is Global History?

Sept. 4   Introduction to the Course

Over the weekend read Wolf, Europe and the People without History, pp. 1-7 and
Kennedy, Preparing for Twenty First Century, chapters I, II.

Week II   The Challenge of the 21st Century

Sept. 8   Defining Global Problems
Sept. 11   Imagining Solutions

To be read by Monday, Kennedy, Preparing, chapters IV, V, VI.

The lectures and discussions this week will be aimed at understanding the shape of the
world we have inherited. We will be looking not only at the accumulated problems, but the
terms that are used to define them such as "development" and "underdeveloped," "affluent" and
"poor," "modern" and "traditional."

Your first paper, due September 15th is a relatively simple assignment. In three pages, define
what you believe to be the key problem facing the world today. You will refer to this paper again
at the end of the course when you will asked to write a final paper explain how this problem
came into existence historically and how, using your own historical understanding, you would
urge the world to solve it.

Part II   The Atlantic World Before 1492

Week III   Old Worlds: Africa and the Western Hemisphere

Sept. 15   Our African Origins
Sept. 18   The First Revolution: Neolithic Agriculture

Readings: Wolf, Europe and the People without History, pp. 24-44, 58-72

Neither Africa or what we now call the Americas were static societies awaiting the magic
wand of European influence. On the contrary, each had their unique character and dynamics,
their own past and their own future. This week we will be trying to understand these unique
civilizations, which would make such vast contributions to the Atlantic world.

Specialized Courses: Chronological: Age of Expansion

Week IV   The Newest World: Europe

Sept. 22   The Rise of Feudal Europe, 800-1200
Sept. 25   Black Death, Peasant Revolts, Crisis of Feudal
Society

Readings: Wolf, Europe and the People without History, pp. 101-125.

By world standards, Europe was a latecomer, dependent and backward in 800. On the margins of what was then the "civilized" world of Eurasia and Africa, this peninsula developed its own unique characteristics: manorialism and a guild economy, feudalism, and the Christian worldview.

Week V   Crisis of Feudalism and the Rise of Commercial Capitalism

Sept. 29   Europe Reformed: Rise of Commercial Capitalism
Oct. 2   The World of Christopher Columbus

Readings: Konig, Columbus: His Enterprise, pp. 9-42

Feudal civilization appeared to be a stable and self-sustaining until the 14th century, when it underwent a massive biological and spiritual crisis. We will look at how this altered medieval economy, undermined feudalism, and prompted apocalyptic visions which resulted in an aggressive expansionism that was to have a huge impact on the rest of the world.

Week VI   From Contact to Conquest

Oct. 6   The Precolumbian Americas
Oct. 9   The Tale of Two Empires: Aztec and Spanish

Readings: Konig, Columbus: His Enterprise, pp. 43-124; Wolf, Europe and the People Without, pp. 131-157

There is a danger in imputing to Europeans too much foresight. They did not so much discover the so-called "New World" as invent it. In the process, they reinvented themselves. We now know that Columbus was not the first European to contact the Western Hemisphere, but he looms so large in our imaginations because he did more than any other person to shape the way we think about the world he had blundered into. It is important to understand Columbus not just as an historical actor, but as representative of a larger dynamic. In your second paper (due Oct. 13) you are to write a four page paper on the way your own views of Columbus have changed and how you would now interpret his actions.

Part III   The Formation of the Atlantic World

Week VII   Colonization and Slave Trade

Oct. 13   From Conquest to Plantation: Trade and
          New Patterns of Labor and Consumption
Oct. 16   Africa and the Slave Trade

Readings: Schievelbusch, Tastes of Paradise, chapters I and II.
           Wolf, Europe and the People Without, pp. 195-208

Once the quest for gold and souls was exhausted, European's began to think of the "New World" as a source of cash crops and raw materials. In time, Europe would become addicted to new world commodities and an Atlantic division of labor and consumption would be created. The Dutch and the English had joined the Portuguese and the Spanish in the creation of new modes of production which required unprecedented amounts of labor. The result was the massive slave trade, which transformed not only Africa and the Americas, but also Europe, where new habits of consumptions were being formed. By following the history of new products -- sugar and tobacco -- we can begin to grasp the many dimensions of this process.

Week VIII   Scientific and Commercial Revolutions
            of the Seventeenth Century

Oct. 20   The Conquest of Mother Nature
Oct. 23   Religious Reformation, Patriarchy, and the Capitalist Work Ethic

Readings: Schievelbusch, Tastes of Paradise, chapter IV
           Merchant, "Production, Reproduction, and the Female"

Already in the seventeenth century, we can begin to see the pattern of north/south inequalities emerging. An Atlantic division of labor was already evident, with Africa contributing the labor, the Americas the land, and Europe the capital. We will look at how knowledge and power came together in the first scientific revolution, producing a new concept of "Nature" compatible with the increasing rate of exploitation of the planet. We will also consider the ways in which the Reformation reinforced the patriarchical organization of household production in Europe, changing the way gender and generation was organized.

Specialized Courses: Chronological: Age of Expansion

Week IX   Industrial Revolution in Europe, 1750-1870

Oct. 27   Preindustrial Europe
Oct. 30   The First Industrial Revolution

Readings: Gillis, "The First Industrial Society"
            N. McKendrick, "The Making of the Wedgewood Factory"
            Schivelbusch, Tastes of Paradise, chapter V

Until the late eighteenth century, Europe was satisfied with its commercial domination of the Atlantic, feeling no great need to expand its domestic production. By 1850 all this had changed, as capitalists took direct control of the means of production, thereby transforming European society and politics beyond all recognition. North America was soon to follow, thus further widening the gap between north and south. You are to write a five page paper on why the industrial revolution first occurred in Europe. It is due on November 4th.

Part IV   The Making of the Modern World

Week X   New Empires, 1870 to 1917

Nov. 3   The Second Industrial Revolution
Nov. 6   The New Imperialism: Moving People and Inventing
         Races

Readings: Gillis, "Birth of the Modern City"
            Wolf, Europe and the People Without, pp. 325-353
            Schivelbusch, Taste of Paradise, chapter VIII

The nineteenth century began with American revolt against the old European empires, moves toward the abolition of slavery, and the promise of free trade. It ended with the renewal of imperialism, new forms of labor discipline, and new mercantilist controls over African and Latin American economies. In 1900, inequalities in economic and military power were so great that it seemed that the self-defined "white race" had established permanent hegemony over virtually the entire globe.

Specialized Courses: Chronological: Age of Expansion

Week XI World Wars and World Revolutions, 1914-1970
Nov. 10 Europe Self-Destructs, 1914-45
Nov. 13 The Rise of the Superpowers, 1945-1970

Readings: Kennedy, Preparing, chapter XI
          Wolf, Europe and the People Without, pp. 361-383

The last hundred years have been marked by massive movements of peoples. They no longer leave their homes as slaves, but their migrations are not exactly voluntary. Pushed by population explosion and poverty, and drawn to constantly changing labor markets, the greater part of the globe's population has become uprooted and proletarianized, redefined into newly invented racial categories more easily exploited for political and economic purposes. The locus of power has also been shifting. Just as hegemonic power seemed to reach its peak, it was undermined by world war (1914-18) which not only exhausted all the great powers in Europe itself, but produced inadvertently two new world powers -- the United States and the Soviet Union -- both of which tried to assume the role of economic and political leadership which the Europeans had forfeited. The United States took the lead among the capitalist powers, while the new Soviet Union tried to create a grand alliance of socialist states.

When in the period 1939-1945 fascism failed to reassert European world dominance, Europe accepted its secondary position, abandoned its empire, and in the post-1945 concentrated on its own internal development, producing its greatest era of prosperity. Meanwhile, the superpowers, engaged in an international struggle for superiority largely at the expense of the Third World, ultimately exhausted themselves through overmilitarization, leading to the ultimate collapse of Communism and the total restructuring of international capitalism.

Week XII Emergence of Multipolar World, 1970-Present

Nov. 17 The Western Economic Miracles, 1950-1970
Nov. 20 Rise of the Japan and the NICs

Readings: Kennedy, Preparing, Chapters VIII, IX, X

The Cold War that can be traced back to 1917 came to a sudden end in 1989 with the collapse of the Soviet Union and the independence of its central European client states. This was greeted in the United States as proof of the superiority of the capitalist system, but this proved an empty victory, for the problems facing the western capitalist countries were only a little less dire than those which had brought down the Soviet system. The environmental crisis knew no political boundaries, and the militarization which had crippled the Soviet economy had was also a cause of the inability of the United States to compete economically with its less militarized allies, Japan and Germany. Already in the 1970s, earning power was dropping and standards of living were leveling out. New social movements, the civil rights and feminist movements, were challenging the established white male power structure. A crisis was looming in capitalist countries as well.

Specialized Courses: Chronological: Age of Expansion

Week XIII The Contemporary Crisis of Global Capitalism

Nov. 24 Crisis of the Superpowers: Vietnam and Afghanistan
Nov. 28 Thanksgiving

Readings: Kennedy, Preparing, Chapters III, IV, V.

The great irony of our time is that the two powers which emerged triumphant in 1945 had been overtaken in two decades by those they had defeated. In the end, neither the United States nor the Soviet Union "won" the Cold War. They became industrial/military giants only to find that demilitarized Japan and Germany outstripped them in less than three decades. We need to understand how this happened. But we also need to understand how the non-industrializing nations of the Third World (the South) were increasing at a disadvantage, and why the gap between North and South has grown in the last two decades.

Week XIV New World Order or Disorder?

Dec. 1 Restructuring of Capitalism in the 1970s and 1980s
Dec. 4 Globalization and the Fate of National Economies

Readings: Kennedy, Preparing, Chapters XII, XIII, XIV

As the bimillenium is only four years away, it seems time to take stock of the fate of the earth. We will be concerned this week not only about the ecological crisis that is upon us, but the growing gap between north and south. Are we headed toward a New World Order or a New World of Disorder? Here is where you can begin to use the history you have learned to think about the present and the future. You will want to return to the first paper you wrote and, using what you have learned, prepare a five page essay on how the problem you originally identified in it came about historically and how it can be resolved in a manner with the historical forces at work in the world today. You will bring this paper to the final exam.

Week XV Review Week

Dec. 8 New World Order or Disorder?
Dec. 11 General Review of the Course

Final Examination will consist of two parts. The first is your paper, the second will consist of an essay question on one of the major historical developments from 1870 to the present.

Specialized Courses: Chronological: Age of Expansion

Allen M. Howard
Rutgers University
World Civilizations: Africa, Europe, Americas

506:114--World Civilizations: Africa, Europe, Americas   Spring 1998

Instructor: Allen M. Howard, Rutgers University
Office: Van Dyck 007a; Tues. 10:00-11:00; Weds. 1:00-2:00 & B.A.
E-mail: <ahoward@rci.rutgers.edu>; Phone: 732-932-7142

Teaching Assistant: Kevin Deuschle
Office Van Dyck 013; Thurs. 11:00-12:00; Fri. 9:30-10:30
Phone: 732-932-7415

Tutors: Malika Alleyne and Joseph Varga

DESCRIPTION AND GOALS OF THE COURSE:

Through lectures, readings, slides, films and discussions this course will explore the history and current condition of the Atlantic world, concentrating primarily on West Africa, Western Europe, the Caribbean, and certain areas of Central and North America. We begin by examining some of the major problems, challenges, and opportunities of the present-day. Then we shift our focus to the pre-1500 Islamic world system and to the economic, political, and cultural dynamics of the above regions during that time. Next we move to the post-1500 period, focusing on how interactions resulted in a massive destruction of the Native American population, created a new Atlantic economic system, and brought other fundamental changes, including environmental changes. The final weeks of the course will be concerned with the modern industrial and political revolutions and the patterns of "development" and "underdevelopment" that are the background to the present world crisis.

The course is historical, but the questions it deals with are starkly contemporary, and we will debate current as well as historical issues.

Topics we will explore include:

--The nature of the Eastern Hemisphere commercial and political systems before 1500; Islam in Africa, Asia, and Europe.

--Atlantic-wide historical forces, including trade, slavery, racism, colonialism and resistance, capitalism, industrialization, rise of the nation-state, and revolution.

--How these forces have affected men and women differently, and the gendered dimension of social, political, economic, and environmental change.

--Ways in which ordinary people have helped shape history; the course focuses heavily on labor and on working people.

--How new societies and cultures have developed through interaction around the Atlantic.

--The "Globalization of Capital" in recent decades and related problems, such as the loss of jobs in New Jersey.

Specialized Courses: Chronological: Age of Expansion

--Some ways in which history provides understanding of current problems of economic inequality and environmental breakdown.
--What you and others might do to organize for a more democratic and just economy and to prevent further environmental decay.

The course is divided into units that coincide with some of these topics. You will receive a study guide for each unit, but will also be expected to pose and answer your own major historical questions.

To be an educated and engaged citizen, one must think about the world at large and be able to express oneself effectively on critical issues. Therefore this course stresses oral and written expression as well as historical knowledge. Historical perspective is the ability to deal with the past analytically, not simply narrating what happened but gaining an understanding of why things have turned out the way they have. Thus history is always interpretation. History also involves empathy and respect for the diverse experiences, values, and outlooks of people. We will spend a good deal of time examining and debating different ways of interpreting the past, and it will be your task to try to understand how others have experienced events and also to develop your own viewpoint on the major issues.

This course will be built around active student participation. All readings should be done by the day assigned.
--20% of the grade will be based on discussion and debates
YOU WILL BE ASKED TO KEEP A LOG OF YOUR CONTRIBUTIONS AND HAND THIS IN REGULARLY
--20 % will be based on short papers that will involve interpretation of readings, linkage of readings and lectures, etc. Such writing will focus on skill building.
--40% of the grade will be based on two longer papers (each 20%)
--20% of the grade will be based on the final exam
TUTORIAL SESSIONS ARE CRITICAL TO THIS COURSE; YOU WILL DISCUSS READINGS/LECTURES, PREPARE FOR PAPERS, AND REVIEW COMPLETED PAPERS. -- Extra credit for well-prepared participation in debates.
--Late papers will be marked down; if a paper has not been handed in by the time graded papers are returned, a written exam will be substituted. More than three unexcused absences will reduce the final grade. Late arrival at class will count as an absence. The final grade will take into consideration the progress a student has made in mastering the material and concepts and in presenting that understanding orally and in writing.

The following books are to be purchased at the Recto & Verso Book-store, 80 Albany St., north of the Albany-George St. intersection:

P. Curtin, The Rise and Fall of the Plantation Complex
M. Leon-Portilla, The Broken Spears
O. Sembene, God's Bits of Wood
D. Wright, The World and a Small Place in Africa

Specialized Courses: Chronological: Age of Expansion

Additional readings and documents handed out in class will provide alternative viewpoints.

In certain weeks we will meet in sections or small groups; a schedule will be provided later.

Jan. 20 --Introduction; The Shape of the Modern World; Some Common Interpretations and Misunderstandings

Unit I: EASTERN HEMISPHERE COMMERCIAL/POLITICAL SYSTEMS BEFORE 1500

Jan. 23 --The Expansion of Islam and the Islamic World

Read: Hrbek and El Fasi, "The Rise of the Islamic World" and "The Coming of Islam" P 1-8
Abu-Lughod, "Islam and Business" in Before European Hegemony P 9-19

Jan. 27 --India, South East Asia, and China Integrated into the Eastern Hemisphere System; Moorish Spain

Read: Abu-Lughod, "The Indian Subcontinent: On the Way to Everywhere P 32-38
Pimenta-Bey, "Moorish Spain.. Academic Sources and Foundation for...Western Universities" P 39-42

Jan. 30 --West African Sudan to 1500; Integration into the Eastern Hemispheric Commercial System; Sustainability Issues

Read: Wright, xi-xv, 3-39

Feb. 3 --The Mali Empire in West Africa; Mali and Niumi in the World System

Read: Boahen, "The Rise and Fall of Mali" in Topics in West African History P27-31
Wright, 40-69

FILM: "CARAVANS OF GOLD" (ALL FILMS WILL BE SHOWN IN VD211)

Feb. 7 --Venice and Genoa Integrated into the Eastern Hemisphere System

Read: Abu-Lughod, "Changes in the System of Trade" P43-48
Davis, Venice: Art and Literature P49-58

TUTORIAL SESSIONS

SHORT PAPER FOR UNIT I DUE FEB. 10

Specialized Courses: Chronological: Age of Expansion

Unit II: <u>EUROPEAN EXPANSION ABROAD; THE CONQUEST OF THE AMERICAS</u>

Feb. 10 --   From Feudal Europe to the Crisis of the 14th Century;
             Sustainability and its Limits
       Read: Power, "The Peasant Bodo" P 59-67
             "Peasants Wars of the 14th Century" HANDOUT
             Curtin, 3-16

Feb. 13 --Meso-America Before 1500; Sustainability and its Limits
       Read: Leon-Portilla, vii-31 (also read appendix)
             Upshur, "Mesoamerica, Formative & Classical Periods" P 79-84 (pages omitted)

Feb. 17 --The Iberians in the Americas; Columbus and Cortez
       Read: Curtin, 17-28
             Leon-Portilla, 32-90

       FILM: "CONFLICT OF THE GODS" from the "BURIED MIRROR"

Feb. 20 --The Conquest of Mexico and Aftermath; <u>DEBATE</u>
       Read: Leon-Portilla, 91-end
             Cortez, <u>Letters from Mexico</u>, P 95-101
             De Las Casas, <u>A Short Account of the Destruction of the Americas</u>, P 85-94
             Curtin, 58-70

TUTORIAL SESSIONS

LONG PAPER FOR UNIT II DUE FEB. 24

Unit III: <u>THE ATLANTIC SLAVE TRADE, THE PLANTATION COMPLEX, AND ISSUES OF
UNDERDEVELOPMENT; AFRICAN-AMERICAN CULTURES AND RESISTANCE</u>

Feb. 24   --Toward a Capitalist Society in Europe; Mercantile Expansion, European Rivalries
             in the Americas
       Read: Curtin, 86-97
             Power, "Thomas Paycocke of Coggeshall" P 102-109

Feb. 27   --Sugar and Slaves: The Plantation Slave Economy and Underdevelopment;
                    Ideologies and Structures of Racism
       Read: Curtin, 46-57, 73-85
             Dunn, "Sugar and Slaves" P 110-116
             Wright, 67-94

Specialized Courses: Chronological: Age of Expansion

Mar. 3   --Africa, the Slave Trade, and Questions about Africa   Underdevelopment
         Read: Curtin, 29-45, 113-143
                Wright, 95-134

Mar. 6   --African-American Communities; Resistance and Revolution
         Read: Curtin, skim 144-157, read 158-169
                Thompson, Flash of the Spirit P 117-125
                Klein, "Creation of a Slave Community and Afro-American Culture" P 126-138
                Bush, "The Woman Slave and Slave Resistance" P 139-149

Mar. 10 --The End of Slavery; Formation of New Societies
         Read: Curtin, 173-206
                Ofonagoro, "The African Presence in North America" P 150-157

TUTORIAL SESSIONS

SHORT PAPER ON UNIT III DUE Mar. 13

Mar. 13 --Pseudo-Scientific Racism; African & African-American Responses
         FILM: "SUGAR CANE ALLEY" DISCUSSION OF FILM AND READINGS

UNIT IV: CAPITALISM AND COLONIALISM: INDUSTRIALIZATION AND THE
WORLD-WIDE COMMODIFICATION AND MOVEMENT OF GOODS AND LABOR; RACE,
ETHNICITY AND LABOR RESISTANCE

Mar. 24 --Debating the Sources of the Industrial Revolution
         Read: Strayer, The Making of the Modern World, P 158-164
                Gillis, "The First Industrial Society" P 165-174
                McKendrick, "The Making of the Wedgewood Factory" P 175-180

Mar. 27 --International Movement of Labor and Capital; Labor Segmentation; New Societies
         Read: Wolf, "The New Laborers P 199-211 (pages omitted)
                Namias, "Philip and Theresa Bonacorsi--Children of the Lawrence Strike" P 212-220
                Shepherd, "Indian Women in Jamaica, 1845-1945" P 221-224

Mar. 31 --Imperialism, Conquest, and Early Colonial Rule in West Africa
         Read: Wright, 135-185
                Sembene, 1-77

Apr. 3   --Economic, Social, and Cultural Changes in the 20th Century
         Read: Sembene, 78-139
                Wright, 170-208

TUTORIAL SESSIONS

Specialized Courses: Chronological: Age of Expansion

Apr. 7   --Women and Working Classes in West Africa and Caribbean
         Read: Sembene, 140-199

Apr. 10--From Protest and Strikes to National Independence in the Third World; World War II and
         the Decline of Europe
         Read: Sembene, 200-245
               Wright, 209-218

Apr. 17 FINAL DISCUSSION OF SEMBENE AND UNIT IV

LONG PAPER FOR UNIT VI DUE APRIL 21

UNIT V: GLOBALIZATION OF CAPITAL IN THE 1970S-1990S--ORGANIZING TO
PROTECT JOBS AND THE ENVIRONMENT WITH A MORE SUSTAINABLE FUTURE

Apr. 21--The Rise of a Consumer Society in the U.S.; The Commercialization of the Prairie, the
         Rain Forest, the Savanna and Other Environments
         Read: Worster, "Dust Bowl: Sodbusting" P 225-240
               Barry, et al., "Agriculture: The New Plantation" P 241-249

Apr. 24   --The Dynamics of Globalization in the 1970s-1990s and its Implications for All of Us
         Living in the Atlantic
         Read: Wright, 219-254
               Readings on reserve at Alexander Library (options will be explained)

TUTORIAL SESSIONS

Apr. 28   --Global Structures and Global Resistance--Discussion
         Read: Collins, What Difference Could a Revolution Make P 250-264
               Readings on Chiapas and West Africa on reserve at Alexander Library (options will
                  be explained)

May 1 --Neo-Malthusian and Alternative Interpretations; --Questions about Economic Justice and
         Environmental Protection
         Read: Poster, "Carrying Capacity: Earth's Bottom Line" P 265-283
               Readings about contemporary environmental issues on reserve at Alexander Library (options
                  will be explained)

DEBATE AND DISCUSSION on the Role of Individuals, NGOs, Corporations, and Governments
    in Building a Just and Sustainable World

MAY 5: Reading Day Review (TUTORIAL SESSIONS--times to be announced)

MAY 7: FINAL ESSAY EXAM

Specialized Courses: Chronological: Age of Expansion

Gyan Prakash
Robert Tignor
Princeton University
The World and the West

PRINCETON UNIVERSITY
Department of History

The World and the West

History 213   Fall 1997
Professors: Gyan Prakash   M/W 2:30
               Robert Tignor

Description: This introductory course aims to provide an understanding of the processes that have divided the modern world into the West and the non-West. While tracing and highlighting the global transformations that organized and hierarchized peoples, cultures, and economies, it emphasizes and locates itself in the history of the non-West to reflect on the formation and the dominance of the modern West. We focus on such themes as: the dynamics of society and polity before the age of European expansion; trade, conquest, and the emergence of the modern West; the political, economic, and cultural forms of western dominance and their effects on colonizing and colonized societies; imperialism, nationalism, and the struggle for nation-states; and neocolonialism, postcoloniality and the legacies of colonial modernity. We explore these themes selectively; instead of attempting a comprehensive survey of world history, we highlight certain regional settings and particular periods to examine the constitution of territories, peoples, and identities in terms of race, "tribe," class, gender, empire, and nation. Such a selective and thematic examination of the making of the modern world-- connecting the formation of the West with that of the non-West--offers another vision of the history of the West, a view from elsewhere--the non-West.

Readings: The readings consist of a text-book, scholarly works, novels, primary documents, and articles (roughly 150 pages per week). The following books are available for purchase in the University Store. Substantial reading assignments will be drawn from these books, but there is also an ample number of each work in the library on three-hour reserve.

Chinua Achebe	*Things Fall Apart*
Joseph Conrad	*Heart of Darkness*
Buchi Emecheto	*The Joys of Motherhood*
M.K. Gandhi	*Hind Swaraj*
Al-Jabarti	*Napoleon in Egypt*
William McNeill	*Polyethnicity and National Unity in World History*
Toni Morrison	*Beloved*
Miguel Leon-Portilla	*Broken Spears*
William Shakespeare	*The Tempest*

Specialized Courses: Chronological: Age of Expansion

L.S. Stavrianos   *The World since 1500* *
Marilyn Young   *The Vietnam Wars*

(* Students not required to purchase, but may do so; there will be several copies on reserve)

Requirements: Mid-term (15%) and Final (35%) exams; preceptorial participation (25%); and four short (approx. 500 words) written assignments (25%).

Schedule

Week 1
9/15   Introduction (T)
9/17   Eurasia in the 1500s (P)
        Vespucci (xerox); Montaigne (xerox); Kennedy (xerox)

Week 2
9/22   The World in the 1500s: Africa (T)
9/24   Spain, Portugal & the rise of Mercantilism (T)
        Stavrianos, 291-363; Shakespeare, *The Tempest*

Week 3
9 /29   European Conquest and Exploration (T)
10/1   European Trade and Empire in Asia (P)
        Stavrianos, 363-395; Leon-Portilla, *Broken Spears.*
        First Written Assignment Due on Wednesday, 10/1.

Week 4
10/6   Silver and Sugar in the Americas (T)
10/8   Slavery in Comparative Perspective (T)
        Stavrianos, 410-430; Morrison, *Beloved.*

Week 5
10/13   Revolutions and Counter-revolutions (P)
10/15   Industrial revolution and colonialism (P)
        Stavrianos, 433-452; 457-479; Al-Jabarti, *Napoleon in Egypt*, 3-118, 133-80.
        Second Written Assignment Due on Wednesday, 10/15.

Specialized Courses: Chronological: Age of Expansion

Week 6
10/20   Changes in the Atlantic Economy and Polity: Latin America (T)
10/22   **Mid-term**
            No reading assignment.

BREAK

Week 7
11/3   New Imperialism and the Colonization of Africa (T)
11/5   Imperialism and metropolitan culture (P)
            Brantlinger (xerox); Conrad, *The Heart of Darkness.*

Week 8
11/10   Imperialism and Resistance: British India and China (P)
11/12   Colonial Societies in Africa (T)
            Achebe, *Things Fall Apart.*

Week 9
11/17   Nationalism in Asia (P)
11/19   Decolonization & Nationalism (P)
            Stavrianos, 504-528, 586-640, 658-666; Gandhi, *Hind Swaraj*; Nehru (xerox).
            Third Written Assignment Due on Wednesday, 11/19.

Week 10
11/24   Nationalism and decolonization in Africa (T)
11/26   Africa since independence (T)
            Stavrianos, 534-541, 666-679; Cesaire (xerox); Senghor (xerox); Fanon (xerox).

Week 11
12/1   National Liberation Movements (P) **Film: Apocalypse Now** (Francis Ford Coppola), 7:30
            pm.
12/3   US and Decolonization (T)
            Young, *Vietnam Wars*, 1-149.

Week 12
12/8   The Postcolonial world (P)
12/10   Summing up (P)
            McNeill, *Polyethnicity and National Unity;* Appadurai (xerox).
            Fourth Written Assignment Due on Wednesday, 12/10.

Reading Period Assignment: Emecheto, *The Joys of Motherhood*

Specialized Courses: Chronological: Long Twentieth Century

Michael Adas
Rutgers University
World History in the Twentieth Century

RUTGERS UNIVERSITY
DEPARTMENT OF HISTORY

506:111
World History in the Twentieth Century
Professor Michael Adas
TAs: Steve Adams, Finis Dunaway, Rebecca Gershenson, Dina Lowy, Steffani Pfeifer & Todd Uhlman
MW6 (4:30-5:50) - Vorhees 105

The Age of Imperialism and the Birth of the Twentieth Century

Sept 4 - Introduction: Darwin's Caution and "The Century of Violence"
Sept 9 - France Fades: Defeat & Cultural Florescence, The Birth of the Consumer Age
Sept 11 - Germany Rises: Strategic and Ideological Contours of the "Modern" MUSIC
Sept 16 - Emerging Giants on the Periphery: U.S. and Russia; A Lament for the Peoples "Doomed to Extinction"
        Reading - Adas, Stearns, Schwartz, *Turbulent Passage*, Prologue; pp 8-16; chap 1 & pp 49-57.
Sept 18 - Global Superpower: Britain and a Racial and Gendered World Order
        SLIDES/MUSIC
        Reading - *Turbulent Passage*, chapter 3.
Sept 23 - DISCUSSION SECTIONS: Colonial Empires, Europe's Civilizing Mission, Racial & Gender Stereotypes
        Reading - Joseph Conrad, *Heart of Darkness* entire.
Sept 25 - China in Crisis; The Rise of Japan as a Global Power
Sept 30 - Picasso's Pivot: The First Challenges of the Colonized
        Reading - *Turbulent Passage*, pp. 57-63; chapter 4; & pp. 220-228; Fischer, *Gandhi*, 1-3.
Oct 2 - DISCUSSION SECTIONS: Worlds We Have Lost: The View from the Colonized World
        Reading - Chinua Achebe, *Things Fall Apart* entire.

The First World War and Its Impact

Oct 7 - Machines over Men: Lost Lessons of The "Great War"
        SLIDES/MUSIC
Oct 9 - "The Peace to End All Peace"; A Time of Inversions
Oct 14 - Wilson vs. Lenin: Paths to Global Recovery
        Reading - *Turbulent Passage* pp. 119-39, 196-201 & 229-37.

Specialized Courses: Chronological: Long Twentieth Century

Oct 16 - DISCUSSION SECTIONS: Failed Peace and America Triumphant: Feminist and Minority Challenges from Within
Reading - Leuchtenberg, *Perils of Prosperity*, Prologue & chapters 1-4 & 9.

Mid-Term Essay **EXAMS** Distributed.

Hollow Victory and Capitalist Crisis

Oct 21 - The Best of Times, The Worst of Times
SLIDES/MUSIC America's Celebration of the Machine Age
The Rise of Stalinism in the Soviet Union
Reading - *Turbulent Passage*, chapter 7. Leuchtenberg, *Perils,* chapters 5-8 & 10.
Oct 23 - Fascist Beginnings: Benito Mussolini and the New Rome
Mid-Term Essay **EXAMS** Due IN CLASS
Oct 28 - The Great Depression; FDR and the Interventionist State
Reading - *Turbulent Passage*, 139-42 & chapter 6.
Leuchtenberg, *Perils,* chapters 11-13 & epilogue.
SLIDES/MUSIC
Oct 30 - The Failure of the Weimar Experiment and the Rise of Nazism; Aryan Racism & the Specter of Genocide
Nov 4 - DISCUSSION SECTIONS: Totalitarianism Nazi Style
Reading - Haffner, *The Meaning of Hitler*, entire.
Nov 6 - From Total War to Genocide: World War II in Europe, the Soviet Union and the Middle East
Nov 11 - **EVENING SHOWING** of Agnieszka Holland's film "Europa, Europa" (Class will meet at 9:00 pm instead of 4:30)
Nov 13 - The Pacific War to Hiroshima
SLIDES/MUSIC
Reading - *Turbulent Passage*, 142-154.

The Atomic Age and the End of the Twentieth Century

Nov 18 - Meanings of the Communist Victory in China
Reading - *Turbulent Passage*, chapter 13.
Nov 20 - The Causes and Impact of the Cold War
Reading - *Turbulent Passage*, chap. 9 & pp. 284-99.
Nov 25 - Decolonization and the End of the European World Order
Reading - Fischer, *Gandhi,* finish.
Turbulent Passage, pp. 238-55 & chap. 9.
Dec 2 - DISCUSSION SECTIONS: The Morning After: Population Explosion, Environmental Degradation, and Cultural Renaissance in the Third World
Reading - *Turbulent Passage*, chapter 12.

Specialized Courses: Chronological: Long Twentieth Century

Dec 4 - The Repudiation of Racism and Victories in the Freedom Struggles: The US, South
Africa, Eastern Europe
SLIDES/MUSIC
Reading - *Turbulent Passage*, pp. 299-305, 346-9.
Dec 9 - DISCUSSION SECTIONS: America Confronts a Revolutionary World; To the Debacle
in Vietnam
Reading - Caputo, *Rumor of War*, entire.
Dec 11 - The End of the Twentieth Century; The Last of Ideology and the Decline of the
Superpowers? Technological Potential and a Planet in Peril
Reading - *Turbulent Passage*, chapter 11 & Epilogue.

All readings listed are required and taken entirely from the following **paperbacks**, which are
available at both the University Bookstore and New Jersey Books.

Adas, Stearns, Schwartz, *Turbulent Passage: A Global History of the Twentieth Century*
Joseph Conrad, *Heart of Darkness*
Chinua Achebe, *Things Fall Apart*
William Leuchtenberg, *The Perils of Prosperity*
Louis Fischer, *Gandhi*
Sebastian Haffner, *The Meaning of Hitler*
Philip Caputo, *A Rumor of War*

Major written assignments for the course will consist of a TAKE-HOME ESSAY AT MID-TERM
and an IN-CLASS FINAL EXAM. In addition, there will be two or three SHORT QUIZZES in the
discussion sections. Credit will also be given for participation in discussion sessions. Discussion
topics are listed in the syllabus and will be outlined in advance. As readings will not be duplicated
in lectures and discussion sections, regular attendance is essential to doing well in the course.

Office Hours -- Van Dyke Hall 116 (932-6747)

(Adas)   Monday 1:30-3:00
                Wednesday 11-12:30
                and by Appointment

190

Specialized Courses: Chronological: Long Twentieth Century

Philip D. Curtin
The Johns Hopkins University
The World and the West: The Revolution of Modernization

THE JOHNS HOPKINS UNIVERSITY
Department of History

Professor Curtin
History 100:496
The World and the West: The Revolution of Modernization
Spring, 1998
Four credits

This course departs somewhat from the traditional pattern of historical study. Instead of relating a series of events that took place in a given period of time in some particular part of the world, it concentrates on a process. That process is the interaction of Western culture and the other major cultures of the world since about 1500. The first half was concerned principally with the period in which Europe gradually changed its position from rough equality with other technologically proficient societies to that of a world leadership. By 1800, Europe was not yet in a position to dominate on a world-wide scale, but it was clearly on the way to industrialization---the first industrial society, which other societies had either to copy or resist.

The present semester will be concerned with the industrial age. The chronological break at 1800 is not sharp. Some forms of interaction, such as the plantation complex, were traced well beyond 1800 during the first semester. Others, arising out of the wholesale migration of Europeans overseas, are mainly a nineteenth-century phenomenon, though their origins must now be traced back to the period before 1800.

The world and the West interacted in many different ways during the past two centuries. Needless to say, all of them cannot be taken up in a one semester course. The lectures and readings will therefore skip around among the multitude of possible examples, concentrating on culture change---on the manner in which people changed their ways of life in response to contact with culturally different environments. This subject not only takes in the non-Western people who respond to the impact of the West; it is also concerned with the changes in Western culture among the settlers who went overseas.

This course used to be taught with taped lectures to convey information, making more time available for actual face-to-face interchange of ideas. The normal weekly pattern was two hour-long discussions, supported by two hours of taped lectures. Most of the lectures have been transformed to be included in book of essays. They will be made available in draft, some rougher than others. Any suggestions that would help improve the final version would be gratefully received.

The tapes for lecture 23 onward are available on loan at the audio visual section of the Eisenhower Memorial Library. They can be played on a standard cassette tape recorder, which makes it possible to stop the lecture, make it repeat, and otherwise control the speed of information. Tape recorders may also be borrowed by those who otherwise have no access to one.

As a way of giving structure to discussion, each discussion session will be opened by student presentations of a "discussion-opener." With few students in the course this semester, the discussion openers can be quite flimsy---little more than an outline of your thought about the problems. Anyone wanting to invent his or her own discussion topic is free to do on consultation.

The lists of additional readings are not to be treated as assignments. They are carry-overs from earlier years, designed to provide a point of departure for students who would like to pursue that subject further at some future time.

TOPIC I - SETTLEMENT

First Week - Introductory

January 16 - Introductory Meeting

Read for Next Week's Discussion:
Marshall G. S. Hodgson, "Interrelations of Societies in History," in Hodgson, *Rethinking World History*, pp. 3-31.
Dean C. Tipps, "Modernization Theory and the Comparative Study of Societies," *Comparative Studies*, 15:199-206 (1973).

Second Week - Population and Settlement

February 2
Discussion based on:
Lecture I - Overseas Settlement before the Napoleonic Wars
Lecture 2 - Growth and Movement of Populations
And on these readings:
Komlos, John, "Nutrition, Population Growth, and the Industrial Revolution in England," *Social Science History*, 14:69-91 (1990).
Schofield, Roger, "The Impact of Scarcity and Plenty on Population Change in England, 1541-1871," in Rotberg and Rabb, *Hunger in History*, pp. 66-93.
McNeill, William H., "Historical Migration in Historical Perspective," *Population and Development Review*, 10:1-18 (1983).
Thistlethwaite, Frank, "Migrations from Europe Overseas in the Nineteenth and Twentieth Centuries," in Rudolph J. Vecoli and Suzanne M. Sinke, *A Century of European Migrations, 1830-1930*, pp. 17-49.

Specialized Courses: Chronological: Long Twentieth Century

Possible Discussion-Openers:
1) Was the European Migration out of Europe mainly a matter of push from European developments, or pull from the advantages to be had overseas?
2) Was there a "mortality revolution" in the nineteenth century, or can European population increase be accounted for better in other ways? If so, what caused it?
3) Was Malthus right?
4) Why was migration across the Atlantic mainly by Africans until the 1840s and mainly Europeans after that decade?

Additional Readings:
Rudolph J. Vecoli and Suzanne M. Sinke, *A Century of European Migrations*, 1830-1930 (Urbana, 1991).
Pieter C. Emmer and Magnus Morner, *European Expansion and Migration: Essays on Intercontinental Migration from Africa, Asia, and Europe* (New York, 1992).
Walter Nugent, Crossings: *The Great Transatlantic Migrations, 1870-1914* (Bloomington: Indians University Press, 1992).

Third Week - European Overseas

February 9 -Discussion based on:
Lecture 3 - Theories and Theorists of Colonization
Lecture 4 - New Colonies of the Nineteenth Century
Lecture 5 - Emigration and Culture Change

And on these readings:
D. F. Sarmiento, *Life in the Argentine Republic,* Chapter 2.
Richard W. Slatta, *Gauchos and the Vanishing Frontier*, pp. 7-29, 180-192.
Duncan Baretta, Silvio R. and John Markoff, "Civilization and Barbarism: Cattle Frontiers in Latin America," *Comparative Studies*, 20: 587-618 (Oct. 1978).
Joseph K. Howard, *Strange Empire*, pp. 23-45, 292-306.
Richard Elphick, *The Shaping of South African Society*, 1652-1840, (2nd ed., 1989), pp. 66- 102.

Possible Discussion-Openers:

1) Did the Wakefieldian theory of colonization serve as a significant guide to what the British actually did overseas, or was it simply an intellectual construct of interest only to the history of European economic thought?
2) Measured by the standards of the time, was Wakefield's theory of colonization good theory? What, for that matter, is the difference between good theory and bad?
3) Based on the process of culture change among the gauchos of the Plata basin and the metis of central Canada, what aspects of European culture were most likely to change beyond the frontiers? What aspects were least likely to change?

Specialized Courses: Chronological: Long Twentieth Century

Fourth Week - The Role of Location in the History of Argentina and South Africa

(February 16 - Presidents' Day Break - No Class)
Postponed class - Discussion based on:
Draft on article by Curtin on Location in Argentine and South African History.
Leonard Thompson, *History of South Africa*, pp. 1-109. (skim as required)
David Rock, *Argentina 1516-1987*, pp. 39-161. (skim as required)
Possible Discussion-Openers:

1) Duncan somewhere gives this definition: "Frontiers are places where no one has an enduring monopoly on violence." Owen Lattimore and Frederick Jackson Turner had different ideas. Which definition has most explanatory value---or "none of the above?

2) Why did the cowboy, the gaucho, the Canadian metis, and the voortrekker all emerge as national symbols?

3) Part of Turner's frontier theory was that open, cheap land made for a safety valve and for a more democratic society. Why was this not the outcome in Argentina or South Africa before 1880? Or was it?

Additional Readings:
H. Giliomee, "Process in Development of the Southern African Frontier," in Howard Lamar and L. Thompson, *The Frontier in History*, pp. 76-119.

TOPIC II - CONQUEST

Fifth Week - The Roots of Imperialism

February 23 - Discussion based on:
Draft Chapters 1 and 2 of "Imperial Rule"
P. D.. Curtin (ed.), *Imperialism*, pp. Ix-xxiii, 1-22 (Cuvier and Knox), 132-65 (Carlyle), 177-191 (Macauley).
D. K. Fieldhouse, *Economics and Empire 1830-1914*, pp, 63-87.
Ronald Robinson, "Non-European Foundation of European Imperialism Sketch for a Theory of Collaboration," in Roger Owen and Bob Sutcliff (eds.), *Studies in Theory of Imperialism,* pp. 117-142.

Possible Discussion Openers:

1) Did capitalism or industrialism cause imperialism?

2) What, if anything, can we learn by reading "the bad ideas of Western man," as represented by Cuvier and Knox?

3) Was either Carlyle or Macaulay correct in his assessment of the situation as he saw it (as represented by the assigned readings)? If not, why not?

Additional Readings:
Further reading in Fieldhouse.
Michael Barratt Brown, *Economics of Imperialism* esp. pp. 39-72.
Mommsen, Wolfgang J. and Jurgen Osaterhammel, *Imperialism and After: Continuities and Discontinuities* (1986).

Sixth Week - Imperialism and Culture Change

March 2 - Discussion based on:
Draft chapters 3 (Politics of Empire) and 4 (Central Asia and South Africa)
Elizabeth Bacon, *Central Asia Under Russian Rule*, pp. 1-28, 92-188.

Possible Discussion-Openers:

1) Were the Russians "successful" colonizers of Central Asia, compared with other colonizers of other territories in the nineteenth and early twentieth centuries? For that matter, what was a "successful" colonizer?
2) Why was the historical development of Soviet Central Asia in the twentieth century a) so different from, or b) so similar to, that of South Africa?

Additional Readings:
Rhodes Murphey, *The Outsiders: Western Experience in India and China* (Ann Arbor, Michigan Press, 1977).

Seventh Week - Mexico and Southern Asia

March 9- Discussion based on:
Draft chapter 5 (Cultural Change in Mexico), and 6 (The Choice of Intermediaries)
Nelson Reed, *The Caste War in Yucatan*, pp. 3-49, 159-226.

Possible Discussion-Openers:

1) Why did the Cruzob retain some aspects of their culture while shedding others in response to an external threat?
2) In the oasis states of Central Asia, and in Bengal, Indonesia, and Malaya, the Europeans introduced changes in government and land tenure, How significant was the difference between European intentions and the outcome? Why?

Specialized Courses: Chronological: Long Twentieth Century

Additional Readings:

The remainder of Reed

Edward Spicer, *The Yaquis: A Cultural History*

Evelyn Hu-DeHart, *Yaqui Resistance and Survival*

Maarten Kuitenbrouwer, "Aristocracies Under Colonial Rule: North India and Java," in C. A. Bayly and D. H. A. Kolff (eds.), *Two Colonial Empires: Comparative Essay on the History of India and Indonesia in the Nineteenth Century* (Dordrecht: Nijhoff, 1986), pp. 75-94.

Spring Break - March 16 to 20 - No Class

TOPIC III - CONVERSION

Eighth Week - Missionary Movements

March 23 - Discussion based on:

Draft Chapter 7 (Missionary Movement) and 8 (Missionaries in East Africa)

Robin Horton, "The Rationality of Conversion," *Africa*, 45: 219-23.

Jessica A. Cope, "Religious and Cultural Conversion to Islam in Ninth-Century Córdoba," *Journal of World History*, 4:47-68 (1993).

Peel, J. D. Y.., "Conversion and Tradition in Two African Societies: Ijebu and Buganda," *Past and Present*, no. 7, pp. 108-417 (November, 1977).

Possible Discussion-Openers:

1) Did the missionary movement cause imperialism, or did imperialism cause the missionary movement, or neither?

2) How different was the rationality of conversion in ninth-century Córdoba and twentieth-century Africa? (Based on Horton and Coope)

3) Is Peel's discussion of conversion in Buganda and Ijebu consonant with what Horton or Coope have to say about conversion in Africa or Muslim Spain? If not, who is right?

Additional Readings:

C. Wrigley, "The Christian Revolution in Buganda," *Comparative Studies in Society and History*, 2: 33-48 (October, 1959).

Holger Bengt Hansen, *Mission, Church, and State in a Colonial Setting: Uganda, 1890-1925* (New York: St. Martin's Press, 1984).

Specialized Courses: Chronological: Long Twentieth Century

Ninth Week - Conversion from Within

March 30 - Discussion based on:
Draft Chapter 10 - Meiji Reforms
Fairbank, Reischauer, and Craig, *East Asia: Tradition and Transformation*, pp.484-558 .

Possible Discussion Openers:

1) Was the Meiji Restoration a revolution in the sense of the French or Russian Revolutions, or was it something else---distinctively Japanese?
2) Was the Meiji "revolution" caused principally by internal or by external pressures?
3) Looking at the range of examples of cultural borrowing in the course (Buganda, Peter's Russia, Cruzob Maya, Yaqui, Japan, Central Asia, etc.) what generalizations are possible about what was borrowed from the outside and why?

Recommended
Jones, E. L., *Growth Recurring: Economic Change in World History* (Oxford, Clarendon Press, 1988).
Jansen, Marius (ed.), *The Emergency of Meiji Japan* (Cambridge: Cambridge Press, 1995)
McClain, James L., John M. Merriman, and Ugawa Kaoru (eds.), *Edo and Paris: Urban Life and the State in the Early Modern Era* (Ithaca: Cornell University Press, 1994).
Macpherson, W. J., *The Economic Development of Japan 1868-1941* (Cambridge: Cambridge University Press, 1987)
Totman, Conrad, *Early Modern Japan* (Berkeley: University of California Press, 1993).

Tenth Week - The Modernization of Turkey

April 6 - Discussion based on:
Draft Chapter 11 - Ottoman Reforms
Zurcher, Erik J., *Turkey: A Modern History* (London: I.B. Tauris, 1994)
D. E. Ward and D. Rustow, *Political Modernization in Japan and Turkey*, pp. 434-468. (Catalogued under "Conference on Political Modernization.")

Possible Discussion-Openers:

1) It has been said that "nationalism" is crucial for modernization. Hence, Japan was able to modernize rapidly because it had "national unity" under the Tokugawa, while Turkey was held back till it could shake off the multi-national Ottoman heritage. Argue forcefully for or against this proposition.
2) Mustapha Kemal seems to epitomize the "great man" theory of history more than any other leader we have studied---even Apolo Kagwa. Was he really a crucial determinant of change, or did circumstances simply make it possible for him to appear to be so?

Specialized Courses: Chronological: Long Twentieth Century

3) It has been argued that Japan "modernized" faster and more fully than the Ottomans and their Turkish successors, yet, paradoxically, Turkey of the 1990s was far more "Western" than Japan. Is this true, if so, how can it be explained?

Additional Readings:
Bernard Lewis, *The Emergence of Modern Turkey.*

TOPIC IV - THE REVOLUTION OF MODERNIZATION

Eleventh Week - The Non-Western Revolt

April 13 - Discussion based on:
Draft Chapter 12 (Resistance and Withdrawal) and 13 (Millennial Movements)
Adas, *Prophets of Rebellion*, xvii-xxvii, 3-91, 183-189.

Possible Discussion-Openers:

1) Were millennial movements a positive or a negative influence on successful modernization? ---or on independence movements?
2) Did any of the revolts in Adas' discussion ever have the slightest chance of succeeding? If so, which? If not, why not?
3) None of Adas's revolts was truly millennial. What makes some revolts against Western influence millennial, while others are not?

Additional Readings:
Peter Worsley, *The Trumpet Shall Sound*, pp. ix-xix, 11-16, 32-48, 75-92.
D, A. Low, *Eclipse of Empire* (1991)

Twelfth Week - "Nationalism": Indonesia

April 27 - Discussion based on:
Lecture 25 - The Indonesian Revolution and its Setting
Lecture 26 - Indonesia Under the Early Republic
Ernest Gellner, *Nations and Nationalism*, pp. 1-38, 137-43.
W. Travis Hanes III, "On the Origins of the Indian National Congress: A Case Study of Cross-Cultural Synthesis," *Journal of World History*, 4:69-98 (I 993)
O. Pflanze and P. D. Curtin, "Varieties of Nationalism in Europe and Africa," *Review of Politics*, 28:129-53 (April, 1960).
Bernard Dahm, *The History of Indonesia in the Twentieth Century*, pp. 20-109

Specialized Courses: Chronological: Long Twentieth Century

Possible Discussion-Openers:

1) Is "nationalism" (by whatever definition) necessary to "modernization" by some definition)?
2) Was nationalism in India inspired by Western culture, or would it have come anyhow, even without the Theosophical Society?
3) Why did "Islamic fundamentalism" fail in Indonesia? Or did it?
4) Why did the PKI fail in Indonesia? or did it?
5) Compare Sukarno with the leaders of Adas's revolts. What accounts for his comparative success?

Additional Readings:
John Darwin, *Britain and Decolonization: The Retreat from Empire in the Post War World* (New York: St. Martin's Press, 1988)
Karl Deutsch, "The Growth of Nations," *World Politics*, 5:168-196.
E. J. Hobsbawm, *Nations and Nationalism since 1780: Programme, Myth, Reality* (Cambridge: Cambridge University Press, 1990).
Anthony J. S. Reid, *Indonesian National Revolution, 1945-50* (Longman: Hawthorn Australia, 1974)

Fourteenth Week - "Nationalism": Ghana

May 4 - Discussion based on:
Lecture 27 - The Creation of a Nation
Lecture 28 - The Creation of a Nationalism
Arnold Toynbee, *A Study of History* (abridgment of vols. vii-x by D. C.Somervell), pp. 144-88, 219-40. (London, OUP, 1957).
Charles Issawi, "Empire Builders, Culture Makers, and Culture Imprinters," *Journal of Interdisciplinary History*, 20:177-196 (1989).

Possible Discussion-Openers:

1) What are the really important differences between the rise of nationalism and the independence movements in Indonesia and Ghana?
3) From the perspective of the seminar's discussions, what is good and what is bad in Toynbee's analysis?

Specialized Courses: Chronological: Long Twentieth Century

Roland Spickermann
University of Detroit, Mercy
20th Century Global History

HISTORY 332 -- 20th Century Global History
Dr. Spickermann
Briggs 349, MWF 12:00-12:50
Fall 1996

Office Hours: Briggs 318, MWF, after 1:00 PM, or whenever the door is open
E-mail: spicker@udmercy.edu or spickermann@earthlink.net

Welcome! This course will cover the history of the whole planet roughly from World War I to the collapse of the USSR. In this period, we can truly discuss global history: the evolution of planetwide economic and political systems, and the assumption/imposition of some degree of Western culture throughout the world.

But these developments occurred neither uniformly nor smoothly: the West itself had trouble with adopting Western values, and with adapting to industrialization and democratization, and the process could only be harder in non-Western areas where these processes were not only turbulent but also foreign. We will be comparing "the West" with "the rest" often, to gain better insight on each. Hang on... this will be a wild ride.

WARNING: students with no background in history (for example, if you have never heard of World War I or the USSR) should think carefully before taking this course. It is certainly possible to pass this course -- and even do well in it -- without such a background, but it is more difficult.

COURSE LOAD:

Now some bureaucratic details. I will assign two papers (ten pages each), a mid-term, a final examination, and (perhaps) the occasional map quiz in this course. However, I also reserve the right to give surprise quizzes, in order to ensure that students are keeping current with the readings. While the combined value of these quizzes will never count as much as a mid-term or a paper, I will factor the quizzes into the total grade. Tentatively, the value of each of the assignments is as follows: papers 20% each, mid-term 20%, final exam 40%.

PAPER #1:	October 4
MID-TERM:	October 23
PAPER #2:	November 25
FINAL:	December 12

Specialized Courses: Chronological: Long Twentieth Century

I do not grade for in-class participation, except in borderline cases. But you should participate, anyway: the more you participate, the better you learn. So: ASK QUESTIONS. CHALLENGE MY INTERPRETATION.

IF YOU DO NOT UNDERSTAND SOMETHING, SAY SO. (Very likely you are not alone in not understanding it.)

While I have not required it, I strongly recommend that you buy and use Strunk's and White's The Elements of Style. Few books will help you with writing as much as this book will.

We will use four books --

1.Eric Hobsbawm. The Age of Extremes. A History of the World, 1914-1991.
2.Eric R. Wolf. Peasant Wars of the Twentieth Century.
3.Theodore H. von Laue. The World Revolution of Westernization.
4.William R. Keylor. The Twentieth-Century World: An International History.

READINGS (except for the first day, for obvious reasons) ARE TO BE DONE BEFORE THE SESSION FOR WHICH I HAVE ASSIGNED THEM.

SCHEDULE OF READINGS:
PART I: THE FRAMEWORK

1. September 4 -- Introductory Discussion - Core Concepts and Themes
(Yes, I know you could not possibly have read these chapters yet.)
von Laue Thesis
von Laue, ch.1 How the Concept Originated
von Laue Appendix

2. September 6 -- The Nature of the West
von Laue, ch.4 The Revolution at Work in Europe
von Laue, ch.15 The United States to 1945: A Most Privileged Nation

3. September 9 -- Pre-20th-Century International Structures and Relations
Keylor, Prologue The Global Context of International Relations at the Beginning of the 20th Century

4. September 11 -- Outside the West: Different Dynamics
Wolf, ch.1 Mexico
von Laue, ch.2 The Political Revolution
von Laue, ch.3 The Cultural Revolution

Specialized Courses: Chronological: Long Twentieth Century

5. September 13 -- World War I
Hobsbawm, ch.1 The Age of Total War
Keylor, ch.1 Germany's Bid for European Dominance (1914-1918)
von Laue, ch.5 World War I

PART II: THE BOLSHEVIK CHALLENGE

6. September 16 -- The Bolshevik Revolution: A Second World Order?
Wolf, ch.2 Russia
von Laue, ch.6 The Communist Counterrevolution

7. September 18 -- Bolshevik Revolution (2): Creating the "Second World"
von Laue, ch.10 Stalinism
Hobsbawm, ch.2 The World Revolution

8. September 20 -- Bolshevik Revolution (3): Creating the "Second World" (2)
Hobsbawm, ch.13 "Real Socialism"
von Laue, ch.17 Building a State in Backward Eurasia

PART III: A BROKEN WORLD, 1919-1945

9. September 23 -- Versailles and Europe: Interwar Economic and Political Relations
Keylor, ch.2 The Peace of Paris and the New International Order
Keylor, ch.3 The Western World in the Twenties: The Era of Illusions

10. September 25 -- Versailles Beyond Europe: the Decline of European Empires
von Laue, ch.8 The Effects of the War Outside Europe
Hobsbawm, ch.7 End of Empires

11. September 27 -- Versailles Beyond Europe: the Rise of Non-European States
Keylor, ch.6 The Confirmation of United States Supremacy in Latin America
Keylor, ch.7 The Confirmation of Japan's Supremacy in East Asia
    Part 1: The Period of Peaceful Penetration

12. September 30 --The Great Depression
Hobsbawm, ch.3 Into the Economic Abyss
von Laue, ch.9 The Great Depression
Keylor, ch.4 The Western World in the Thirties: The Illusions Dispelled
    Part 1: The Collapse of the World Economic Order

13. October 2 -- Fascism and Nazism: Anti-Traditional, Anti-Modern
Hobsbawm, ch.4 The Fall of Liberalism
von Laue, ch.7 The Fascist Counterrevolution

14. October 4 -- Anti-Fascism: Liberal and Marxist Alliance
PAPER DUE!
 Hobsbawm, ch.5 Against the Common Enemy
 Keylor, ch.4 The Western World in the Thirties: The Illusions Dispelled
        Part 2: The Collapse of the European Security System

15. October 7 -- World War II in Europe
 von Laue, ch.13 Hitler's Germany
 von Laue, ch.14 World War II
 Keylor, ch.5 Germany's Second Bid for European Dominance (1939-1945)

16. October 9 -- The Holocaust
 Guest Speaker: Mr. Martin Loewenberg

17. October 11 -- Discussion of Genocide, a 20th-Century Phenomenon
 (no readings)

18. October 14 -- World War II in Asia
 von Laue, ch.11 Japanese Expansion
 Keylor, ch.7 The Confirmation of Japan's Supremacy in East Asia
        Part 2: The Period of Military Expansion (1931-1941)
        Part 3: The War in Asia (1941-1945)

19. October 16 -- MIDTERM

PART IV: A DIVIDED WORLD, 1945-1991

20. October 18 -- Postwar Western Trends 1945-1973
 Hobsbawm, ch.9 The Golden Years
 Keylor, ch.15 The Far East: The Road to the New Co-Prosperity Sphere
        Part 1: The Miracle of Japan

21. October 21 -- Postwar "Second World" Trends
 von Laue, ch.18 The Strains of Catching Up

22. October 23 -- Social Changes in the West: the West's Further "Westernization"
 Hobsbawm, ch.10 The Social Revolution 1945-1990
 Hobsbawm, ch.11 Cultural Revolution

23. October 25 -- Cold War - Confrontation, 1945-1962
Keylor, ch.8 The Formation of the Bipolar World in the Truman-Stalin Era (1945-1953)
Keylor, ch.9 Coexistence and Confrontation (1953-1962)
    Part 1: Eisenhower's "New Look"
    Part 2: The Post-Stalin "Thaw"
    Part 3: The Anomaly of Berlin

24. October 28 -- Cold War - Coexistence, 1962-1985
Keylor, ch.10 Detente and Multipolarity (1962-1975)
Keylor, ch.12 The Resurgence of East-West Tension (1975-1985)

25. October 30 -- Postwar Western Economic Development 1973-1991
Hobsbawm, ch.14 The Crisis Decades

26. November 1 -- Cold War - General Overview
Hobsbawm, ch.8 Cold War
von Laue, ch.16 The United States after 1945: Exceptionality Eroded

PART V: THE "THIRD WORLD", 1945-1991

27. November 4 -- Decolonization / Independence: Creating the "Third World"
Hobsbawm, ch.12 The Third World
von Laue, ch.21 The Burden of Development

28. November 6 -- Political Mobilization in the Third World
von Laue, ch.19 The Bandung Generation
von Laue, ch.22 The United Nations as an Agency of Westernization

29. November 8 -- America and Latin America: Noncolonial Dependence
Keylor, ch.9 Coexistence and Confrontation (1953-1962)
    Part 4: The United States and Latin America in the Crisis Years
Keylor, ch.13 Latin America's Quest for Development and Independence
Wolf, ch.6 Cuba

30. November 11 -- The Chinese Revolution (1) - Peasant Revolution in Red
von Laue, ch.12 China -- Toward the "Yanan Way"
Wolf, ch.3 China

31. November 13 -- The Chinese Revolution (2) - State-Building and Forced Industrialization
Keylor, ch.11 The Rise of China and the Cold War in Asia
von Laue, ch.20 Chairman Mao

32. November 15 -- Vietnam - Third World Revolution and Cold War Battleground
Wolf, ch.4 Vietnam
Keylor, ch.11 The Rise of China and the Cold War in Asia
    Part 4: The United States and Indochina

33. November 18 -- Algeria: Islamic Resistance to the West / Africa: "Neo-Colonialism"?
Wolf, ch.5 Algeria
Keylor, ch.14 Africa: From Independence to Dependency

PART VI: THE END OF THE "SHORT CENTURY"

34. November 20 -- The Third World as a Cul-de-Sac
Hobsbawm, ch.15 Third World and Revolution
Wolf Conclusion

35. November 22 -- Revolutions of 1989/91 -- Collapse of the Second World
Hobsbawm, ch.16 End of Socialism

36. November 25 -- Revolutions of 1989/91 (2) - Europe's Resurrection
PAPER DUE!
Keylor, ch.16 Moscow, Washington, and the End of the Soviet Empire
Keylor, ch.17 The Resurrection of the European Idea

37. November 27 -- The "Newly Industrializing Countries" -- Out of the Third World
Keylor, ch.15 The Far East: The Road to the New Co-Prosperity Sphere
    Part 2: The Gang of Four and Asean
    Part 3: The Deng Revolution in China
Keylor, ch.18 Asia at the Crossroads
Keylor, ch.21 Latin America: Democracy, Free Markets, and Regional Stability

November 29 THANKSGIVING HOLIDAY

38. December 2 -- Third World Still: Africa and the Middle East after the Cold War
Keylor, ch.19 Africa on Its Own: Ethnicity, Autocracy, and Underdevelopment
Keylor, ch.20 The Middle East: Progress toward Regional Reconciliation

39. December 4 -- Prospects for the 21st Century
von Laue, ch.23 The Human Condition at the End of the 20th Century
Keylor, ch.22 A New Multilateralism?
Hobsbawm, ch.19 Towards the Millennium

40. December 6 -- REVIEW

FINAL EXAM: Thursday, December 12, 11-12:50

IV.

Specialized Courses: Thematic

Specialized Courses: Thematic

Jane Hathaway
Ohio State University
Marginal Groups in the Non-Western World

HISTORY 694: MARGINAL GROUPS IN THE NON-WESTERN WORLD

Spring 1996 T,R 9:30-11:30 Journalism 371

Professor J. Hathaway
Office: Dulles 144 ph: 292-7138/2674 (dept. office)
  e-mail: hathaway.24@osu.edu
Office hours: T, R 1:00-2:30

Description and objectives: This is a lecture and discussion course comparing and contrasting the treatment of marginal groups and minorities in the major civilizations of the non-western world from roughly the 16th through the 20th centuries. Our goal is to determine to what extent different cultures used common criteria to define, address, and, in some cases, create marginal groups. We shall take up four groups: 1) ethnic and religious minorities, 2) women, 3) military slaves (mamlōks) and eunuchs, and 4) the infirm and disabled. The major regions covered will be the Middle East, Africa, India, the Far East, and Latin America. Inevitably, however, not all regions will receive equal treatment due to varying amounts of literature on each topic. Instead, the course will pursue a broad topical approach so as to encourage comparison and an integrated view of marginality during a critical period in history. Whenever possible, we shall read recent studies so as to gain an idea of the direction historiography is taking.

Written assignments:
1) **Two papers** of 6-8 pages each, due **in class Tuesday, April 23, and Tuesday, May 21**. The first paper will compare the status of a marginal group in at least two culture areas. The second paper will be a critical comparison of two films viewed in class. Detailed descriptions of the paper assignments will be distributed in due course.
2) A **take-home final examination**, to be distributed in class **Thursday, May 30**. The exam will consist of two short essay questions and one long essay question. You are to write it in one two-hour bloc of time, not counting proofreading and fact-checking. The completed exam is due **by 5:00 p.m. Monday, June 3**.

Grading: class participation 15%
            papers 60% (30% each)
            final 25%

Late work: All assignments are due on the dates specified above. Late work will be downgraded by one letter grade for each day it is late. Work that is four or more days late will not be accepted. I do not give incompletes. If you are unable to complete the quarter's work on schedule, be prepared to turn in what you have accomplished or accept an "E". Exceptions to this policy will be made only in dire circumstances (e.g., serious illness, death in the family), which **must** be documented.

Specialized Courses: Thematic

Cybertip: You are invited to visit the History Dept.'s home page on the Worldwide Web at http://www.cohums.ohio-state.edu/history/. There you will find "Tips for History Students," information about the department's courses and programs, career information, and links to other interesting material.

Class format: The first hour of each Tuesday class will be devoted to a lecture presenting an overview of the week's topic and introducing the major debates and questions in the literature. The second hour and the Thursday class will be devoted to discussion of readings, a guest speaker, or viewing and discussing a film, as appropriate.

Readings:
The following books are required for the course and are available at SBX, Longs', and the University Bookstore:

Kenneth J. Andrien and Rolena Adorno, eds., Transatlantic Encounters: Europeans and Andeans in the 16th Century (Berkeley, Los Angeles, and Oxford, 1991)
Mark R. Cohen, Under Crescent and Cross: The Jews in the Middle Ages (Princeton, 1994)
Serena Nanda, Neither Man Nor Woman: The Hijras of India (Belmont, CA, 1990)
Leo Spitzer, Lives In Between: Assimilation and Marginality in Austria, Brazil, West Africa, 1780-1945 (Cambridge, 1989)

These books have also been placed on closed reserve in the Main Library, along with the following books:

C.E. Bosworth, et al., eds., The Islamic World from Classical to Modern Times: Essays in Honor of Bernard Lewis (Princeton, 1989)
Nigel Cameron, Barbarians and Mandarins: Thirteen Centuries of Western Travellers in China (Hong Kong and New York, 1970)
Orlando Patterson, Slavery and Social Death: A Comparative Study (Cambridge, MA, 1982)

As a rule, readings not included in the required texts will be handed out in class the week before they are to be read.

Suggestions for reading: Always read critically. Ask yourself what the author's attitude and approach to his topic are and whether these remain consistent throughout the text. Check the notes, bibliography, and acknowledgments, if available, to see what sources the author uses and to whom he is beholden. If you read two or more texts on a given topic, compare the authors' handling of their material.

Specialized Courses: Thematic

Schedule of Readings and Activities

Mar. 26 Introduction to the course

Mar. 28 Defining marginality
Library research presentation by Dr. David Lincove - Main Library, Room 124

H.F. Dickie-Clark, The Marginal Situation: A Sociological Study of a Coloured Group, Chs. 1-2
Spitzer, Lives In Between, Ch. 5

Apr. 2, 4 Ethnic minorities and ethnic tensions
Film: Our God the Condor (4/2)
Guest speaker: Hakan Özoþlu (4/4)

Spitzer, Ch. 4
Andrien and Adorno, eds., Transatlantic Encounters, Chs. 6, 7
Hakan Özoþlu, "State-Tribe Relations: Kurdish Tribalism in the 16th- and 17th-Century Ottoman
    Empire"
Isabel Fonseca, "A Reporter at Large: Among the Gypsies," New Yorker 25 September 1995, pp.
    84-97

Apr. 9, 11 Religious minorities
Guest speaker: Professor Stephen Dale (4/9)

Cohen, Under Crescent and Cross, entire
Spitzer, Ch. 3

Apr. 16, 18 Foreign visitors and residents
Guest speakers: Professors Kenneth Andrien and Carter Findley (4/16)
Film: Black Robe (4/18)

Andrien and Adorno, Transatlantic Encounters, Chs. 3, 5, 8
Carter V. Findley, "An Ottoman Expedition to Europe, 1889: Ahmed Midhat and Madame Gülnar"
Cameron, Barbarians and Mandarins, Ch. 8

Specialized Courses: Thematic

Other readings on ethnic and religious minorities (for your information):
David Crowe, A History of the Gypsies of Eastern Europe and Russia (New York, 1995)
Stephen Dale, Islamic Society on the South Asian Frontier: The Mappilas of Malibar, 1498-1922
(Oxford, 1980)
Allan G. Grapard, The Protocol of the Gods: A Study of the Kasuga Cult in Japanese History
(Berkeley, 1992)
Robert Haddad, Syrian Christians in Muslim Society (Princeton, 1970; reprint Westport, CT, 1981)
Philip S. Khoury and Joseph Kostiner, eds., Tribes and State Formation in the Middle East
(Berkeley, Los Angeles, and Oxford, 1990)
Avigdor Levy, ed., The Jews of the Ottoman Empire (Princeton, 1995)
Bernard Lewis, The Jews of Islam (Princeton, 1986)
H.S. Morris, The Indians in Uganda (Chicago, 1968)
Norman A. Stillman, The Jews of Arab Lands: A History and Source Book (Philadelphia, 1979)
_____, The Jews of Arab Lands in Modern Times (Philadelphia, 1991)

Apr. 23, 25 Mamluks and Janissaries
First paper due Apr. 23

David Ayalon, "The Muslim City and the Mamluk Military Aristocracy," in Ayalon, Studies on the
Mamluks of Egypt (London, 1977), 312-319
Jere Bacharach, "African Military Slaves in the Medieval Middle East: The Cases of Iraq (869-955)
and Egypt (868-1171)," International Journal of Middle East Studies 13 (1981): 471-95
J.A.B. Palmer, "The Origin of the Janissaries," Bulletin of the John Rylands Library 35, 2 (1953):
448-81
Speros Vryonis, Jr., "Seljuk Gulams and Ottoman Devshirmes," in Vryonis, Byzantium: Its Internal
History and Relations with the Muslim World - Collected Studies (London, 1971)
Jane Hathaway, "The Military Household in Ottoman Egypt," International Journal of Middle East
Studies 27, 1 (1995): 39-52
Orlando Patterson, Slavery and Social Death, Chs. 2-3 and pp. 299- 314

Other readings on mamluks and Janissaries:
David Ayalon, "Aspects of the Mamluk Phenomenon," I-II, Der Islam 53, 2 (1976): 196-225; 54, 1
(1977): 1-32
(See Ayalon's collected studies in Studies on the Mamluks of Egypt, The Mamluk Military Society,
and Outsiders in the Lands of Islam: Mamluks, Mongols, and Eunuchs [London, 1977, 1979,
1988].)
Amalia Levanoni, A Turning Point in Mamluk History: The Third Reign of al-Nasir Muhammad
ibn Qalawun (1310-1341) (Leiden, 1995)
Bernard Lewis, Race and Slavery in the Middle East: An Historical Enquiry (New York, Oxford,
1990)
Michael Winter, "Turks, Arabs, and Mamluks in the Armies of Ottoman Egypt," Wiener Zeitschrift
für die Kunde des Morgenlandes 72 1980): 97-122.

Specialized Courses: Thematic

Apr. 30, May 2 Women in history and historiography
Guest speaker: Professor Claire Robertson (4/30)
Film: Small Happiness: Women of a Chinese Village (5/2)

Marilyn Boxer and Jean Quataert, eds., Connecting Spheres: Women in the Western World, 1500 to the Present (New York, 1987), Introduction
Joan Scott, "The Problem of Invisibility," in S.J. Kleinberg, ed., Retrieving Women's History: Changing Perceptions of the Role of Women in Politics and Society (Oxford, New York, Hamburg, Paris, 1988)
Claire Robertson and Iris Berger, eds., Women and Class in Africa (New York, 1986), Introduction, Ch. 6
Claire Robertson and Martin Klein, eds., Women and Slavery in Africa (Madison, WI, 1983), Introduction
Paula Sanders, "Gendering the Ungendered Body," in Beth Baron and Nikki Keddie, eds., Women in Middle Eastern History: Shifting Boundaries in Sex and Gender (New Haven, 1992)

May 7, 9 Women in society and politics
Film: Fire Eyes (5/7)

Irene Silverblatt, Moon, Sun, and Witches: Gender Ideologies and Class in Inca and Colonial Peru (Princeton, 1987), Introduction, Ch. 5
Leslie Peirce, The Imperial Harem: Women and Sovereignty in the Ottoman Empire (Oxford and New York, 1993), Introduction, Ch. 5
Jonathan Berkey, "Circumcision Circumscribed: Female Excision and Cultural Accommodation in the Medieval Near East," International Journal of Middle East Studies 28, 1 (1996): 19-38
Nigel Cameron, Barbarians and Mandarins, Ch. 17

Other readings on women:
Leila Ahmed, Women and Gender in Islam: Historical Roots of a Modern Debate (New Haven, 1992)
Lois Beck and Nikki Keddie, eds., Women in the Muslim World (Cambridge, MA, and London, 1978)
Gail L. Bernstein, ed., Recreating Japanese Women, 1600-1945 (Berkeley, 1991)
Jack Goody, The Oriental, The Ancient and the Primitive: Systems of Marriage and the Family in the Pre-Industrial Societies of Eurasia (Cambridge and New York, 1983)
Jane Hathaway, "Marriage Alliances among the Military Households of Ottoman Egypt," Annales Islamologiques 29 (1995): 133-149
Cheryl Johnson-Odim and Margaret Strobel, eds., Expanding the Boundaries of Women's History: Essays on Women in the Third World (Bloomington, IN, 1992)
Claire Robertson, Sharing the Same Bowl? A Socioeconomic History of Women and Class in Accra, Ghana (Bloomington, IN, 1984)
Wiebke Walther, Women in Islam from Medieval to Modern Times (Princeton, 1995)

Specialized Courses: Thematic

Marilyn R. Waldman, et al., eds., <u>Understanding Women: The Challenge of Cross-Cultural Perspectives</u> (Columbus, 1992)

May 14, 16 Eunuchs

Orlando Patterson, <u>Slavery and Social Death</u>, pp. 314-31 (Note the context in which the eunuchs are presented.)

Shaun Marmon, <u>Eunuchs and Sacred Boundaries in Islamic Society</u> (Oxford and New York, 1995), Chs. 2, 4

Serena Nanda, <u>Neither Man Nor Woman</u>, entire

Other readings on eunuchs:

Mary M. Anderson, <u>Hidden Power: The Palace Eunuchs of Imperial China</u> (Buffalo, 1990)

David Ayalon, "Eunuchs in the Mamluk Sultanate," in Myriam Rosen- Ayalon, ed., <u>Studies in Memory of Gaston Wiet</u> (Jerusalem, 1977). Also in <u>The Mamluk Military Society</u>.

_____, "On the Eunuchs in Islam," <u>Jerusalem Studies in Arabic and Islam</u> 1 (1979): 67-124. Also in <u>Outsiders in the Lands of Islam</u>.

Jane Hathaway, "The Role of the Kḫzlar Aḫasḫ in 17th-18th Century Egypt," <u>Studia Islamica</u> 75 (1992): 141-58

_____, "The Wealth and Influence of an Exiled Ottoman Eunuch in Egypt: The Waqf Inventory of ᶜAbbas Agha," <u>Journal of the Economic and Social History of the Orient</u> 37, 4 (1994): 293-317

Taisuke Mitamura, <u>Chinese Eunuchs: The Structure of Intimate Politics</u> (Rutland, VT, 1970)

May 21, 23 The Infirm and Disabled
Film: <u>Plagued</u>, Part IV (5/23)
Second paper due May 21

Evliya Çelebi, <u>Narrative of Travels in Europe, Asia, and Africa in the 17th Century</u>, ed. and trans. Joseph von Hammer-Purgstall (London, 1834), Vol. I, Part 1, pp. 174-5; Vol. II, pp. 10-11, 30- 1

Alexander Russell, <u>The Natural History of Aleppo</u> (London, 1794), Vol. II, Book 3, Ch. 5; Book 5, Chs. 3-5; Book 6

Fedwa Malti-Douglas, "<u>Mentalités</u> and Marginality: Blindness and Mamluk Civilization," in C.E. Bosworth, et al., eds., <u>The Islamic World: Essays in Honor of Bernard Lewis</u>

Specialized Courses: Thematic

Other readings on the infirm and disabled:
Michael Dols, The Black Death in the Middle East (Princeton, 1977)
Steven Feierman and John M. Jansen, eds., The Social Basis of Health and Healing in Africa
(Berkeley, 1992)
Nancy Gallagher, Egypt's Other Wars: Epidemics and the Politics of Public Health (Syracuse, 1990)
_____, Medicine and Power in Tunisia (Cambridge and New York, 1983)
Fedwa Malti-Douglas, Blindness and Autobiography: "Al-Ayyþm" of Taha Husayn (Princeton,
1988)
William H. McNeill, Plagues and Peoples (Garden City, NY, 1976) - a study of the role of epidemics
in history

May 28 Reading and review

May 30 Marginality, subalternity, and world history
Take-home final exam distributed

Gyan Prakash, "Subaltern Studies as Postcolonial Criticism," American Historical Review 99, 5
(Dec. 1994), 1475-90
Frederick Cooper, "Conflict and Connection: Rethinking Colonial African History," AHR 99, 5
(Dec. 1994), 1516-45
Eric Wolf, Europe and the People Without History (Berkeley, Los Angeles, and London, 1982),
Introduction, Afterword

Take-home final exam due by 5:00 p.m. Monday, June 3.

Specialized Courses: Thematic

Tamara Hudec
University of Pennsylvania
The World: Modern Problems from a Global Perspective

The World:
Modern Problems from a Global Perspective

History 011- 900
Summer 1997
Tuesdays 4:30 - 7:40

Tamara Hudec
Office Hours: By Appointment
E-Mail: hudec@sas.upenn.edu

This course explores the types of global connections that have shaped the world over the past two centuries. We will begin by firmly grounding ourselves in the present and considering the notion that, more than ever, we live in a "global" age. Why is world history more popular now than it was ten years ago? How does our current fascination with globalization color our understanding of the past?

Working backward in time, we will confront issues such as nationalism, revolution, colonialism, slavery, capitalism, migration and the impact of religion and technology on human communities as we examine the extent to which the movement of people, goods, and ideas has "globalized" the world. As we consider these processes, we will focus on locales around the world and consider the interrelation between global and local issues.

To help you explore the range of possibilities for historical inquiry, I have incorporated a wide variety of source materials into the course. We will use film, material culture, literature, oral history, documents, commentaries, textbooks, the WWW, memoirs, commentaries from both inside and outside a culture, and take a trip to the Morris Arboretum to gain insight into historical methods. I have also scheduled a series of short guest presentations to introduce you to other teachers in the history department and to broaden the range of perspectives you will encounter in the course.

Requirements

Class participation and current event reviews: 40%
Project and presentation: 35%
Map presentation: 10%
Take-home final: 15%

Specialized Courses: Thematic

Course Materials

Books available for purchase (House of Our Own, 3920 Spruce St.)
Jorge Amado, The Violent Land, (New York: Avon, 1988)
Geraldine Brooks, Nine Parts of Desire: the Hidden World of Islamic
     Women (New York: Doubleday, 1996).
Basil Davidson, The Black Man's Burden: Africa and the Curse of the
     Nation-State (New York: Random, 1993).
Richard Price, Alabi's World (Baltimore: John Hopkins Press, 1990).
Jonathan Spence, God's Chinese Son: the Taiping Heavenly Kingdom of
     Hong Xiuquan (New York: W.W. Norton, 1996).

*All course readings will also be available at the Rosengarten Reserve Library.

Course Outline and Assignments

20 May) Introduction: Living in a Global World
          Library tour: Using Lexis/Nexis and the Wilson Index
          Individual meetings to discuss possible project designs.

27 May) The "Clash of Civilizations" and the "End of History"
          Guest presentation: Sources for world history on the Internet
                    -- Scott Roberts
          * Project proposal due
          Read:
                    Fukuyama, "The End of History?"
                    Huntington, "No Exit -- The Errors of Endism,"
                    Huntington, "The Clash of Civilizations?"
                    Kurth, "The Real Clash,"

3 June) Culture and Power: "Cultural Colonialism"
          Museum Visit: Native Americans (p)reserved in time and space
          Montage: Cinematic visions of "Indians"
          *Current events review #1
          Read:
                    Creighton, "Maintaining cultural boundaries . . . ."
                    Silko, Storyteller (selections)
                    Churchill, From a Native Son (selections)

Specialized Courses: Thematic

10 June) Inside/Outside: Interpretations of Islam and Gender
Guest presentation: Women in Islam -- Beshara Doumani
*Current events review #2; Source list for project
Read:
> Brooks, Nine parts of desire: 1-76; 167-200; 225-239
> Haddad and Smith, "Women in Islam . . .."
> Guindi, "Feminism comes of age in Islam."
Begin "People in Motion" mini film fest, My Beautiful Laundrette

17 June) People in Motion: Migration and/or? Diaspora
Film fest continues -- El Norte
Guest presentation: What is a diaspora? -- Savita Nair
*Current events review #3
Read:
> Hanif Kureishi, "The Rainbow Sign."
> Salman Rushdie, "The New Empire within Britain."

24 June) Nationalism: "The Black Man's Burden"
Slide show: Nationalism and African images of Europeans (Related
  museum trip in July, date TBA)
Guest presentation: The impact of nationalism on Africa --
  Speaker TBA
*Current events review #4; Project progress report
Read:
> Basil Davidson, The Black Man's Burden: 197-322.
> Rudyard Kipling, "The White Man's Burden."

1 July) Ideology and International Politics: the Culture of the Cold War
Guest Presentation: The US and the Cold War-- Frank Gavin
Individual meetings to discuss project progress report
*Current events review #5
Read:
> Extracts from the Black Book of Polish Censorship
> "The Censor Speaks--'I, the Censor,'"'
> Vçclav Havel, "The Power of the Powerless,"
> Milan Kundera, "Nobody Will Laugh,"
Begin: Amado, The Violent Land

8 July) Global Capitalism: Cash Crops and Consumption
Arboretum Visit: Botany and the technology of imperialism
*Current Events Review #6
Read:
> Amado, The Violent Land
> Sydney Mintz, Sweetness and Power (selection)

14 July) Imperialism/Colonialism: the Opium Wars and China
      Guest Presentation: Opium in China --Paul Howard
      *Current Events Review #7; Outline for project presentation
      Read:
              Spence, God's Chinese Son: 3- 125
              and as much of the remainder of the book as possible.

21 July) Slavery and Resistance: Rebellion in the Caribbean
      Guest Presentation: The Haitian Rebellion -- Gene Ogle
      Musical Selections from Tambours de la terre: Afrique; Amerique
      *Current Events Review #8
      Read:
              Price, Alabi's World: xi-xx pp 3-40, 79-116, 274-278
              and as much of the remainder of the work as possible.

28 July) Exploration, Race and the Enlightenment
      *Project Presentations
      Read:
              Excerpt from The Resolution Journal of Forster
              LinnÄ, Excerpt from The System of Nature
              Kant, Excerpt from Physical Geography
              Hegel "Geographical Basis of World History."

5 August) What is World History?
      Survey of world history textbooks
      *Project Presentations
      Take-home final distributed at end of class

NB -- Final version of project and take-home final must be in my box in the
      history office NO LATER THAN 5:00 PM on Monday 11 August 1997.

Specialized Courses: Thematic

David Northrup
Boston College
Africa's World, Part I: 1400–1825

Hs 079. Africa's World, part I: 1400-1825
Professor David Northrup
Carney 169
Boston College
Fall 1996
Office hours: TTh 9-10, 3-4

"Africa's World" examines modern world history from an African vantage point. This term studies how, in the period 1400-1825, Africa's long-standing relations with the Islamic world and Asia were overtaken by growing European power and how, through the Atlantic slave trade, Africans were established in the Americas. It also examines how the liberal and industrial revolutions helped end slavery and the Atlantic slave trade.

The course fulfills the university core requirement in history (first half) and Cultural Diversity. It may also count toward the Black Studies and the International Studies minors.

REQUIRED BOOKS   Abbreviation
Kevin Shillington, History of Africa, revised edition (St Martin's)   Shillington
Basil Davidson, ed., African Civilization Revisited (Africa World Press)   Davidson
David Northrup, ed., The Atlantic Slave Trade (D. C. Heath/Houghton Mifflin))   AST
David Northrup, "Readings for HS079-Africa's World -I" (Coursepack in Bookstore)   Readings
Philip D. Curtin, The Rise and Fall of the Plantation Complex (Cambridge Univ. Pr.)   Curtin

Specialized Courses: Thematic

DATE	UNIT TOPIC	LECTURE	READING ASSIGNMENTS
9-3		Introduction	
9-5	I. AFRICA	North Africa to 1600	Shillington 66-77, 157-69
9-10	& ISLAM	West Africa to 1600	Shillington 78-106, 181-88; Davidson 91-118
9-12		Eastern Africa	Shillington 107-15, 122-31; Davidson 127-45, 169-75
9-17	II. AFRICA	Africans in Renaissance Europe	Curtin 1-16
9-19	& EUROPE	West Africa meets the Portuguese	Curtin 29-45; Davidson 118-24, 203-7, 211-20, 229-31
9-24		Eastern Africa and the Portuguese	Shillington 131-37, 146-53; Davidson 145-65, 175-200
9-26		South Africa and the Indian Ocean	Shillington 212-20; Davidson 305-9
10-1		Africans' Impressions & Responses	readings 1-12
10-3		Europe's Strengths	Readings 13-24
10-8		Review	
10-10		MID-TERM EXAM	
10-15	III. AFRICA	Europe and the Americas	Curtin 17-28, 46-70
10-17	& THE	Origins of the Slave Trade	AST 1-35; Curtin 73-85; Davidson 223-26
10-22	ATLANTIC	How Many? By What Means?	AST 67-95; Davidson 250-71
10-24		Africans as Importers	Shillington 170-80, 197-206; Readings 25-30; Curtin 113-43, 208-11
10-29		The Middle Passage	AST 37-54, 97-132
10-31		Africa's Strengths	Shillington 188-96, 153; Davidson 277-85; AST 133-73; Curtin 126-28
11-5	IV. AFRICA	Slave Societies in the Americas	Curtin 98-110; Readings 31-34
11-7	& THE	Liberal Revolutions	Curtin 144-57; Readings 36-37
11-12	AMERICAS	Slave Revolution and Revolts	Curtin 158-69; AST 203-17; handout (2 pp.)
11-14		Industrialization and Abolitionism	AST 175-202; Davidson 271-72, 274-77
11-19		Emancipation in the British Caribbean	AST 203-17, Curtin 173-88
11-21		Africans in the Americas	
11-26		Emancipation in the USA: Global Comparisons	
12-3		Europeans and Muslims in Africa	Curtin 189-206; Readings 35-36
12-5		The Columbian Exchange	
12-18 (Wed.) @9 a.m.		Final Exam	

REQUIREMENTS

Grades will be based upon exams (mid-term 20%, final 30%), other written work (35%) and participation (15%).

Written Work: Each student must submit at least three essays of about 1000 words, each summarizing and interpreting the themes of one part of the course. Essays should make good use of the information and ideas presented in the assigned readings, discussions, and lectures. If all four essays are submitted, the best three grades will be counted. Due dates and topics are: 9-17 Africa and Islam; 10-8 Africa and Europe in the 16th century; 11-5 Africa and the Atlantic Slave trade; 11-21 Africans in slavery and emancipation in the Americas.

Participation: Students will be evaluated on the following; 1) physical presence (including punctuality); 2) Quality of responses to professor's questions about the daily reading, 3) Quality of questions posed. To receive maximum credit for participation it is quite important that each day's reading assignment be prepared carefully before class.

In preparing reading assignments learn personal, group and place names and use the maps in the textbooks to learn their locations. It is strongly recommended that students whose background in modern European history is weak buy or borrow (and read) a textbook on that subject.

Specialized Courses: Thematic

QUESTIONS FOR DISCUSSION DAY-BY-DAY
9-5   When and how was Islam established in North Africa? What changes did Arab and Islamic influences bring?
9-10   What were the most important features of Mali? What impressions did outside observers have of Mansa Musa and of the empire of Mali? How much was Mali influenced by Islam? In what ways were Songhay, the Hausa States and Bornu affected by Islam? What were their relations with other Muslim states? Describe urban life and learning. Discuss the class structure.
9-12   Compare the influence of Islam and Christianity in the northeast quadrant of Africa. Who are the Swahili? What is their importance? Describe their contacts outside of Africa. What was the importance of Great Zimbabwe and Kilwa?
9-17   Describe Portuguese impressions and actions in West Africa, especially at Elmina and Benin.
9-24   Compare Portuguese activities in Ethiopia, along the Swahili coast, and in the Mutapa empire. Explain how Portuguese motives and the circumstances of the Africans influenced Portuguese actions.
9-26   What significance did the Cape Colony have for European penetration of Africa and of the Indian Ocean?
10-1   What impressions did Africans form of Europeans? Do African impressions of Europeans seem more naò ve than European impressions of Africans? Why (not)?
10-3   What political, military, economic, social, and cultural strengths and weaknesses did early modern Europe possess?
10-15   Compare the impact of Spain in the Caribbean with that of Portugal in Africa before 1550. Account for the differences.
10-17   How did the slave trade begin in the Kingdom of Kongo? What do Williams, Jordan, and Davis agree upon? What do they disagree most about? Can their differences be resolved?
10-22   Why is it important to know the volume of the African slave trade? Why are calculations of the volume controversial? How were slaves obtained in Africa in the eighteenth century?

Specialized Courses: Thematic

David Northrup
Boston College
Africa's World, Part II: c. 1800–present

Hs 080: Africa's World, part II: c. 1800-present
Professor David Northrup
Carney 169
Boston College
Spring 1997
Office Hours: TTh 9-10, 1-2

"Africa's World" examines modern world history from an African vantage point. The second half looks at how, after 1800, Africa was drawn deeper into industrializing Europe's orbit, culminating in the European conquest of Africa at the end of the 19th century. It then explores how Africans regained their independence by uniting their nationalist activities and actions with the global forces of Pan-Islamic, Pan-African, socialist, and nationalist movements arising in Asia, Europe, and the Americas. The final section assesses Africa's relations with countries & cultures on other continents in the second half of the twentieth century.

The course fulfills the university core requirement in History (second half) and in Cultural Diversity. It may also count toward the Black Studies and the International Studies Minors.

REQUIRED READING [* = requested for O'Neill Reserve Room]	Abbreviation
Bulliet, et al. The Earth and Its Peoples, vol. C. (Houghton-Mifflin)	Bulliet
Kevin Shillington, History of Africa (St. Martin's)	Shillington
"Readings for Africa's World -II" (Bookstore)	Readings
Buchi Emecheta, The Joys of Motherhood (Heinemann Educational Books)*	Emecheta
Alan Paton, Ah, But Your Land is Beautiful (Scribners)*	Paton
Tepilit Ole Saitoti, Worlds of a Maasai Warrior (Univ. of California)*	Saitoti

Specialized Courses: Thematic

TOPIC SCHEDULE AND READING ASSIGNMENTS

1-14		Introduction	
1-16	I. AFRICA,	African Revival and European Intrusion	Shillington 226-32, 258-74, 278-88
1-21	INDUSTRIAL	Trade and Secondary Empires	Shillington 232-57; Bulliet 736-45
1-23	-IZATION	The Industrial Revolution	Bulliet 652-77
1-28	&	Explorers, Missionaries, and Conquerors	Shillington 289-316
1-30	IMPERIALISM	Colonial Rule in Africa - I	Shillington 332-62
2-4		Case Study of Colonial Rule: Nigeria	Emecheta, all
2-6		Colonial Rule in Africa - II: Settler Colonies	Shillington 317-31, 338-39
2-11	II.	Africans in the Americas after Slavery	Readings #1 & 2; Bulliet 720-24
2-13	THE GLOBAL	TBA	
2-18		Pan-Africanism: Back to Africa	Readings #3, #4, #5
2-20	ROOTS OF	Pan-Islamic Movements	Bulliet 766-75, 870-73. 878-82; Shillington 381-85
2-25		Mid-Term Exam	
2-27	AFRICAN	The Example of Asia	Bulliet 746-66, 776-91
3-4 & 6		Spring Vacation	
3-11	LIBERATION	Radical Revolution: Russia	Bulliet 855-70
3-13		Radical Revolution: China	Bulliet 914, 918-25
3-18		Europe Left, Right, and Center	Bulliet 873-78, 884-911
3-20	III.	Gandhi and South Africa	Bulliet 926-32; Shillington 361-63, 403-7; Readings #6
3-25	AFRICAN	Protest in the 1950s in South Africa	Paton, all
4-1	LIBERATION	Independence of African Proprietary Colonies	Readings #7; Shillington 363-80, 390-93
4-3	MOVEMENTS	Independence of African Settler Colonies to 1965	Shillington 380-82, 385-89
4-8		Wars of Liberation in Southern Africa	Shillington 393-406, 428-32
4-10		The Cold War and Liberation in Southern Africa	Readings #8; Bulliet 942-75
4-15	IV.	Constructing New Nation and Economies	Shillington 407-28
4-17	NEW AFRICAN	Constructing New Identities	Saitoti, all
4-22	SOCIETIES &	Africa and the World	Bulliet 977-1026
4-24	IDENTITIES	African Women and Liberation	
4-29		TBA	

REQUIREMENTS AND GRADES

Grades will be determined by the mid-term exam (20%), three required papers (15% each), participation (10%), and the final exam (25%). In the grading system in use at Boston College A (4.0) is awarded for work that is exceptional in its quality and originality, B (3.0) represents work that rises above the minimum required, C (2.0) denotes work that is minimally acceptable in accuracy and understanding, while D (1.0) signifies work falling below minimal standards. F (no credit) = failure.

Written Work: Each student must submit three essays of about 1000 words each analyzing three of the four case studies. Essays should make good use of the assigned readings and classroom discussions and lectures. If you write on all four topics, the best three grades will be counted. Due dates and topics are:

2-4 The Joys of Motherhood is set in the British colony of Nigeria. What opportunities and constraints did colonial rule impose? How did Africans cope with these circumstances?

Specialized Courses: Thematic

2-18 Africa and African America: How were some Africans under colonialism and some African Americans after slavery rediscovering and redefining their images of each other and their relations up to 1945?

3-25 What were the tactics, coalitions, and goals of the 1950s movement in South Africa? What were its strengths and weakness?

4-17 What opportunities and constraints does living in the modern world provide to an African like Saitoti? How successfully does he cope with these circumstances?

Participation: Students will be evaluated on the following; 1) physical presence (including punctuality); 2) the quality of responses to professor's questions about the daily reading, 3) the quality of questions posed. To receive maximum credit for participation it is quite important that each day's reading assignment be prepared carefully before class. In preparing reading assignments learn personal, group and place names and use the maps in the textbooks to learn their locations.

Specialized Courses: Thematic

Zenon V. Wasyliw
Ithaca College
Twentieth Century Global Revolutions

Zenon V. Wasyliw
Muller 427
274-1587
e-mail: Wasyliw@Ithaca.edu

Fall 1996
Office: MWF 12:15-1:15
TTH 5:20-6:20
and by appointment

Twentieth Century Global Revolutions
11-273-01

Twentieth century revolutions created a complex and dynamic global community on the eve of the twenty first century. A revolutionary transformation in western everyday life and values in response to the insecurities of industrialization and a scientific "modernization" process initiated a reconceptualization of traditional cultural values and worldviews. Political, scientific, philosophical, economic, social and cultural thoughts and conditions changed rapidly. Europeans provided idealistic revolutionary solutions to these complex transitions and tensions. Those who followed the Eighteenth and Nineteenth century ideologies of Liberalism/Capitalism, Nationalism, Marxism and their offshoots attempted to create and apply utopian models in the socially and culturally diverse world of the twentieth century. Political/ ideological revolutions inevitably had to deal with global cultural realities and the outcomes were far from ideal.

Revolutions are not strictly political and ideological in nature. Revolutions of this century became revolutionary struggles to culturally transform the values and everyday life of global multicultural societies to fit European utopian ideological parameters. In actual revolutionary practice, conflicting cultural values of unique global societies became the base of revolutionary activity. Current and future global revolutions will involve expanded perceptions of cultural tension that go beyond state boundaries.

This course will offer a comprehensive survey of twentieth century global revolutions. We shall first analyze the underlying causes, theories and models of revolutions. We shall then evaluate specific revolutions and revolutionary movements. European conditions and activities will be examined with special emphasis placed upon the Russian/Soviet revolutions. The Chinese Revolution will be evaluated within the context of a western revolutionary model implemented and modified by a non-western people, with special emphasis placed upon evaluating the Chinese Cultural Revolution. The post World War Two period introduced a global revolutionary movement of decolonization. India's Gandhi proposed a unique, non-violent path of civil disobedience, which many view revolutionary. We shall evaluate Gandhi's model and judge its implementation in the United States by Martin Luther King.

Revolutions occurred with greater frequency in the latter half of the twentieth century. We shall begin with an overview of conditions on the African continent and then specifically appraise revolutionary conditions in Nigeria and South Africa followed by Latin American revolutions in Cuba and elsewhere. The Middle East (or South West Asia) provides examples of new revolutionary cultural formations and directions based upon traditional values. We shall appraise the most recent revolutions in Eastern and Central Europe and evaluate current and future revolutionary trends and movements that transcend state borders but are culturally based: music, popular culture, gender relations, consumerism, spirituality, the media and new technologies.

Textbooks: The following books are required for this course and may be purchased at the college bookstore.

ACHEBE, Chinua. No Longer at Ease.
DEFRONZO, James. Revolutions and Revolutionary Movements.
FISCHER, Louis. Gandhi: His Life and Message.
KAPUSCINSKI, Ryszard. The Soccer War.
SCOTT, John. Behind the Urals.
ZHENHUA, Zhai Red Flower of China.

General twentieth century global history textbooks will be placed on library reserve for background use.

Requirements

1. Regular attendance is expected of all students. College policy allows only three unexcused absences. Absences will adversely affect the comprehension of course material and one's grade. Students are expected to have read the assigned readings and participate in class discussion. **Please remember that attendance will influence your grade!**

2. Each student will complete two interpretive essay examinations and a final comprehensive examination. The essays will be conceptual in nature and will test the students' comprehension and analysis of the material covered in class and the readings.

3. Book critiques are another component of course requirements. Students must complete two critiques. Three critiques may be turned in and the best two calculated into the final grade, or students may turn in only two critiques all of which will be calculated. The following authors will be critiqued: The first a choice of either Scott or Zhenhua, the second, Fischer or Achebe. Due dates are listed in the Topics and Assignments section of the syllabus. The following book critique guidelines will be followed.

Specialized Courses: Thematic

The book critique will consist of four sections:

1. Introduction: Introduce the author's main thesis and themes. Include a brief summary of what the critique will specifically examine.

2. Provide a brief historical, geographical background and setting.

3. Select three or more main themes and events you have analyzed as being most significant and support them with specific examples.

4. Provide a critique of the work's strong and weak historical and stylistic points. Decide how the book relates to the Global Revolutions course and recommend an appropriate readership.

4. Cooperative learning. The course of the Chinese Revolution will be assessed by group presentations and discussions of Son of the Revolution. Appointed student communes will accomplish this task with the appropriate revolutionary zeal. A concise communal written report will also be required. More specific instructions will be forthcoming.

5. The writing of essays, critiques and papers follows specific criteria and all sources must be properly documented. Carefully read the sections of the syllabus dealing with plagiarism and writing papers.

Grading:

All work must be completed to earn a passing grade!

Two book critiques worth 20%		40%
Midterm examination	15%	
Final examination essays		30%
Qualitative class participation		15%
		100%

Miscellaneous:

1. Films reinforce materials covered in class and should be appropriately analyzed.
2. Make up examinations (for those with a valid excuse) will be given at the professor's convenience.
3. Please stop by during scheduled office hours or by appointment to discuss course material or life in general.

Specialized Courses: Thematic

DATE	CLASS NO.	TOPICS AND READING ASSIGNMENTS
28 Aug.	1.	Introduction and Course Expectations What is a Revolution? Definitions and Theories DeFronzo, Chapter 1
2 Sept.		Labor Day
4 Sept.	3.	Science, the Industrial Revolution and Challenges to the Traditional Order The Development of Revolutionary Ideologies and pre-Twentieth Century Revolutions
9 Sept.	4.	The World-System of Development, Western Imperialism and Global Cultural Revolution
11 Sept.	5.	World War One: Catalyst for Revolution? Begin reading <u>Behind the Urals</u>
16 Sept.	6.	The Russian Marxist Revolution in Theory and Practice at Home and Abroad DeFronzo, Chapter 2
18 Sept.	7.	The anti-Culture Cultural Revolution and Social Transformation
23 Sept.	8.	At What Cost Cultural and Social Revolution? Discussion of <u>Behind the Urals</u>
25 Sept.	9.	Interwar Europe in an Age of Uncertainty, and the Rise of Totalitarianism <u>Behind the Urals</u> Book Critique is Due! Begin reading <u>Red Flower of China</u>
30 Sept.	10.	Fascism, Hitler's Germany and the Racial Revolution: the Holocaust and Its Legacy.
2 Oct.	11.	A New World Order and Revolutionary Transformation in East Asia: Japan, the West and Origins of the Chinese Revolution
7 Oct.	12.	Communal Presentations on the Course of the Chinese Revolution

Specialized Courses: Thematic

9 Oct.	13.	Communal Presentations and a Critical Evaluation of <u>Red Flower of the Revolution</u>
14 Oct.	14.	An Analysis of Mao and the Great Chinese Cultural Revolution Begin Reading <u>Gandhi</u>
16 Oct.	15.	Western Colonialism and the Periphery: Revolutionary Paths towards Political and Cultural Independence: The Vietnamese Revolution, DeFronzo, Chapter 4 MIDTERM Examinations are Due!
17-18 Oct.		Semester Break
21 Oct.	16.	India: Colonialism, the Struggle for Independence and New Identities. Gandhi and the Establishment of India and Pakistan
23 Oct.	17.	A Critical Evaluation of <u>Gandhi</u> and Discussion: Are Gandhi and Non-violent Civil Disobedience Revolutionary?
28 Oct.	18.	The American Civil Rights Movement and Cultural Identity: Peaceful or Violent Revolution? Begin reading <u>No Longer at Ease</u>
30 Oct.	19.	The American Cultural Revolution of the Nineteen Sixties The <u>Gandhi</u> Critique is Due
4 Nov.	20.	Western Colonialism in Africa and Revolutionary Paths Towards Independence
6 Nov.	21.	Internal African Revolutions: In Search of Stability DeFronzo, Chapter 8
11 Nov.	22.	Cultural Revolution in Nigeria and South Africa. Discussion of <u>No Longer at Ease</u>
13 Nov.	23.	The Middle East (South West Asia) and Cultural Revolution: Turkey and Iran Compared DeFronzo, Chapter 7
18 Nov.	24.	The Arab World and the Establishment of Israel <u>No Longer at Ease</u> is Due
20 Nov.	25.	Is the Cuban Revolution a Model for Latin America? DeFronzo, Chapters 5 and 6

Specialized Courses: Thematic

25-29 Nov.		Thanksgiving Read The Soccer War
2 Dec.	26.	Discussion and Analysis of "The Harder They Come" and the Urban Revolutionary
4 Dec.	27.	The Revolutionary Restructuring of Gender Relations
9 Dec.	28.	Discussion and Analysis of The Soccer War. The 1989-1991 Revolutions in Eastern and Central Europe: The Triumph of Culture Over Ideology
11 Dec.	29.	Future Global Cultural Revolutions: A Conceptual Reflection
16 Dec.	30.	Examination Week

The West and the World
A History of Civilization

KEVIN REILLY

"Reilly's text is the most teachable . . . one of the best conceived chronological narratives of world history . . . leaves students with a much more sophisticated vision of the global past and present." —*Lynda Schaffer (Tufts University)*

This text engages students and provokes discussion by presenting the past through the prism of current and perennial issues. Interpretive chapters on such topics as gender, religion, war, ecology, and nationalism create both thematic narratives and the strands of a larger chronological account. The book makes great ideas accessible, explores major historical turning points, and reveals the dynamic of increasing global interactions (trade, migrations, etc.). It also compares cultures and civilizations while giving voice to individual lives.

VOL. I: FROM THE ANCIENT WORLD TO 1700
Volume I explores perennial issues. Gender relations are examined across the neolithic and urban revolutions. Issues of class, civility, and citizenship come to life in a history of Middle Eastern, Mediterranean, Chinese, and Muslim cities. Ideas of love and sex are compared in European, Japanese and Indian history. The social dislocations of empire are compared in Rome and China. The Crusades are viewed through Muslim as well as Christian sources. In addition the seventeenth-century scientific revolution is compared with science in China and the Muslim world.
ISBN 1-55876-152-7   368 PP.   PAPERBACK, $19.95

VOL. II: FROM 1500 TO MODERN TIMES   *(FORTHCOMING 1999)*
Topics of Volume II are designed for a study of world history since 1500. The method is vivid and comparative. Economics and ecology, racism and nationalism, individuality and mass culture are explored. Studies of individuality in the Protestant Reformation and Neo-Confucianism, race in the U.S. and Brazil, apartheid and segregation, and the ecology of peanut farming in Africa and of plastics in the post-war U.S. help to delineate the contours of the West, the world, and the modern.
ISBN 1-55876-153-5   444 PP.   PAPERBACK, $19.95

Kevin Reilly, Raritan Valley Community College, is co-founder and first president of the World History Association. He is editor of several books and book series, including Readings in World Civilization. He has taught at Columbia, Rutgers, and Princeton Universities.

Napoleon in Egypt

ABD AL RAHMAN AL-JABARTI;

TRANSLATION BY S. MOREH;

INTRODUCTION BY ROBERT TIGNOR;

ESSAY BY EDWARD W. SAID

"[Al-Jabarti] resents the French invasion, ridicules their claim to be a defender of the faith, rejects their belief in liberty and equality, despises their lack of morality and personal hygiene, but approves their efficiency, common loyalty and cooperation, and wonders at their technical and scholarly abilities. There was much he admired in these uncouth barbarians who even had a translation of the Koran in their luggage. . . . Al-Jabarti's work has been a treasure house . . . Moreh's editing and translating can serve as a model to other scholars."

—Journal of the American Oriental Society

"Superlative translation . . . excellent commentaries . . . witty illustrations . . . exactly the right length for classroom use . . . inexpensive"

—World History Bulletin

The book is an Arab view of a turning point in modern history. Napoleon's conquest of Egypt in 1798 was the first contact between a Western power with imperial goals and an ancien régime of an African society. Sheik Al-Jabarti's chronicle is a unique combination of historical narration and reflection combined with daily observations about the atmosphere in Cairo and the mood among the local population.

The French view of these events is described by Napoleon's secretary; **Edward W. Said**, Columbia University, provides a stinging critique of French preoccupation with Egypt and the resulting cultural 'Orientalism.'

Abd al Rahman Al-Jabarti (1754–1825) was a renowned Arab historian and writer. **S. Moreh**, Hebrew University, is one of the world's leading experts on Arab literature. **Robert Tignor**, Princeton University, places Jabarti's account in historical context in his introduction.

ISBN 1-55876-069-5   HARDCOVER, $28.95
ISBN 1-55876-070-9   PAPER, $16.95
196 PP., ILLUSTRATED WITH 40 LINE DRAWINGS

Ancient African Civilizations
Kush and Axum
STANLEY BURSTEIN, EDITOR

This book examines two ancient African civilizations, Kush and Axum, which were the most highly developed civilizations south of Egypt, but are often overlooked in modern texts.

Stanley Burstein has researched, compiled, and translated with commentary the most significant Greek and Roman sources concerning Black Africa. The result is a fascinating book about the people of the southern part of the Nile Valley, the gold mines of Nubia, the Hellenistic city of Meroë, capital of the Ethiopian Empire of Kush with its own highly developed culture (300 BC–300 AD). The texts include a report about Nubian soldiers in a Roman frontier army.

Axum is best known as one of the oldest capitals of the ancient Ethiopian empire (100–500 AD). The texts in this book describe the Red Sea trade and the rise of Axum, the birth of the Axum Empire (Sudan and Ethiopia), the conversion of Axum to Christianity, and the Axumite civilization on the eve of the Middle Ages. The illustrations include reproductions of excavations of pyramids, temples, Roman baths, and palaces from Kush and of the well-preserved highrise buildings and stone obelisks from Axum.

Stanley Burstein, California State University, Los Angeles, is author of *Graeco-Africa: Studies in the History of Greek Relations with Egypt and Nubia* and other books.

ISBN 1-55876-147-0   HARDCOVER, $29.95
ISBN 1-55876-148-9   PAPERBACK, $16.95
196 PP.   JUST PUBLISHED

Story of the Jamaican People

PHILIP SHERLOCK AND HAZEL BENNETT

The last general history of Jamaica was published in 1960. Since then the country has become an independent nation and has developed a new sense of national identity out of the experience of 450 years of European colonization, African slavery, and the transplanting of immigrant populations from India, China, Lebanon, and Syria.

The Jamaican people have never accepted what was presented to them as the history of Jamaica. The heroes of the British Empire are not their heroes, and their battlefields are in Jamaica, the Caribbean, and Afro-America, wherever Afro-American freedom fighters have struggled for liberty.

A new interpretation of the Jamaican experience is long overdue. In this book, Sir Philip Sherlock teams up with documentarian Dr. Hazel Bennett to tell the story of the Jamaican people from an Afro-Jamaican rather than a European perspective. Africa is at the center of the story; by claiming Africa as homeland, Jamaicans gain a sense of historical continuity, of identity, of roots—an experience they share with fifty million Afro-Americans throughout the Americas and across four centuries.

This is a book for the 1990s and beyond; for the present generation and generations to come; for Jamaicans at home and abroad; and for all Afro-Americans who are descendants of the great diaspora.

Philip Sherlock, former Vice-Chancellor of the University of the West Indies, is author of *A Short History of the West Indies*. **Hazel Bennett** is the former Head of the Department of Library Studies of the University of the West Indies.

ISBN 1-55876-145-4   HARDCOVER, $48.95
ISBN 1-55876-146-2   PAPERBACK, $19.95
486 PP. ILLUSTRATED   JUST PUBLISHED

Ibn Battuta
in Black Africa

SAID HAMDUN AND NOEL Q. KING, ED. AND TRANS.

This book is one of the most important documents about Black Africa written by a non-European Medieval historian.

" . . . lively translation . . . outstanding introduction . . . appealing illustrations . . . useful maps. . . ." —*World History Bulletin*

Abu Abdalla ibn Battuta (1304–1354) was one of the greatest travelers of pre-modern times. He traveled to Black Africa twice. He reported about the wealthy, multi-cultural trading centers at the African East coast, such as Mombasa and Kilwa, and the warm hospitality he experienced in Mogadishu.

He also visited the court of Mansa Musa and neighboring states during its period of prosperity from mining and the trans-Saharan trade. He wrote disapprovingly of sexual integration in families and of a "hostility toward the white man." Ibn Battuta's description is a unique document of the high culture, pride, and independence of Black African states in the fourteenth century.

"Ibn Battuta's narrative allows us to look at that country through eyes unlike our own. For once, sub-Saharan Africa is viewed without the intrusion of colonialism and racism, as just another corner of a large and fascinating world. . . . This book provides much food for thought, combined with the simple pleasure of a good travel tale well told." —*The Boston Globe*

Noel Q. King, University of California, Santa Cruz, is the author of Religion in Africa and numerous other books. Said Hamdun teaches at the University of Nairobi. **Ross Dunn**, San Diego State University, author of The Adventures of Ibn Battuta provided an introduction to this edition.

ISBN 1-55876-087-3   HARDCOVER, $28.95
ISBN 1-55876-088-1   PAPERBACK, $16.95
166 PP.   ILLUSTRATED

DATE DUE

MY 03 '03			

Demco, Inc. 38-293